OROMO WITNESS

OROMO WITNESS

by Abdul Dire

Flexible Press
Minneapolis, Minnesota
2020

Opinions expressed are those of the author. The events and conversations in this book have been set down to the best of the author's ability based on research and personal interviews.

ISBN- 978-1-7339763-5-0

Cover design by William Burleson
Cover photo by Lauren Lombard

Editors:
William E Burleson, executive editor
Daniel Schuette
Vicki Adang, Mark My Words Editorial Services, LLC

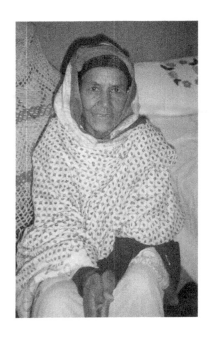

To my maternal grandmother,
Fatuma Sheikh Ahmed, who opened
the doors of education for me.

CONTENTS

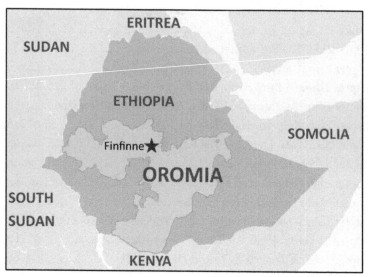

Oromia Region of Ethiopia (post 2010).

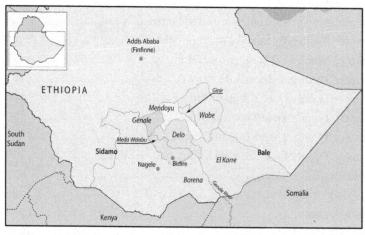

Map of the Bale province of Ethiopia (1960s).

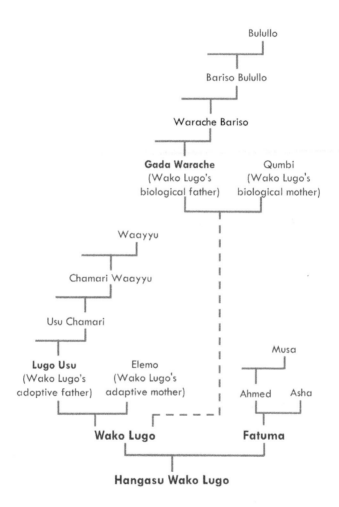

PREFACE

History is written by the victors.
Oral history is spoken by the people.
This book represents the voice of the people.

I WROTE THIS BOOK for three reasons.

First, I was dismayed and angry. There are virtually no documents or books that capture the Bale Oromo's struggle. The few snippets I have been able to find are inaccurate and written from the perspective of the oppressor. I wanted to correct this injustice.

Second, I wanted to tell a specific story. My maternal uncle, Hangasu Wako Lugo, experienced the Bale Oromo's struggle in many ways. His father, Wako Lugo, was an early architect of the Bale Revolt. His uncle General Wako Gutu was the supreme leader of the Rebellion. Hangasu was a young boy during the armed struggle of the 1960s, a leader and key contributor in the 1970s and 1980s, a witness to and participant in the elections of 1994. He is now in exile living abroad. His story provides a glimpse into the struggle of the modern Oromo people.

Finally, I wanted my children to know where we came from. My children are second-generation immigrants. Because they primarily speak English, they would otherwise have no access to this important history.

As one of the world's ancient countries, Ethiopia (along with Liberia) maintained her status as the only historically independent African country (apart from a five-year occupation by Italy). Therefore, Ethiopia is considered Africa's oldest independent "republic." Ethiopia's population is currently estimated at more than 110 million, making it the second most populous African country after Nigeria and the twelfth most populous in the world. Its modern ethnic composition includes: the Oromo, Amhara, Tigre, Sidama, Somali, Afar, Gurage, Walayta, Hadiya, and many other small groups. The Oromo people are the single largest ethnic group in the country, representing more than 40 percent of the population. The Amhara and Tigre are the next largest ethnic groups; combined they represent 32 percent of the population.

The Oromo people were invaded and incorporated into the modern Ethiopian Empire during the reign of Emperor Menelik in the late 1800s. The Oromo people resisted northern Tigre-Amhara rule at different places and times. This book focuses on the Bale Oromo People's Struggle that took place during the 1960s. This ordinary people's movement challenged the Emperor Haile Selassie's government. Haile Selassie was deposed by his own military junta in 1974. The new Derg government fell under communist influence for seventeen years. In 1991, the Derg regime collapsed, and the Ethiopian People's Revolutionary Democratic Front (EPRDF), which was dominated by the Tigray People's Liberation Front (TPLF), took over the country.

First established in 1992, Oromia is one of the ten regional states that constitute modern Ethiopia. It spans the eastern, central, and western part of Ethiopia. The Oromia Regional State has twenty-one zones (the equivalent of provinces). The Bale and Borana zones account for almost 50 percent of

Oromia's total area. Madda Walabu, a district located in the southernmost tip of the Bale zone, is an important place in Oromo history: It was the center of the spiritual, cultural, and political system of the Oromo people.

To write this book, I had to go outside traditional research routes and find living witnesses, veterans of and eyewitnesses to the Bale Oromo's struggle. Many of these witnesses are now in their 70s, 80s, and 90s, and their numbers are starting to dwindle. They had never been asked to share their stories, and they were more than willing to share. Their willingness to share inspired me to record their stories, and their testimonies and memories provide the main content for this book. Because this is primarily an oral history, I have not included footnotes. Because my people were predominantly pastoralists, they didn't use the Gregorian calendar. Unless events took place at the same time as other world events, it was difficult to identify the exact dates for many of the events. Thus, dates in this book are my best estimates. Because I conducted the research and the interviews in Oromo language, translating the exact meaning and context into English isn't always possible. I have done my best to faithfully capture the essence of what was said.

As I began to study our history, I realized how much more is yet to be explored, how many more stories of struggle, of the ways individuals and communities have overcome seemingly insurmountable difficulties, are yet to be written. My hope is this book will inspire others to write, build on this work, and lead the way in preserving history for the next generation.

CHAPTER ONE:
THE RESTAURANT

IN THE WINTER OF 2006, I was a senior at the University of Minnesota. One night, my uncle Hangasu asked me to give him a ride home from his work. Hangasu is more than my uncle; he is also a father figure, a mentor, and a friend. Hangasu worked a second shift in a restaurant on Lake Street in Minneapolis, Minnesota. During the first shift, he worked for St. Paul Public Schools in the food services department. Hangasu worked two jobs to put food on the table and pay the bills so his children could focus on school instead of work. Hangasu and his wife, Maryam, have eight children: three daughters and five sons. On weekends, Hangasu served and guided the American-Oromo Community of Minnesota's board of directors.

It was five minutes before midnight the night I drove on the snowy Minnesota roads to pick up Hangasu. I had not picked him up at the restaurant before, and I didn't know what to expect. I parked the car on the street and knocked on the door. The restaurant had closed hours earlier. I looked through the window. Hangasu was the only person I could see. He came and opened the door for me. He was wearing a blue apron over his normal sweater, and he was holding a mop. "Give me five minutes," he said. "I'm almost done." He went back to what he was doing, mopping the floor. I could see he took his job seriously. He was obsessive about cleanliness, checking every inch of the floor to make sure he didn't miss a spot.

By this time, I was in tears. I couldn't look at him anymore. I rushed out of the building and returned to my car. I cried. I knew he was working, but I had never asked what his job was. He was sweeping the floor so we could attend school.

I wasn't crying because there is anything wrong with mopping the floor. Hangasu knew what he was doing. He was investing in his children's future. What shocked me was the chasm between the picture I had of Hangasu and the job he was doing at the time. In my mind, Hangasu was a pioneer Oromo leader. Yet, he swallowed his pride to enable his children to go further, and I admired him for that. He valued work and impact over words. He took a long-term view. As of 2020, in addition to his eight children, Hangasu had twelve grandchildren. When the family arrived in Minnesota in 2000, Hangasu made each child promise that at a minimum they would earn a bachelor's degree. I too was part of this deal, and as a senior in college, I was very close to that goal.

As I drove my uncle home that night, we didn't talk much, mostly because I was hurting inside. The next morning I got curious. How did we get here? What life experiences shaped Hangasu to be who he is today? Why was education a priority for him? These questions propelled me to learn more about Hangasu and the circumstances that shaped his worldview.

CHAPTER TWO:
HANGASU

HANGASU WAKO LUGO WAS BORN in 1956 in Bidire, a small village in the Bale zone of modern-day Oromia. He was born in an area called Dallo, near the northern banks of the Ganale River. He grew up in a rapidly changing Ethiopia.

Hangasu has been a living witness of the Oromo movement since he was born. He literally grew up in the battlefield during the Bale Rebellion. Hangasu accompanied his father wherever he went, and that included the battlefield. When he was just 10 years old, he sat and listened in on exclusive executive meetings where major military decisions were made during the Bale Rebellion. He met Emperor Haile Selassie in person three times, and he argued with him about education twice as a teenager. He observed Colonel Mengistu Haile Mariam up close at his house and struck up a casual conversation with him. In the early 1970s, Hangasu was the right-hand person for Magarsa Bari (one of the founders of the Oromo Liberation Front [OLF]). Hangasu worked with the Oromo elders and leaders such as Haji Adam Saddo and Haji Abdullahi Ganamo in the Bale prairies. He was held in one of the harshest Somali prisons along with Adam Jilo (a key figure in the Bale Oromo movement). After he was released from prison in 1983, he accompanied General Wako Gutu (the supreme leader of the Bale Revolt) in a military expedition and saved the general's life. In the 1990s, after the communist regime was toppled, he ran for a House seat representing Dallo, his home district. He quickly learned the election was anything but fair.

Despite this background and his broad experience, Hangasu avoided assuming leadership positions, which one might expect of someone with his experience, insight, and foresight. He could have led any Oromo political organizations of his choice, but he didn't. The only time he tried was when he ran for the parliamentary House seat in 1994, a race he lost.

After that there were many instances where he was the natural successor or was expected to take up the role. Every time, he turned down these opportunities and nominated somebody else. When General Wako Gutu died, many younger members of the executive committee insisted he accept the nomination to succeed the general. Some even threatened to leave the organization if he didn't step up to lead it. Still he refused, saying there were people older than he who had spent much longer time in the field with the general than he had.

When I asked him why he never took on a leadership role, Hangasu told me he believed that power corrupts. "Leadership requires fundamental toolsets: First, there must be a law that regulates everybody including the leader himself. The law must be democratic, and the law must specify that nobody is above the law," he said. "Second, there must be an organization in the fullest meaning of the word. At the end of the day, everybody is required to protect the interest of the organization, not the interest of any one individual, and the organization must outlast its leaders. As far as I can see, we [the Oromos] lacked both of these fundamental tools. Without these tools, frankly, I wouldn't trust myself to fulfill my duty."

"In the meantime, I want to work in the background to help others," he continued. "I want to focus my attention on humanitarian work in the area of education."

That's how I know my uncle. Tirelessly focused on and working for the betterment of his community, his family, and his people. But the question remains, how could this reluctant leader, who had seen and experienced so much over his lifetime, now be mopping floors late at night in a Minneapolis restaurant?

*

Hangasu's father was Wako Lugo. Wako Lugo was 6 feet tall and had a strong build. His face always looked serious; his eyebrows were dark and dense. An assistant to Wako Lugo, who'd spent many years with him in the 1970s, described him as "a lion nobody messed with." Despite his outward appearance, his people remembered him for his wisdom and generosity to all.

Wako Lugo Usu was born in 1905 just after Dallo had been forced to join the Ethiopian Empire. His uncle, Waayyu Teesso, was one of the first of the southern Oromo to accept Islam. Hangasu's grandfather was the last of an ancient line of religious leaders practicing a faith that predated both Islam and Christianity in Dallo. The father of his father's father led an Arsi Oromo pastoral society.

As with Hangasu's relatives, many of his children, nieces, and nephews would live lives as refugees. The Oromo diaspora followed the political turmoil that came when Ethiopia transitioned from an empire to a communist state and a system dominated by northerners, who were apparently indifferent to the rights of the Oromo people in the south.

Wako Lugo had two families, a biological family and an adoptive one. At the start of the twentieth century, Lugo Usu—the last known Qaallu, or spiritual leader, of Rahitu in Dallo—and his wife, Elemo, had a daughter, but they wanted a son.

Everything they tried failed. As was customary in those days, Lugo Usu appealed to his friend and clan member Gada Warache. Gada had four boys and two girls. Gada gave his 7-year-old son, Kadir, to Lugo to adopt. Kadir refused and ran back to his mother's house. When his father reproached him, little Kadir cried fiercely and refused to return.

Lugo Usu came up with another proposal. He told Gada, "I want your unborn son from your wife Qumbi Wako Bonayya." This was not a typical request, even for that period. Gada saw the desperation in his brother, gathered himself, and said, "You don't know if it will be a boy or a girl." Lugo replied, "I will beg God to make this baby a boy." Gada agreed to the proposal.

When Lugo went back to his wife, she immediately announced to her friends, "*Akka Waaqaa hin beekanii, haadha Waaqoo naan jedhaa.*" Simply translated, this means, "You don't know how God works, just call me the mother of Wako." Apparently, she had named the unborn baby Wako.

A few months later, in 1905, Qumbi gave birth to a boy. Gada and Qumbi quickly transferred the baby boy to his new, eager parents. Elemo and Lugo confirmed his name as Wako. Thus it was that Wako Lugo Usu would grow up in the house of Qaallu. Wako Lugo would inherit the legacy of resistance from his adoptive father, Lugo Usu, and emerge as the leader of the Bale Oromo Revolt, a legacy that Hangasu would continue and built upon by connecting the Bale Oromo's cause with the national Oromo struggle.

CHAPTER THREE:
A BRIEF HISTORY OF THE
OROMO PEOPLE

THE OROMO PEOPLE WERE invaded and incorporated into the modern Ethiopian Empire during the reign of Emperor Menelik in the late 1890s. The Oromo people resisted the northerners, Tigre-Amhara rule, at different places and times. For example, Arsi Oromos in Arsi province resisted the Menelik conquest militarily, but they were overpowered because the emperor was backed by the colonial powers who put modern weapons at his disposal. After he won militarily, to deter those who resisted him, Menelik mutilated the hands of their men and the breasts of their women. He gained the rest of the territories unchallenged.

In 2014, the Oromia regional government erected the Anole Monument as a tribute to those who were brutally massacred and mutilated. It took 120 years for the Arsi Oromo to openly speak and display this tragic Ethiopian history. Some unprogressive Ethiopians still deny the event took place. This denial to confront the harsh history is one of the impediments to the country's progress in the present day.

The Oromo people live in the central and southern highlands and constitute the largest ethnic group in Ethiopia—estimates range from 40 percent to 45 percent of the population—in an ethnically diverse country. There are more than eighty ethnic groups speaking more than eighty languages. The Oromo and Amhara have been the largest groups, with Amhara making up most of the ruling class.

It is difficult to know the true population of the Oromo; successive imperial governments attempted to downplay the country's ethnic diversity. The Amhara had alliances with Shawa Oromo elites through faith and marriage. These assimilated elites participated in the country's administration and military affairs. The only way an Oromo could integrate into the Ethiopian government was to convert to Christianity. Therefore, a large number of Oromos in the north and central highlands accepted Orthodox Christianity as a means of integration and as a way for the elite collaborators to ally with the northerners. Hangasu's southern Oromo ancestors lived outside the northern establishment.

During the reign of Emperor Haile Selassie, although there were at least as many Muslims as Christians in the country, the total Muslim population in Ethiopia was virtually unknown. Although Haile Selassie preached religious freedom, his policies and actions contradicted this. In the Ethiopian media of the time, Ethiopian Muslims were referred to as "Muslims in Ethiopia," as if they didn't belong. Because the media was controlled by the government, it was only reinforcing the will of the emperor. Under Emperor Haile Selassie's Amhara hegemony, it was a crime to write in Oromo, all Oromo print media were banned, and the Oromo language was banned from being used on the radio (it was said to break the radio and was therefore not fit for radio broadcast).

In the rural, pastoral south, there was no mixing of culture and no intermarriage with the north. Since the early twentieth century, rural towns in the pastoral south have been predominantly Muslim. Very few Muslims assimilated to get an education and advance their lives. To gain higher education, one had to give up the Oromo language—Afan Oromo—for Amharic, the only recognized state language.

The northern Amhara and the southern Oromo were in constant conflict. The southern Oromo opposed just about everything the northerners stood for. The northerners cared about expanding their influence, controlling the population, and exploiting resources from the south. The southern Oromo continually resisted, striving to control their own destiny and live with dignity on their ancestral land.

The Oromo system of governance was known as the Gada system. In the late nineteenth century, before the introduction of Islam and Christianity in the south, the Arsi Oromo followed the way of life and governance of the Waaqeffannaa and Gada (or Gadaa), the equivalent of church and state.

In the Waaqeffannaa belief system, the people believed in one god—Waaqa—the creator and sustainer of all things. They prayed to Waaqa for all their needs. The people had a small number of principles for interacting with others. They believed in justice and fairness. They believed in avoiding *chubbu*, which means "sin" or "wrongdoing to others." The Qaallu was the spiritual leader of the community. The Qaallu had a principal wife, chosen from a specific tribe. Only children born of the principal wife had the "purest blood" and were deemed qualified to inherit Qaallu.

Gada was an egalitarian, democratic system of governance that had been practiced for hundreds (and possibly thousands) of years. Every tribe had a Gada Council that managed its affairs. Every male who was of age had full rights to elect and to be elected to the Gada Council, which functioned like town hall meetings in New England. The Gada leaders, Abbaa Gada, managed the affairs of all tribes collectively. Between tribes, the Gada leaders would discuss all matters and reach a consensus. The Gada leaders recognized people in the community who demonstrated exemplary acts of service and punished people who didn't live up to expectations or committed crimes.

In Waaqeffannaa and Gada system, people were required to follow the decision of their tribe. In exchange, the tribe provided protection and insurance to its citizens. While the Abbaa Gada presided when the Gada Assembly met, the Qaallu was the spiritual leader but also played a political role. Although the Qaallu institution no longer exists in its original form today, the Oromo national flag (black, red, and white) was adapted from the Qaallu turban.

The Qaallu was the most honorable and most fair person in the community. No major decision could be made without his approval. The title of Qaallu was passed down to the spiritual leader's sons. The Qaallu had high status, was considered pure, avoided sins, was always careful, and spoke only the truth. The Qaallu did not participate in wars and was not even allowed to carry metal because it could be used as a weapon for hunting and warfare. The Qaallu was not allowed to raise cattle, farm, or do business. These activities were done *for* Qaallu. The Qaallu would bless and preside over local gatherings and would declare the consensus of the community's final decision.

Before the invasion of northerners, the Oromo people governed themselves through this Gada system—locally and regionally. However, the northerners' conquest disrupted this life. The Oromo institutions were systematically weakened and replaced by the Amhara rule.

Emperor Menelik of Ethiopia implemented his Amhara rule through Melkanyas. Melkanyas were northern settlers sent by the emperor to administer the native Oromos in the south. They were also referred to as *neftenya,* which means "rifleman." Their job was to execute the emperor's orders in partnership with northerner civilian administrators. Natives were obligated to build shelter for and provide provisions to these Melkanyas. Every major tribe leader's house was assigned a Melkanya. Practically, the Melkanyas were the landlords, and the natives were their slaves.

Empowered by the emperor, the Melkanyas looted the natives' properties and raped their women. They disrespected the native population, including their leaders. The natives had no means to fight back. At the same time, the natives could not accept living under this kind of humiliation.

*

Midmorning in a pastoral society is a busy time. Pastoralists milk cows around 5 or 6 in the morning, then let them out for grazing, and bring them back around for the second milking midmorning.

One morning while the Qaallu, Lugo Usu, sat outside his humble mud hut watching over his cattle and his wives busy milking them, the Melkanya assigned to Lugo's house came.

The Melkanya walked right past Lugo without acknowledging him. To Lugo's surprise, the Melkanya entered his main house. To Lugo, this was an act of war—a stranger from a government he never really accepted had entered his bedroom. To Lugo, home was not simply where he stored his valuables; it was also his sanctuary. This was the equivalent of breaking into the emperor's residence. After all, he was the leader of his people. If he accepted this public humiliation by letting his sacred residence be assaulted, the rest of the population would do the same.

Lugo was furious. But there was no system for Lugo to bring his perpetrator to justice. Under Ethiopian rule, the Melkanya was the rule and ruler. Nobody would listen to Lugo; in fact, he could be punished for daring to sue the king's soldiers. The Oromo Gada system didn't apply to the alien settlers, and the settlers didn't care about what they perceived as the backward system of the Oromo government.

So Lugo took the matter into his own hands. He went to his kitchen, picked up his spear, and waited. A few minutes later, the Melkanya left the house with a container full of honey in one hand and butter in the other hand. Lugo threw his spear directly into the Melkanya's stomach. The spear went straight through the man. He lay on his back, crying for his life. Lugo withdrew his spear and shouted, *"Akka dammaa fi dhadhaa agarte, way na agarte."* Roughly translated, this means "You saw honey and butter, but I was nonexistent to you."

When I heard this, I said, "He did what? He killed a man for stealing some food?" My uncle was frustrated by my question.

"You're missing the point," he said. "Lugo's judgment to kill was not about what the soldier stole. Rather it was about drawing a line to protect his own dignity because his people would emulate him."

My uncle further explained that Lugo's reaction was a turning point in Arsi Oromo's resistance to Ethiopian rule in many ways. First, Qaallus were not allowed to carry arms, let alone kill with them. The fact that Qaallu (who was regarded as a saint in his society) killed a settler meant the northerners' subjugation had gone too far. As a leader of his people, Lugo declared resistance by leading the way. He broke the codes of Qaallu to leave behind the legacy of resistance. He went from a saint to a resistance leader.

Secondly, no Oromo had ever killed a Melkanya in the region. The tribe was concerned about the king's wrath and appealed to the government to forgive the mistake. The local government, wanting to calm things down, called it an accident and buried the issue. The local government's decision to let Lugo free was also strange. Perhaps the government chose the region's stability over revenge for one careless and greedy soldier.

Finally, for the natives across the region, Lugo's act signified that the settlers' exploitation was no longer bearable. People throughout the region started finding creative ways of eliminating the Melkanyas assigned to control them. One of these ways was to trick the Melkanya into joining them on a hunting trip by promising glory and riches.

With comfortable lives and few worries about provisions, the Melkanyas had begun picking up hobbies from the locals. This included hunting. The natives had always loved and admired hunting as a way to distinguish themselves. For example, killing a lion was a big deal because it required both bravery and skill. Killing an elephant was an even bigger deal; elephants are more valuable prey and more difficult to hunt because they are very in tune with their surroundings and know when hunters enter their territory. People sought the title of "elephant killer."

Hunting lions and elephants brought glory and title; it also had an economic motivation. Lion skin was valuable. Elephant trunks and tusks were extremely valuable, albeit contraband. The Melkanyas wanted to gain the glory and riches from hunting lions and elephants.

On one occasion, a group of Oromo took one of the Melkanya to hunt elephants. It could take days or weeks to find them. This particular group was hunting in a place called Filtu, south of the Ganale Doria River, near the Ethiopian-Somali border.

When the natives and Melkanya reached the place, they separated into small groups of two to three people and set up camp. Each group made its own fire to provide light, heat, and a way to cook. They had finally reached the elephants' land and had a big day ahead of them. They went to sleep.

One of the natives, unable to sleep, saw that the Melkanya in his group was in a deep sleep. He noticed that there was a long rope coming from where the Melkanya slept. Melkanyas wore long pieces of cloth (similar to a rope) around their waist to store their ammunition. The man alerted his friend, then got up and put the end of the rope into the fire. The rope began to burn. Minutes later, when the flames reached him, the Melkanya jumped up and began running around, not fully aware of what was going on.

Back in those days, early 1900s, the Oromo people wore animal skin as a jacket. The native who had thrown the Melkanya's rope onto fire took out his leather jacket and waved it at the Melkanya to fan the flames. By this point, the Melkanya was totally engulfed in flames. The native kept waving his leather at the Melkanya, shouting, "Oh, my lord is burning! Let me help you!" The Melkanya burned to death.

Another technique the natives used was to set up the Melkanya. The natives, knowing which elephants and lions to hunt and which to avoid, would send the Melkanya to the wrong side of a dangerous elephant. The elephant, with its strong sense of smell, would sense the human danger and attack and kill the Melkanya. One Arsi Oromo who had done such a thing had to explain why his Melkanya didn't return. The Oromo cried out in Afan Oromo:

> *"My lord, My lord,*
> *You took a bull during your period,*
> *You took a buck during your period,*
> *You took container full of butter during your period,*
> *You took container full of honey during your period,*
> *There is nobody that didn't experience your injury."*

Assuming the native was crying over his friend's death, the Melkanya comforted him, saying, *"Ay homaa miti"*—"no worries."

The native replied, *"Isa ka du'eef hin boohu; isin ka hafeef booha malee."*—"I am not crying for the dead one; I am crying for you (the one that is still alive)."

The Melkanyas didn't speak Afan Oromo well. They were usually at a disadvantage because they had no clue what the natives were saying. These kinds of opportunistic resistance, which had been started by Lugo Usu, continued throughout the region.

*

After Lugo Usu passed away, his cousin Waayyu Teesso was crowned the next Qaallu. During this time, Islam was being introduced in the Dallo area. People who accepted Islam were punished by beating and considered *gosa keessaa bahe,* meaning "he left the tribe." It was the tribe's responsibility to bring that person back to his sanity.

Every tribe had multiple groups of eight young men, called *saddeeta.* The *saddeeta*'s role was to carry out the decision of their tribal leaders. In this case, when a person had confirmed to Islam, either through admission or a manifestation of the pillars of Islam (such as the five daily prayers), the tribe would send *saddeeta* to tie up the person and bring him for public punishment. He would be tied to the ground with his back and chest exposed. The *saddeeta* would pick new, long, straight branches of an *ulee* tree. Four saddeeta would stand on one side of the man, and four on the other side; they would beat the person until he either rejected Islam or collapsed.

Despite this violent penalty, many in the tribe who heard about Islam considered changing their way of life to the new religion. Most hid it from the community for fear of their tribe's punishment and loss of tribal protection. Things changed when Waayyu Teesso, the Qaallu of the Rahitu clan, accepted Islam. As Qaallu, he could not be persecuted like an ordinary person.

The tribe was confused about what to do and finally decided to allow him to become a Muslim. When the news of Waayyu Teesso's acceptance of Islam spread through the area, people who had wanted to accept Islam but had been afraid to do so asked the Qaallu for protection. He gave it, and within a few short years, almost the entire population of Arsi Oromo in Dallo had accepted Islam.

On one of his trips from village to village, Waayyu traveled on horseback with his friend Intale Shonko. A few hours into their trip, they realized they had been followed by two Melkanyas. Intale kept observing the two armed settlers. He told Waayyu that the Melkanyas had been following them since they left the village and asked what they should do. Waayyu immediately dismissed Intale's concern by answering his question with another question: "Are you afraid that these Amharas are going to kill us?"

Waayyu's dismissal of the threat posed by Melkanyas was a grave mistake. The Melkanyas were not bound by local ethics. They had no respect for Waayyu's culture or values. In fact, the Melkanyas despised his way of life. They tolerated Waayyu's advocacy for his people and his refusal to accept Christianity. However, for him to accept Islam was an insult to the government that wanted to impose its rule and religion on the natives. To make the matter worse, Waayyu had used his status to extend immunity to those who accepted Islam. The Melkanyas couldn't take it any longer. As Waayyu and Intale rode their horses down the hill into the Dayyuu River, the two

Melkanyas opened fire from behind. Waayyu was hit and died on the spot. Intale ran for his life. He escaped and lived to tell the story.

The community was devastated by the Melkanya's assassination of their leader, Waayyu. His assassination was not a random, impulsive action by the settlers. Every major decision like this was made by the emperor himself. Once again, the people had no means to bring the perpetrators to justice. For now they could only mourn. But you can imagine the rage inside the community. Their beloved leader had been killed by the settlers before their eyes.

Wako Lugo was most affected by this tragedy. He was a teenager at the time. He considered Waayyu a father figure. Waayyu loved him and often took him to various meetings with government officials and to tribal gatherings. Young Wako Lugo despised the settlers for taking Waayyu away too soon and pondered the day he would avenge Waayyu's death.

Waayyu had two sons, but his children were not old enough to be Qaallu. His brother Muhammad-Gada was crowned the next Qaallu. Muhammad-Gada was extremely handsome. People throughout the region talked about his beauty constantly. To this day, both women and men talk about his beauty. This is very unusual because Arsi Oromo people of the time were not known for complimenting each other about anything.

On his inauguration, sometime in the early 1930s, Muhammad-Gada immediately embellished his name by adding his new title: Muhammad-Gada-Qaallu. By this time, most Oromos in Dallo had stopped believing in the Qaallu institution; instead, they'd replaced Qaallu with an imam, a Muslim spiritual leader. Nevertheless, Muhammad-Gada-Qaallu continued to be the leader of his people, advancing the legacy of resistance started by Lugo Usu.

CHAPTER FOUR:
RESTORING OLD TRIBAL TIES AND FORGING NEW ONES

THE RAHITU CLAN LIVED IN DIFFERENT parts of the Bale zone. Muhammad-Gada-Qaallu lived in the Dallo and Madda Walabu areas, but the majority of the Rahitu clan lived in the Ginnir district, where there is a whole area named after them. The leader of the Rahitu in this region was Sultan Nuho Dadhi. "Sultan" was his title. It means "ruler" or "leader" of a sovereign state.

Sultan Nuho heard about the newly crowned Qaallu of Dallo and wanted to renew and strengthen their connections. Sultan Nuho sent a message to Muhammad-Gada-Qaallu, extending his congratulations and inviting him to Rahitu for a state visit.

Muhammad-Gada-Qaallu consulted his advisors and elders. The elders of Dallo knew about Sultan Nuho. He was a wise man and a seasoned leader who interacted not only with other Oromo and Somali tribes but also with the Arabs. Muhammad-Gada-Qaallu was known for his good looks and bravery, but he was not an eloquent speaker. The elders decided Muhammad-Gada-Qaallu should be accompanied by one other person who could compensate for this weakness. For this task, the elders chose Dire Irressa, the master of rhetoric.

Dire Irressa is my paternal grandfather. My paternal grandmother told me he was a tall, dark-skinned, bald man of a strong build. When I was a child, she used to hold my shoulders and say, "You're tall like him." I'm not that tall nor bald, at least not yet. But I appreciated her intentional effort to build my morale and emotionally connect me with my grandfather. She repeatedly told me that my grandfather was a very wise person. My grandmother made me realize that he was an important person even though I never got the chance to meet him. My father didn't get the chance to get to know him either.

Other than hearing stories from my grandmother, I had limited access to my paternal grandfather's history. My uncle Hangasu heard some stories about Dire from his father because Dire and Wako were friends. My uncle would describe my grandfather as an attorney general of the region. I also interviewed Adam Jilo, who admired Dire's eloquence as a young man growing up in Dallo. He told me that Dire was recognized in his community for his mastery of oral communication, logical argument, wisdom, and diplomacy. "By augmenting Muhammad-Gada-Qaallu with Dire, the elders wanted to ensure the Dallo Rahitu were well represented when they met with Sultan Nuho," Adam Jilo said.

The Dallo elders gave Muhammad-Gada-Qaallu and Dire rules of engagement for their meeting with Sultan Nuho. They told Muhammad-Gada-Qaallu to not respond to the Sultan directly. Instead, he was to ask Dire how to respond, then tell Nuho whatever Dire said.

Armed with these instructions, Muhammad-Gada-Qaallu accepted the invitation; he and Dire rode off on horseback to Rahitu. After a week of travel, the two reached their destination. Sultan Nuho welcomed them and threw a big feast for their reception. He invited the entire local Rahitu tribe to meet them.

This kind of meeting was usually conducted under a tree because there was no hall large enough to accommodate the population. The *oda* tree (sycamore) was considered an official symbol of the Oromo people because they used to conduct all of their affairs under this type of tree.

The locals were eager to hear from the new guests. They focused their attention on Sultan Nuho Dadhi, Muhammad-Gada-Qaallu, and Dire Irressa. Nuho announced to all, "These are our brothers from Dallo. They came to see you all."

Sultan Nuho asked two initial questions, then followed with two more. Dire told Gada how to respond every time.

Nuho: "When an obstacle hits one in the toe, where do you feel the pain?"

Gada whispered: "Dire, how should we respond?"

Dire: "You feel the pain in the thigh."

Gada: "You feel the pain in the thigh."

Nuho: "This big tree that we are sitting under, if you hit the trunk, where does it shake?"

Gada: "The branches shake."

Nuho: "The toe is the one that is hit. Why do you feel the pain in the thigh?"

Gada: "Because the roots are connected!"

Nuho: "The trunk of the tree was what was hit. Why did the branches shake?"

Gada: "Because its foundation is one."

Nuho declared: "The peak of Dhamole is Galbi. The origin of Rahitu is Galbi. That is the whole truth as God is witness!"

With those words, the meeting concluded. Nuho's message was intended to make sure the Dallo Rahitu did not forget where they came from and understood that their survival depended on each other. Whoever harmed them would be harming their brothers, wherever they happened to live. They were to stay connected and support each other as needed because their roots were connected and their foundation was one.

At the follow-up private meeting, the leaders also discussed the problems at hand, the subjugation of their people by the northerners and the natives' options for fighting back diplomatically and militarily. Nuho and his people experienced the same brutality from the settlers. They agreed to never allow the northerners' exploitation of their people. Muhammad-Gada-Qaallu and Dire returned to Dallo with more determination to stand up for their people.

Then tension between the northerners and southerners grew. The Arsi Oromos in the south saw the northern Amhara rule as a form of colonialism. The northerners saw the people in the south as backward pagans who should be ruled over and exploited. The Arsi Oromos in the south resented the situation.

The 1936 invasion of Ethiopia by Italy was a major assault on the emperor and the country's sovereignty. The invasion disrupted the status quo. The country lost its independence, and the emperor fled the country.

*

Before discussing the Italian period, it is important to understand the situation on the ground in the Bale and Sidamo zones of Ethiopia. Alliances were made among the different tribes to protect one another.

The Ganale River separates the Bale zone from the Sidamo zone (now Borana and Guji zones). Hangasu's family and extended family lived around this river. This river will be the center of the Bale Revolt in the 1960s.

The Ganale River was treated like an international border by its surrounding inhabitants in the days before Hangasu was born. In fact, the Oromo tribes who inhabited opposite sides of the river considered it *malkaa-seeraa*—a border river. Crossing it was not a trivial matter. Those who lived on the other side of the river were considered adversaries or, at the least, rivals.

My uncle told me a story about his biological great-grandfather, Warache, that illustrates this rivalry across the border and how tribes rewarded those who displayed courage and service to their people. Warache was a huge man (imagine

Shaquille O'Neal) who loved to chew tobacco. Tobacco was the trend of the time but was under attack because of the spread of Islam. Warache was one of the few who continued to chew tobacco. Those who accepted Islam made fun of his tobacco chewing habits and called him *galadi*, a Somali word meaning "nonbeliever."

On one occasion right before the rainy season, Warache led a raid south of the Ganale River. When he returned with cattle and other spoils, he found the river had overflowed its dry season banks. There was no bridge. The only way across the river was to swim, a risky proposition given the strong currents and the depth of the water. Being so tall, Warache could walk across the river. He could carry all his friends on his shoulders, and so he did, going back and forth to get everybody, but leaving those who had made fun of him on the other side. They begged him, "Brother Warache, please, please help us!" He took a lump of tobacco, chewed in front of them and spitted on his own palm. He then told them, "I can only help you if you lick this tobacco from my hand." They all licked, and he helped them cross the river.

The people went back to their village and told this story to the community. As a recognition for saving many lives from the enemy and the water, Warache was given the title *Wayyicha*, making him immune from any future punishment. This special honor for Warache and his family meant nobody could complain about him. If someone made a mistake and hid in Warache's house, that person would also be immune from any persecution by the tribe.

*

To understand the Bale Revolt, one must understand the Oromo population around the Ganale River and their relationship with the Somali tribes who lived in the same area.

Three major Oromo tribes lived in the Bale and Sidamo regions of Ethiopia: the Arsi, the Borana, and the Guji. These tribes are considered brothers. Each had its own territory; rivalry was the consequence. The Arsi tribe of Oromo inhabited the north side of the Ganale River, while the Guji and Borana tribes of Oromo inhabited the south side of the river. North of the Ganale was the Bale zone. South of the Ganale was the Sidamo zone. A tribe crossed the river at their own risk. No tribal law protected those who crossed from the opposite side. The only reason one tribe would cross to the other side was to raid another tribe to gain spoils (mostly cattle). The tribes took turns raiding one another at opportunistic times.

The Arsi tribe followed Islam. The Borana and Guji predominantly followed *Waaqeffanna*—the traditional Oromo way of life.

On the Bale side (particularly in the Madda Walabu district), other tribes lived with the Arsi Oromo. The story of their arrival was well remembered through oral history. According to the legend, some two hundred years ago, three Somali tribes (the Karalle, the Gurraa, and the Ajjuuran) migrated to Madda Walabu—the center of decision-making for the Oromo region—because of famine and drought in their country. The three tribes requested asylum from the Gada leaders.

The Arsi Gada leaders opened their homes to support the new immigrants. The leaders asked the community to collect food and drinks and cattle and goats to assist them. The Somalis and Oromos spoke common Cushitic languages (Afan Oromo and the Somali language are said to share up to 40 percent of their vocabularies), so they had a natural affinity. The Gada leaders wanted to fully integrate them into their community.

The Arsi tribe put together a "citizenship ceremony." The Arsi tribes and leaders attended. The Gada leaders granted full citizenship to each of the three Somali tribes. Each tribe was combined with another Arsi tribe: The Karalle tribe of Somali was combined with the Rahitu tribe of Arsi; the Gurraa tribe of Somali was combined with the Daawwee tribe of Arsi; and the Ajjuuran tribe of Somali was combined with the Wachaale tribe of Arsi.

Each new tribe was given a symbolic gift from the Gada leaders of Arsi. The gift was called *meedhicha*—a piece of animal skin. The gift was a kind of citizenship certificate. They were supposed to hang the gift on the wall of their houses. It was said that the leader of the Gurraa tribe threw away the gift right after the ceremony. He said, "I don't believe in this Arsi-Waaqeffanna thing; this is what nonbelievers do." While some Arsi still followed Waaqeffanna, the Somalis were Muslims and didn't agree with some of the cultural things the Arsi did, including giving *meedhicha* as a gift or citizenship certificate. Ever since, the Gurraa tribe has been known as a rebellious tribe. The Oromo elders still refer to this incident whenever somebody says or does something that is not culturally savvy. However, the Arsi and the Somali still had a lot in common.

As citizens, the Somali tribes became a fully integrated part of the Arsi community. The Arsi tribe is divided in two: Sikko and Mando, usually articulated as Sikko-Mando. Now the three Somali tribes—Karalle, Gurraa, and Ajjuuran—were called Sikko-Mando. They were guaranteed protection from external attacks. They were asked to strengthen kinship with the tribes they combined with and to fulfill the obligation of their fellow tribesmen. They were to fully integrate themselves into the community by learning Afan Oromo and adopting the new culture. They could do business and raise animals without any limitation. After a few years, the Arsi and Somali tribes were inseparable. They had bonds through marriage and business.

The Arsi and Somali tribes were allies living north of the Ganale River, and the Guji and Borana tribes were allies living on the south side of the Ganale River.

The Gutu Usu family was the first from the Bale Arsi tribe to cross the Ganale River with the intention of living permanently on the other side. Four other Arsi families joined them on this venture. The reason for the move was to explore the abundant grazing land for their cattle. The areas near the south side of the river were uninhabited because they were in the danger zone for sudden attacks from the other tribes.

At this time, Lugo Usu had passed away. His brother, Gutu Usu, was an old man. Wako Lugo was the adult in the Gutu family. Because Wako Gutu (the son of Gutu Usu) was a teenager, Wako Lugo played the role of an older brother. For the Arsi of the time, moving the entire family across the enemy line was a crime punishable by the tribe. It was a crime to put yourself or your family in danger. The Arsi elders summoned Gutu and demanded he bring the family back to Bale for their safety. He said, "We are not going back. I can defend my family. I won't seek your help." He simply refused the demands of his tribe.

The Arsi tribe didn't have power on the other side of the river, so the tribe left him alone. A year passed, and the Gutu and other families were still safe. More and more families decided to move to the other side in search of better and bigger grazing land for their cattle. The new families stayed together, still loosely organized as the Arsi tribe of Sikko-Mando.

The alliance, or lack thereof, of these different Oromo and Somali tribes would later be exploited by the Haile Selassie regime to divide and subjugate the people in the region.

CHAPTER FIVE:
EMPEROR HAILE SELASSIE

EMPEROR HAILE SELASSIE ASCENDED to power in 1930 after Empress Zawditu died. He had been Zawditu's regent and heir apparent since 1916. Haile Selassie's original name was Ras Tafari Makonnen. His father, Ras Makonnen, was the governor of the Harar province of Ethiopia. Haile Selassie ruled Ethiopia from 1930 to 1974. During this time, he dealt with the second Italian invasion internationally and a few peasant rebellions domestically.

While serving as Zawditu's regent, Haile Selassie managed to have Ethiopia join the League of Nations, a precursor to the United Nations, in 1923. The League of Nations was an international diplomatic group established after World War I to solve disputes between countries before they erupted into open warfare.

Italy had long held a colonial interest in East Africa. It had occupied Eritrea and some parts of Somalia since 1885. In 1895, the first Italo-Ethiopian war broke out over a "misunderstanding" of language in the Wuchale treaty. Italy believed the treaty gave them protectorate power over Ethiopia, whereas Ethiopia believed the treaty gave Italy no such power. In 1896, Ethiopia, led by Emperor Menelik II, decisively won the war at the battle of Adwa. Thus, Ethiopia remained an independent, sovereign country free from European colonization.

Forty years later, in 1935, the second Italo-Ethiopian war began. Italy already occupied Eritrea and Somalia, leaving Ethiopia as the obvious next victim. The League of Nations was unable to stop the war, partly because of European power dynamics. France and the United Kingdom, which dominated the league, wanted to keep Italy from joining forces with Nazi Germany. So France and the United Kingdom allowed Italy to do what it wanted to in Ethiopia. Ethiopia was isolated. Emperor Haile Selassie mobilized his army as much as he could, but the country was poorly prepared to fight Italy this time around.

On May 5, 1936, Italy took the capital, Addis Ababa (also known as Finfinne*). Emperor Haile Selassie was exiled and fled to Palestine and eventually to England. Mussolini named King Victor Emmanuel III of Italy the emperor of Ethiopia.

Italy's invasion of Ethiopia was bad for the sovereignty of Ethiopia, but ironically it was good for the subjugated Oromo people in the south. For the Arsi Oromos in the south, the invasion gave them a break from the oppressive regime. They didn't know much about the Italians, but they were open to change and willing to listen. Because the Arsi Oromos didn't resist the invasion, the Italians offered them a "free election" and freedom to use their own language in court and media. Both of these things were banned under the northerners' rule.

---

* The world knows the capital of Ethiopia as Addis Ababa. Addis Ababa means "new flower" in the Amharic language. The city's original name was Finfinne, meaning "natural spring" in the Oromo language. Both names are valid. Because this book is ultimately about amplifying the voice of the people, from here forward, I refer to the city as Finfinne.

*

In early 1936, far from Finfinne, Ethiopia's capital, life was good for the Arsi tribe on the Sidamo side of the Ganale River. The Arsi had only occasional clashes with the Guji or Borana tribes, mostly over grazing land and water. The Gutu family had limited interaction with the Ethiopian government on the Sidamo side. They mostly minded their own business and their cattle. Then, seemingly out of the blue, Italy invaded the country. The Amhara administrators and Melkanyas were driven out of the region. The Borana and Guji tribes stood with the Amhara and opposed Italy.

As Haile Selassie administrators, army, and supporters were driven out by the Italian army, the Arsi, now greater in number, saw an opportunity. The Arsi tribe decided to ally itself with Italy on the principle that the enemy of my enemy is my friend. The Arsi resisted Amhara rule when they were in Bale and were happy to see the Amharas and their Melkanyas driven out. The Arsi saw Italy's occupation of their country as temporary.

Years later, Hangasu asked his father, Wako Lugo, why they allied with Italy. His father responded, "We believed the white men wouldn't stay in the country forever. Sooner or later they will realize they don't belong here. On the other hand, we believed the Amhara would never leave the region and would subjugate our people permanently. These Amharas looked like us." Therefore, the Arsi Oromos in southern Ethiopia chose to ally with Italy, accepting short-term colonization for long-term liberty from both Italy and Haile Selassie's feudal system.

For their part, the Italians promised to bring about change. They promised that each community would have its own representative, elected by the people, rather than a representative appointed by Emperor Haile Selassie's government. However, though they preached self-representation and election, the Italians had a different idea about representation. When they invaded Ethiopia, they brought a militia called *banda*. These were Somali-recruited soldiers. Italy wanted these *banda* leaders to represent the people: Their definition of "self-representation" meant that *Somalis* loyal to the Italians would administer local affairs. This would allow the Italians to keep tabs on the region. The Somali leaders didn't pretend to represent the people, so the Arsi people complained to the governor for representation from their own people. The Italian governor of the Sidamo region agreed to establish real representation and elections.

Before the election, Italy had a peculiar way of selecting candidates in this part of the country. When a candidate was nominated by the community, the candidate was brought to the governor for an introduction. This meeting always took place in the governor's office, where the candidate was alone with the governor. As soon as the candidate entered the office, the governor would extend his hand for a handshake. When the candidate approached the governor and extended his hand, the governor would withdraw his hand and punch the candidate in the face, then beat the candidate while he remained confused. Candidates would go back to their community crying and extremely embarrassed. After this happened to a few candidates, nobody wanted to work with the Italians.

The governor wanted to discourage locals from running for office to represent their people; local representation would ruin his plan to put his *banda* in charge. The Arsi were not okay with this though. They wanted to hold the governor accountable for his words. They did not want a *banda* government and intimidation. They wanted a real election.

The Arsi Oromos needed a strong leader to represent them. However, they ran out of candidates. They had already brought a few candidates to the governor, but after the surprise beatings, none had wanted to go back. The Arsi got together and discussed how to address the governor's behavior. They wanted representation, but they didn't like how the Italian governor was treating their people. They had never seen this type of behavior with the Amhara settlers. The Amharas made them pay taxes and looted their properties, but they didn't beat up their representatives. The Arsi wanted someone who could stand up to the Italians. They decided to send Wako Lugo. They believed he was their last resort. He certainly wasn't the type to take a beating from the Italians.

The Arsi elders approached Wako Lugo with the proposal. They explained that there was nobody else who could stand up to the Italians and fairly represent them. Wako refused the offer, saying, "I am busy. I can't even attend to my cattle. I don't have children, as you know. I only have one daughter. I myself need help to tend my business."

The elders said, "If your problem is children, we will take care of this for you. Leave this to us." The elders believed that if they sincerely asked God for their needs or the needs of their people, God would respond in their favor.

One morning the Arsi elders secretly gathered all the community leaders and headed to Wako Lugo's house. The elders entered his house. Wako Lugo was completely shocked. This was part of the Arsi tradition, practiced only under desperate situations. When so many elders showed up at your house unannounced, it meant they were desperate. Whatever they need, the host must give it to them right away. The elders asked Wako Lugo to calm down and sit with them and simply repeat, "Amen." They collectively asked God to grant Wako more children. The famous line was, *"Kophee ilmaan teetii addaan haa wallaalan."* It means, "May your children multiply!" Wako figured out exactly what the elders were up to. He quickly slaughtered oxen for the elders and turned the gathering into a party. There and then, Wako accepted the elders' proposal to represent his people.

The next morning, as was customary, Wako went to introduce himself to the governor as the people's representative. This time everybody in the community wanted to know what was going to happen between Wako and the governor. People stayed close to the office for the news. As Wako entered the office, the governor stood behind his office table. The governor extended his hand. Wako approached, not knowing which way the interaction would go. When Wako extended his hands, the governor withdrew his hand and shouted, *"Vaffanculo!"* and tried to throw a punch as he usually did. Wako didn't speak Italian, but he gathered enough from the governor's body language and physical aggression to figure out the governor's intentions. Wako caught the governor's hand in midair, then punched the governor, throwing him all the way to the wall. The governor—who was likely stunned from Wako's strike—stayed near the wall for a few moments. Wako watched the governor and was prepared to punch him again, thinking that the Italian would rise and fight him. To his surprise, the governor stood, smiled, and shook his hand, this time shouting *"Bono, bono, bono!"* The governor gave Wako many gifts as a gesture of good faith and their agreement to work together.

Wako returned to his people, who were waiting outside, with gifts from the governor. The people celebrated. Just as the elders expected, Wako didn't let them down. A few days later, the governor announced that an election would be held to select the representative for the Arsi. The governor prepared one of the *banda* as a candidate, AbduRahman Muhammad Sheeka. The other candidate was, of course, Wako Lugo.

The election was conducted in a public meeting by raising hands. On the day of the election, the two candidates were introduced. The governor assigned people to count hands when the name of the candidate was called. The governor said, "Who here votes for AbduRahman Muhammad Sheeka?" Only one vote was recorded. Next, the governor said, "Who here votes for Wako Lugo?" Everyone except one raised their hand. The governor took Wako's hand and raised it, announcing "Wako— *Bono*! AbduRahman—*Blash*!"

At that moment, Wako Lugo launched his career in public service. Overnight he reluctantly went from an ordinary citizen to people's representative. Through this service, he earned the title of Ra'is Wako! (*Ra'is* means "leader" in Arabic.) His popularity and influence grew beyond the Sidamo zone. People loved his generosity and fairness. He was equally liked by the Arsi and Somali-Ethiopians.

Italy's invasion created a power vacuum in southern Ethiopia. Italy ruled Ethiopia for five short years. During this time, the locals had a break from the oppressive Ethiopian rule that had previously subjugated them. People experienced a different kind of governance. They also had access to rifles and ammunition from both the Italians and the Somalis.

The Oromo people spoke their own language in court to resolve their disputes. There was an Oromo-language program on the radio. All of these things had previously been banned by the Ethiopian government. Oromos didn't want to lose the temporary freedom they'd experienced under Italian rule. They wanted to do everything they could to prevent the return of Haile Selassie.

While in exile in England, Haile Selassie had sought the support of the Western democracies for his cause. He had little success until the Second World War began in September 1939. On June 10, 1940, Italy's Benito Mussolini declared war on France and Britain by attacking British and Commonwealth forces in Egypt, Sudan, Kenya, and British Somaliland. In August 1940, the Italian conquest of British Somaliland was completed. On April 6, 1941, British and Ethiopian troops drove the Italians out of Finfinne and restored Emperor Haile Selassie as head of the Ethiopian government.

Haile Selassie's return to throne in 1941 was celebrated by the Ethiopian feudals and their international allies, who saw Italy's invasion as an assault on one of the oldest countries in the world.

For the Arsi Oromos in the south, his return was a nightmare. It meant the northerners' rule was back, which meant colonialism was back. The Arsi Oromos were not about to accept that. At the same time, the emperor wanted to punish those who had sided with the Italians and to reward those who had fought for him during the invasion.

In what seemed like a sudden move to the locals, the Italians left the country. This news was as bad for the Arsi Oromos as it was for the Italians. The Arsi couldn't imagine accepting the Amhara rule again. As soon as the Italians were gone, Wako Lugo decided to return to his original home of Bale. He appointed his cousin Chamari Gutu to represent the people in his place. He knew the only place with a chance of resisting Amhara rule was Bale.

Bale was geographically isolated because of the Ganale, Welmal, and Wabe rivers, as well as mountains and forests. The Bale people were also more ethnically homogeneous and were determined not to accept Amhara rule. Wako moved back to Bale with his family permanently. By this time, he had married a second wife and had two boys in addition to his eldest daughter. The Arsi Oromo elders' blessing had worked.

Haile Selassie reinitiated the feudal system established by Emperor Menelik II after he had invaded and incorporated the region into modern Ethiopia in the late 1890s. Under the feudal system, the population was divided into two groups: landlord and tenants. The northerners (Amhara and Tigre) became landlords, and the native southerners became tenants.

On the Bale side, Muhammad-Gada-Qaallu (the gorgeous) had been the people's representative during Italy's occupation. He had worked alongside the Italians as the people's representative, just as Wako Lugo had. In 1943, after the Italians left and the Ethiopians returned to restore their power, Muhammad-Gada-Qaallu organized an army of between sixty and seventy men to prevent the return of the Ethiopian army to Dallo. He gathered his people at the Welmal River, in a place called Melka-Roqa, located north of the Madda Walabu district.

The Ethiopian army was unaware of the planned ambush. When they reached Melka-Roqa, Gada's army fired at their military vehicles. The army jumped from the vehicles and positioned themselves to fight back. Muhammad-Gada-Qaallu's army was already in place and had been watching them the whole time. After a brief but intense fight, the Welmal River was full of dead Ethiopian soldiers. The few soldiers who'd survived the battle fled in their military vehicles. Ethiopians soldiers were called "Amhara" by the locals in those times. Thus, on that day, the locals from Dallo changed the name of that location from Melka-Roqa to Melka-Amhara. Muhammad-Gada-Qaallu and his army celebrated their victory.

Witin a few days, the Ethiopian army returned with reinforcements. By this time, Gada's army had returned home. The Ethiopian army reoccupied Dallo and Madda Walabu without resistance. After the military secured the territories, the government sent civilian administrators to return things to the status quo. Gebre Selassie, one of the civilian leaders appointed by the emperor who was on the run and in hiding during the Italian period, returned to power. His first priority was to persecute those who had supported the Italians and had been involved in the Melka-Amaaraa battle. Because he was from the area, he quickly discovered the whereabouts of Muhammad-Gada-Qaallu and his men. He had them all arrested and sent to the Goba prison.

My grandfather, Dire Irressa, wanted to try a different approach. He sought a diplomatic route for resolving the regional conflict. He organized the elders of Dallo to appeal for Muhammad-Gada-Qaallu's release and to request the removal of Gebre Selassie from the government post he held. For this mission, he took the elders to Goba to speak with Gebre Selassie's superiors.

Dire made the case that the military encounter with Muhammad-Gada-Qaallu at Melka-Roqa was a misunderstanding. Dire explained, "The people of Dallo and, for that matter, the people of Bale want peace. However, Gebre Selassie is propagating instability in the region through his vindictive impulse, and peace can't be achieved under these circumstances. We demand two things: One, release Muhammad-Gada-Qaallu; two, replace Gebre Selassie with somebody we can work with on a peace accord. If these two demands were met, we are prepared to pay taxes, and things will go back to normal."

Dire and his peers were told to stay in Goba and wait until these superiors received an official decree from the emperor. A few days later, Gebre Selassie arrested Dire and his comrades, and they joined Muhammad-Gada-Qaallu in the Goba prison. The emperor had no interest in negotiating; he wanted to crush everyone who showed the slightest sign of rebellion. The elders were held there for a decade without any due process.

My grandmother went back and forth between Bidire and Goba, bribing this official and that official to no avail. The emperor ordered their execution by hanging in 1960. By then, the emperor was paranoid perhaps because of the attempted coup d'état in the capital city by his own Imperial Guard. He eliminated all his opposition at once, regardless of whether they were connected to the coup or not. That decade concluded with the assassination of Bale leaders who sowed and carried the flame of resistance to protect the dignity of their people. The graves of those heroes are nowhere to be found to this day. But their sacrifices didn't go to waste. Their brethren continued the struggle.

I never had the chance to know my grandfather, Dire Irressa. He was imprisoned for a decade and then assassinated. Neither did my father get the chance to get to know him; my father was my grandfather's only child and an infant when my grandfather was jailed. My grandmother raised my father alone. She was kind and intelligent. She maintained relationships with some of Dire's close friends like Wako Lugo and eventually persuaded Wako to arrange for his daughter to marry her son, a proposal Wako Lugo gladly fulfilled.

CHAPTER SIX:
WAKO LUGO AND THE RESISTANCE

WHEN WAKO LUGO RETURNED to Bale, specifically to Dallo, he remained popular. People talked about his generosity and fairness in Nagele, Sidamo, when he represented his people to the Italians. He was quickly appointed to be the people's representative for his clan— Rahitu—in Dallo. He reluctantly accepted and continued his public service. His primary responsibilities were to strengthen the relationship between the government and the general population and to collect taxes. People in Dallo were primarily pastoralists, not farmers. The tax on pastoralists was not as clear as it was for farmers. Comparatively, the pastoralists paid fewer taxes than did the landowners. The Melkanyas and emperor's administrators exploited this loophole by adding bribes on top of the taxes. They kept the bribes for themselves.

When it came time for tax collection, Wako Lugo would ask the exact amount due from his constituents and pay their taxes from his own wealth; then his constituents would pay him directly. Most people in Dallo didn't want to deal with the government.

Wako was loved both by the government and the people. The government loved him because he paid taxes immediately. This was unusual because other representatives would have to go to each person and collect the taxes and then pay the government, which took time. The people loved Wako because he didn't chase them for their taxes; they could pay him at their convenience. Because of this arrangement, most people voluntarily paid double or triple what he had paid on their behalf.

Wako continued to serve on behalf of the people in the Dallo district in the Bale zone. For the first time in his adult life, he was exposed to the ugly side of the Ethiopian feudal system. His father had told him stories of how the Ethiopian government had abused local natives and attempted to subjugate the Oromo people prior to Italy's invasion, but this was the first time Wako experienced it directly. He remembered when Melkanyas killed his dear uncle, Waayyu. Wako was a teenager then. Now, he witnessed firsthand the abuses the northern settlers were committing against local citizens on a daily basis. Haile Selassie personally appointed people he trusted and who demonstrated loyalty to him to different areas of the country. Empowered by the emperor himself, his governors and representatives acted like gods. They expected the locals to serve them like they were kings.

Amharization was one of the key policies Emperor Haile Selassie implemented to win over the critical population. Amharization primarily meant forcing people to accept Orthodox Christianity and adopt the Amhara culture and language. These policies helped the Amhara regimes expand their influence in Oromo regions. This policy worked in the predominantly Oromo regions of Wollo and Shawa; today Wollo is not considered part of the Oromo region because the Wollo people were systematically disconnected over time and swallowed by the Amhara and Tigre. The Wollo remain a threatened minority, subjected to ongoing ethnic cleansing and theft of their lands because it has been effectively cut off from the rest of the Oromo territories. Though they lost significant people and land, the Wollo through sheer determination and conscious acts of resistance have managed to maintain their language, culture, and ways of life.

The assimilated Shawa Oromo elites played a key role in helping spread Amharization. Amharization was a way to impose the Amhara hegemony by ensuring that the entire population would be controlled by one institution—the Ethiopian Orthodox Church. The emperor himself sat at the helm of the church, allowing him to benefit and extend his power. From the emperor's perspective, the plan was sound. After all, it had largely worked in Wollo and Shawa. Surely it would work in other parts of the country as well. His country was all one kingdom, correct?

Not so fast.

In the Bale zone, the government began implementing this one-size-fits-all Amharization policy. The Ethiopian government wanted to tap into the organizational structure of the Oromo people. The Oromo people in general, and particularly the Bale people, were a communal society. People were organized under the Gada system of governance. Each tribe was represented by a tribal leader, who was appointed and confirmed by the tribe. The tribal leaders had a council of elders who advised them on the issues of the time.

The Ethiopian government's assumption was that if the tribe leader could be convinced to accept Amharization, whether through position, bribes, promises of riches, friendship with the emperor, or whatever it took, the rest of the population would follow suit. This would allow the government to control the entire population with minimal resources and without bloodshed.

What the government overlooked or underestimated was that almost all the people in the Bale zone were already Muslims. Amharization would not only require them to change their way of life, it would also mean changing their religion. The notion of replacing the religion they had chosen for themselves with the religion of an oppressor they neither liked nor respected was unthinkable. Therefore, they would rather die than convert to Christianity or adopt the Amhara culture.

Even though the government offered lucrative jobs, impressive titles, and generous wealth to the tribal leaders to convert to Christianity, this attempt was dead in its tracks before it even began. In the entire Bale zone, only three people converted to Christianity to get ahead and gain government jobs.

The Amharization plan would have worked if everyone in the country believed in one religion, spoke one language, and revered the same leaders. But the people of Ethiopia didn't follow the same religion. People followed Christianity, Islam, and traditional religions like Waaqeffanna. The people of Ethiopia didn't speak one language; they spoke more than eighty languages. Each ethnic group had its own language and culture. The emperor's plan dismissed the country's diversity and blindly imposed the Amhara hegemony.

The government felt defeated, at least in Bale, because the Amharization didn't work. The government shifted its efforts toward controlling the population through force. The governors and other administrative and military officials were fully empowered to subjugate the population to their will by abusing, beating, jailing, or killing them if necessary. One way the government attempted to subjugate the people was by assigning several settlers from the north to every village. The settlers, police, and administrative officials together executed the will of the emperor.

A key duty of these officials was to collect taxes from the native population. Tribal leaders were responsible for collecting the taxes from their tribesmen and turning the money over to the government officials. It was not easy for the tribal leader to go to everybody in his tribe to collect the tax. It meant he had to leave his work and family, and he had to do so without pay. If taxes were delinquent, the tribal leader and his constituents would go to prison and have to pay a delinquency fee in addition to the taxes. Sometimes, if the taxes were delinquent and could not be paid locally, the tribal leader had to go to the higher authorities at the zone level and pay bribes to the officials; these bribes could be even more expensive than the taxes and delinquency fees themselves.

Part of the reason for making it hard for people to pay taxes was to humiliate the natives, especially their tribal leaders. The government was already bureaucratic, but these officials added more layers to show the people their Amhara superiority. They were so arrogant that they wouldn't even accept taxes from someone like Wako Lugo, who was willing to pay the government from his own wealth to avoid delinquency and time wasted chasing his tribesmen for taxes. Wako himself had to regularly pay bribes to these officials so he could pay the taxes. These officials were often younger, entitled, and hubristic Amhara or Tigre settlers and administrators; paying bribes to these men was an insult and humiliation to the tribe leaders and to Wako's people. These officials and settlers viewed the population as backward and therefore deserving of subjugation. If that was the message the government officials wanted to propagate, the people of Bale heard it loud and clear.

The people of Dallo (and perhaps more generally, the Oromo people in southeast Ethiopia) felt powerless. The larger population in Dallo became a sitting duck. This contrasted with the settlers, who maneuvered throughout the region freely, armed and empowered by the government. There was no court in which the natives could find justice. Instead, they were often humiliated on their own land by foreigners. The natives started convening secret meetings to find solutions to their predicament. One thing was clear: The natives refused to accept inferiority on their own land. They knew full well that they were born free and would not accept subjugation by foreigners. They agreed to silently eliminate the settlers.

The natives planned a series of silent attacks in key towns and villages to deter the settlers from attacking the natives. The hope was that once the settlers no longer felt safe, they could be driven from the region. The natives had the advantage of numbers; there were far more of them than settlers and administrators.

Sometime in the mid-1950s, the natives carried out a silent attack throughout the Dallo district. They'd secretly plotted to eliminate all the settlers in their area in a single night. To achieve this, every head of household who had a settler assigned to his house would kill the settler on the agreed-upon night.

Settlers moved around freely during the day and relied on the natives for food and shelter in the evenings. The settlers ordered whatever they wished, and the natives had to deliver. One of the foods the settlers craved most was lamb and its fat tail. The natives slaughtered sheep when they wanted to impress the settlers; the settlers took this gesture as an honor.

The natives thought they could turn the settlers' love for lamb tail to their advantage. From experience and ancient folklore, the natives knew that eating lamb fat in excess, especially for dinner and when followed by sleep, had a comforting and drowsy effect. By feeding the settlers fatty lamb meat, the settlers would be weakened. This would allow the natives to strike the settlers with their knives before they could grab their rifles.

This plan was carried out in many villages and was quite successful. Travelers passing through spread the word about the settlers' deaths, which played to the natives' advantage. Within a few days, everyone in the district would know what had happened. Village leaders had eyes and ears everywhere. Culturally, the Oromo people loved news. People would literally sit on major roads to get information. When a traveler passed on a road or through a village, the locals would ask who he was, where was he coming from, where he was going and why, and what the big news was. The traveler would gladly share all he knew while enjoying a drink or food offered to him before he continued his journey.

In one of the villages near Bidire town, called Qarari, one such plan was put into motion by Wako Lugo. There were three settlers in this village. The three heads of households in the village (Wako and his two friends) met in secret and decided on the night and exact time to execute the plan.

That evening they each slaughtered the fattest sheep they could find. They each fed their settlers the lamb meat, especially the fatty tail. Wako sat with his settler and encouraged him to eat more. He probably told the man how special that sheep had been to him. Relaxed and drowsy, the settlers went to bed before midnight. When the appointed time came, the natives gave the signal to strike. This was the moment they had prepared for. Their knives were sharp, and the night was pitch-black.

Wako walked into the house where the settler was and immediately killed him with one strike to the neck. His friend next door did the same. But his other friend struggled. The settler woke up and resisted. The friend called Wako for help, saying, "My brother, Wako, the settler overcame me! He is on top of me, please *help*!"

Wako ran to help. In the darkness, Wako swung his knife at the settler's head. To his horror, his friend cried out, saying, "My brother, you finished me!" Seconds before Wako entered, the settler had rolled to the bottom, knowing Wako would expect him to be on top. His ploy worked.

Wako engaged the settler in hand-to-hand combat as his friend lay dying on the floor. Minutes later, the settler was dead, and Wako turned his attention to his friend. He and other friends tried to help their injured brother, but his injury was too serious.

That morning on his deathbed, Wako's friend summoned his tribe's elders. He explained to his people what had happened: that Wako had come to help but was not at fault. He commanded his tribe to honor his wishes and bury this issue with him. Later that day, the man died, and his tribesmen complied with his wishes. The community came together and made peace with each other and said farewell to the deceased.

Wako was devastated. He cried all night long and blamed himself for the rest of his life, even though there was nothing he could have done to prevent the unfortunate outcome.

Killing a settler was an act of resistance. The community justified it based on what these settlers had done to them. The settlers had humiliated them on their own land, robbed them, looted their property, and entered their homes (their sacred place) as they wished and when they wished. The natives believed they had the right to defend their homes, property, and dignity.

In fact, Wako's father, Lugo Usu, was the first person to kill a settler who had disrespected him and looted his house some forty years earlier. Lugo's action had a ripple effect in spreading resistance throughout the region. Of course, Wako remembered when Melkanyas killed his dear uncle, Waayyu, the leader of his community. At a minimum this event was about avenging his uncle. However, more broadly, the goal was to drive the settlers out of the Bale rural areas before they established a strong foothold. When examined more than half a century later, these acts of resistance had achieved their goal; northern settlers never really settled in the Bale rural area. That made Bale different from the rest of the regions—*its people never yielded to the oppressors from the north.*

Life continued after the event in Wako's village. Within a day or so, the news of the dead native and the three disappeared settlers reached the local government. The administrators, who still respected Wako, initially ignored the rumor that he was behind the attacks. There was no evidence to prosecute him. In addition, the natives would never give up one of their own— especially Wako, who'd taken care of them and stood for them in tough times.

With time, higher-ranking administrators got more suspicious about Wako's intention. The attacks on settlers continued throughout the region. The administrators suspected he had to know something about the ongoing attacks in his district. He denied knowing anything about the assaults. Eventually Wako's relationship with the government grew sour.

*

As the chief of Dallo, Wako traveled to cities to interact with businesspeople, governors, and government representatives. He was very aware of what was going on in Ethiopia. Among the businesspeople he met was a merchant named Sheikh Ahmed

Musa. Sheikh Ahmed was an ethnic Tigri-Werji. The word Tigri comes from the Arabic term *tijaari*, which means "merchant." The tribal name *Werji* indicates their ancestral homeland. Tigri-Werji, therefore, means merchant of Werji.

To this day, all Werjis are Muslims. Sheikh Ahmed Musa came from a family of *ulama*—religious educators and teachers of Islam. Sheikh Ahmed's ancestors lived in the Shawa province in Dalatti, Sabbata, and Gaara Rogge. Sheikh Ahmed had two brothers, Ibrahim and Dawud. Their father, Musa, passed away when they were little. Ibrahim, the oldest of the three, traveled as a teenager to Wollo province (Dawe Woreda) in the northeastern part of Ethiopia to study Islam. At the time, Wollo was the epicenter of Islamic studies.

After a few years of study, Ibrahim decided to return to Dalatti to teach his people what he had learned. The Werji people adhered to the Islamic traditions apart from one ritual that didn't quite fit the Islamic tradition: drinking during special occasions.

Ibrahim had forgotten about this drinking ritual while away from his hometown. When he returned, Ibrahim was shocked by the behavior of his tribe. On special occasions such as weddings, people drank intoxicants called *qaribo* (also known as barley wine). After one of these weddings, the young Ibrahim gathered his tribe and advised them to stop drinking wine because it was prohibited in the Quran. Everybody nodded and moved on.

Ibrahim believed they would heed his advice, but the tribe's response was one of understanding. They acknowledged they should probably not drink, but nobody took him seriously. After all, he was a little boy. Ibrahim had underestimated how deeply ingrained the ritual of drinking during weddings was in the community.

Another wedding came along. To young Ibrahim's surprise, his people drank just as they had before. It was a full-fledged drinking party. This time Ibrahim walked into the middle of the wedding party and asked for the people's attention. "Didn't you promise me that you would stop drinking?" he asked.

By now, the intoxicated elders were annoyed and responded, "Get out of here! How dare you talk to us like this? Who do you think you are?" They reproached him with an Oromo proverb: "*Osoo baala hin baasin, qoree baase,*" meaning that Ibrahim was like a tree branch that grew thorns before growing leaves. They used this proverb when someone overstepped their cultural boundaries.

Ibrahim decided to migrate away from the tribe he believed was indulging in a prohibited ritual. The next morning he took his two brothers, Ahmed and Dawud, and headed south. He settled in Bale province, Sinana Dinsho Woreda. He found that Bale was more receptive to the teachings of Islam. Ibrahim began teaching Islam and eventually became one of the most-recognized scholars in Bale. He was known as Haji Ibrahim of Bale. Ahmed studied the religion under his brother's wing. He earned the title Sheikh Ahmed. The term *sheikh* is a title given to someone who studied the religion beyond the basics, while the title *haji* is given to someone who performed pilgrimage (hajj) to Makkah. Sheikh Ahmed decided to become a businessman, continuing the ancestral tradition. Dawud (later Haji Dawud), the youngest brother, stayed at home to help his mother when she joined them in Bale.

Wako admired the Werji merchants' business ethics and adherence to the Islamic faith, and he proposed to marry Fato, Sheikh Ahmed's daughter. Fato was born in 1930 in a village called Oborraa in Sinana Woreda, five years before the second Italian invasion and occupation of Ethiopia. She was the middle child of nine. She was barely 5 feet tall, light skinned, a fast walker, and sharp of mind and tongue. If she had practiced law, very few attorneys would have dared to challenge her. She could instantly dominate any conversation with witty comments or authoritative commands.

Wako had already built a reputation for himself as a hero and chief of his people. His proposal to marry Fato was quickly accepted. Sheikh Ahmed agreed to wed Fato to Wako sometime around 1950. Fato was approximately 20 years old when they married; Wako was 45. Fato was from a merchant family and lived in a city. Wako was a pastoral chief. The two married in

Goba, Bale. As was Werji tradition, on the wedding day when the groom leaves with the bride, the ushers sang a cultural song. During this ceremony, somebody from the bride's side hides and sprays red pepper into the groom's eyes—one last (painful) memory of the wedding day for the groom. Fato's family was excited to witness this moment. They wanted to see Wako Lugo, the great chief of Arsi, in tears.

When the moment came, Wako galloped through the line of wedding attendants on his horse with his bride at his back. The bride's family had no chance to spray the pepper. Wako had studied the culture and spared his eyes. Later that day, his friends told him what he did was culturally insensitive. He responded by saying, "They should look for their next victim; as for me, I escaped their little scheme."

The couple moved to Bidire in the Bale zone of Ethiopia. Fato had two children. Their daughter, Zamzam (my mom), was born in 1953; their son, Hangasu, in 1956. As was common in a pastoral community, their exact birth dates are unknown.

CHAPTER SEVEN:
HANGASU'S EARLY LIFE

A T BIRTH, HANGASU'S FATHER named my uncle Ahmed; his mother named him Hangasu. According to tradition, more names are better because they show a family's love and affection for the child. Other family members and even neighbors chime in too. Fato's brother, Sheikh Yahya, wanting to reconcile the two names given to his newborn nephew, came up with the name Ahmed-Berq. *Berq* is an Arabic term for lightning, just as *Hangasu* is in Oromo. Hangasu emerged as the most popular name because it was unique. When Hangasu learned about his three names, he, too, preferred Hangasu and kept it because nobody else had that name. It felt very special to a young boy who wanted to be different. As is the custom in that part of the region, parents were addressed as the father or mother of their eldest son. As such, people addressed Fato as *Haadha Hangasu*, the mother of Hangasu.

Fato saw two generations grow up in Bidire in the house where my uncle was born. Even though, as children, Hangasu and Zamzam witnessed the Ethiopian government and Bale fighters bomb their home in Bidire and almost burn it to the ground, Fato would live to tell her grandchildren, "Your uncle Hangasu was born right here under this big branchy *garbi* tree."

Fato was a woman of strong will. She didn't believe in delegating anything. She cooked for herself and her guests into her late eighties and early nineties. She loved telling folk stories to her grandchildren and great-grandchildren at night.

Bidire was a small, old town. Three roads lead away from Bidire: north to Dallo Manna, east to Madda Walabu, and west to Nagele, Borana. In those days, they were all dirt roads. During the rainy season, they would be thick with mud and difficult to travel. To the south, the middle of the countryside was a short walk away.

Bidire had many dogs. It was easy for Hangasu and his friends to feed the dogs and lure them to go hunting. Like his father, young Hangasu loved hunting. Hangasu and his friends would train the dogs to hunt monkeys, pigs, and any other prey they could find. They made arrows from branches and would signal the dog by throwing the arrow toward the prey.

There was no formal education in Bidire. Instead, Hangasu was enrolled in religious education like many children in his town. There, he learned how to read and write the Quran in Arabic. After school, he and his friends would make a ball out of torn socks stuffed with papers and other clothes and play soccer or *doorso*, where they rolled a hollow wheel or rim called a *korbo* like a moving tire. In doorso, the participant threw a wooden spear, aiming to pass the arrow through the hollow section. Hangasu would cherish these wonderful memories his entire life. For the remainder of his days, his face filled with joy whenever he reminisced of these days as a child in Bidire.

From an age before Hangasu could remember, Wako took him on his trips from village to village to attend tribe gatherings. Hangasu loved his father and wanted to please him very much; during these journeys, Hangasu started *salah*, the Muslim five daily prayers, with his father. For the rest of

Hangasu's life, the *salah* always brought up the memory of his father.

On these trips Hangasu matured beyond his young years, listening to the discussions among the elders. He was naturally inquisitive and asked many questions that his father patiently answered.

Through this quality time spent with his father, their relationship grew strong. Hangasu knew he was special in his father's eyes. Hangasu would recall, "When my dad wanted something, he would call me first. Only if I was not around to respond would he call other children." Hangasu added, "Part of it was, back in the days, I slept pretty lightly. I would hear when my dad called—even if it was in the middle of the night. My brothers had a deep sleep." The fact that his father spent extra time with him and that he called him first before calling his siblings validated to Hangasu that his father loved him very much.

Hangasu also recalled, "My father used to discipline his kids." Discipline meant a beating. He confessed, "My dad never disciplined me. I do not know why." My mom, Zamzam, confirmed this story with a minor correction. "There was one time," she said. "I don't remember what Hangasu did, but my dad did beat him. It was a total surprise to us all. We never saw him beat Hangasu before."

That night Wako's horse was eaten by a lion. Wako would never again beat Hangasu. My mom thought, "He must be *qaallu*." By that, she meant he was special. Maybe there was a reason her father never disciplined him. In ancient times, people observed their surroundings and were in tune with their environment. There were very few distractions. Coincidences, like that of Hangasu getting beaten by his father and the horse getting eaten by a lion on the same night, would be analyzed. People would look for the connection between the two events.

At a very early age, Hangasu learned what his father liked and what he did not like. Hangasu recalls his father hated lies, cowardice, stealing, *cubbu* (the harming of an innocent person, animal, or environment), and stinginess. Hangasu recalled, "When my dad gave commands to his children or the public, he spoke very clearly. If he saw something was wrong, he couldn't ignore it. He would take it upon himself to correct it on the spot." This meant confronting the wrongdoer and bringing justice to the victim.

I would say the same thing about Hangasu today. If he encountered a situation where injustice was done to others or to himself, he would address it head on. He would speak truth to power, even when speaking the truth wouldn't serve him well. As the old adage goes, "like father, like son."

Hangasu also observed that his father took special care of the poor and guests. "Guests and travelers regularly stayed at his house." His father would slaughter a cow for the guests, which was a show of his generosity. If the family happened to have *sadaqa*, a charity feast for neighbors, friends, and the needy, his father would personally serve the guests.

Wako Lugo would divide the guests into three groups: adult men, adult women, and children. This was not typical, according to Hangasu. Traditionally, there were only two groups: men and women, and children ate with the women.

Hangasu was curious, so he asked his father why he separated people into three groups. His father responded, "Women usually don't eat when they are with their children. Children are ruthless. They would eat their portion and their mother's portion." That made sense to Hangasu. There is a saying in Amharic that roughly translates to: "Eat and sleep before you have children." With Wako's way, women were able to eat in peace. Quite a surprise, coming from Wako Lugo, the masculine, battle-tested elephant killer.

Wako Lugo was certainly great at people management. He was known for his honesty, integrity, and generosity. He loved his people and his land. Hangasu's observations of his father's treatment of others helped shape his view of the world.

CHAPTER EIGHT:
THE FORCED EVICTION

B Y THE EARLY 1960S, Emperor Haile Selassie was an international celebrity. He was considered an elder statesman in Africa. In 1923, he managed to enlist Ethiopia in the League of Nations (the predecessor to the United Nations). Haile Selassie gained international fame in 1936 when he gave a speech before the League of Nations against Italy's aggression. The league was unable to help. While Haile Selassie lost the League's support, he won the world's sympathy. In 1963, Haile Selassie was the chief founder of the Organization for Africa Union (OAU), which is headquartered in Ethiopia's capital, Finfinne.

Haile Selassie also developed a special relationship with the United States. Between 1954 and 1973, Selassie made six official state visits to the United States. During these visits he met with four US presidents: Dwight D. Eisenhower, John F. Kennedy, Lyndon Johnson, and Richard Nixon. The US–Ethiopian relations were outlined at Kagnew Station, a military base in Eritrea. Ethiopia gave the United States a long-term lease of

Kagnew Station. In return, the United States pledged to provide economic and military assistance to Ethiopia. During the 1950s and 1960s, the United States trained and equipped Ethiopia's army.

But domestic challenges were looming for the emperor. In 1960, his own Imperial Guard attempted a failed coup d'état. The coup stemmed from the lack of political and economic progress. Factions within his government saw a huge gap between what the future should be and where Haile Selassie was headed: maintaining a system where the church and government owned everything and people prostrated themselves to another human being—the emperor.

Haile Selassie's behavior toward his subjects was fascinating during this time. To those beneath him on the hierarchical scale (everybody in the country), his behavior remained aloof and majestic. The emperor usually received visitors while seated in a room with one chair: his own. Everyone stood while addressing him. He demanded strict protocol. People had to bow (prostrate themselves) before addressing him as "His Majesty Janoy." In the presence of his subjects, Haile Selassie behaved every bit as a god descended to earth, projecting a culturally protected aura of power and divinity.

*

Far from the capital city, in the Sidamo zone, the situation was more explosive. The Arsi Oromo who lived in the city of Nagele were ordered to return to Bale or leave the country.

On July 1, 1960, Somalia gained its independence from Italy, and the Somali Republic was formed. Ethiopia prides itself on being the only African country to never be colonized (despite the fact that Italy ruled the country for five years; Ethiopians, especially the elites, don't recognize the Italian rule) and on the fact that they defeated the Italians twice. This was, of course, the external game—Ethiopia wanted to be viewed as a role model of independence for the rest of Africa. The internal game was very different. The emperor was insecure. Ethiopia was a vast land with diverse communities. These lands and people were held together by force and cunning negotiation. For example, the Ogaden region of Ethiopia was moved to Ethiopia's territory during the colonial period in 1889 by King Melelik II after lengthy negotiations with the colonial powers (Britain, France, and Italy). The southeast region of Oromia was also incorporated into Ethiopia around the same time by force.

The Ethiopian government understood that an independent Somalia meant a destabilized Ethiopia. The government knew that Somalis lived in Ethiopia in large numbers, and the government wanted to limit their influence in Ethiopia. The government in Nagele decided the best course of action was to remove the Somalis from Nagele. That meant the Somalis must go back to Somalia.

The city of Nagele Borana, in the Sidamo zone, was a melting pot even back then. All kinds of ethnic groups lived there: the Oromos (Borana, Guji, Arsi), the Amharas, the Somalis, the Gurages, the Worjis, the Konsos, the Kambatas, and more. In those times, people had tribal alliances that protected them from internal and external enemies. For example, the Arsi Oromos had alliances with the Somalis. The Arsi in Bale had already made a few Somali tribes one of their own through alliance and integration. The Arsi Oromos and the Somalis shared one religion—Islam. On the other hand, the Borana Oromo and the Guji Oromo never really welcomed the Arsi Oromo in the Sidamo region. They felt that the Arsi Oromos had taken over their land and continued to spread Islam, which they opposed. The Sidamo zone-based Ethiopian government understood this tribal dynamic well.

With this knowledge at hand, the government declared that the Somalis needed to leave Nagele City immediately and return to Somalia. Most of the people ordered to leave had lived in Nagele almost all their lives. The Arsi Oromos intervened and objected to the declaration. They said, "Somalis are our brothers. They are not going anywhere."

This was what the government had wished for all along—to see the Arsi Oromo ally themselves with Somalis. The government amended the declaration. "Somalis must go back to their country, Somalia; Arsi Oromos must return to Bale. Neither the Somalis nor the Arsi Oromos belong here." To the Arsi Oromos, this sounded as though an invader from the north was telling them to leave their home. Bale, or Sidamo, is all Oromo land. The Arsi Oromos thought if anyone should leave the city, it should be the Amhara government. They were the ones who didn't belong.

The Arsi Oromos ignored the government's order to evacuate the city. At the same time, the Arsi Oromos held secret meetings to come up with potential solutions. They knew that sooner or later the government would use force to implement its orders. After a series of secret meetings in Sidamo and in Bale (Madda Walabu), they came to a conclusion: They agreed to defend themselves. Several people bought guns to protect their families.

Meanwhile, the Ethiopian government heavily armed the Borana and Guji Oromos with rifles to drive out the Arsi Oromos. The Ethiopian government had learned a few tricks from the colonial powers, including that of dividing and conquering the Oromo people. Borana and Guji executed the commands of the Ethiopian government against their own brothers. They killed children and women wherever they found them. A man named Isaaq Sude was killed and skinned, and his head was delivered to the family.

The Arsi Oromos held an emergency meeting where they decided that Arsi families must return to Bale because they didn't have enough power to withstand the government force. The few guns they had were assigned to escort the families to Bale. The Arsi considered their eviction an act of war. Because the same government that displaced them from Nagele also ruled Bale, they sought a permanent solution. One of the solutions was to send people to Somalia to request arms support.

*

Wako Gutu Usu was a cousin of Wako Lugo (uncle to Hangasu). Lugo Usu and Gutu Usu were brothers. Wako Gutu was a resolute and unwavering 38-year-old. He was 6 feet, 8 inches tall and physically fit. He had a natural inclination and intuition for the military. As a teenager, he had been obsessed with guns; he taught himself self-defense and practiced shooting.

Wako Gutu emerged to the public arena in 1962. He was a fierce opponent of the declaration to evacuate Nagele. The government called one more meeting at the Nagele military camp to make its message—that the Arsi Oromos must evacuate Nagele voluntarily or be forced to evacuate by bullets— absolutely clear. The government held a meeting in the military camp to intimidate the families and ensure their obedience.

Wako Gutu faced the government head-on at this meeting. He exchanged a few words with the Ethiopian military commander, Colonel Zawde Tilahun, and the governor of the Sidamo zone, Taddese Tageny. Colonel Zawde asked the people, "What is your problem? Didn't we ask you to evacuate the city?" Wako Gutu stood up and said, "You are our problem. You are killing our people. Looting our properties. This is our land! Why don't you leave?"

Digging in his heels, Colonel Zawde said, "The killing of your people and the confiscation of your properties won't stop until you leave. If you don't leave voluntarily, we will make you leave by force."

The people couldn't hold back their frustration. Together they shouted, "We won't leave our land!" underscoring Wako Gutu's message.

The meeting got disorderly. People started talking loudly and moving away from the gathering. Colonel Zawde picked up his loudspeaker and yelled, "Shut up and sit. Nobody can leave these barracks!" He called for the army to guard the gate. People begrudgingly complied, knowing the brutality of the Ethiopian army.

Wako Gutu ignored the order to stay. Instead, he headed straight toward the gate as one of his friends, Abdullahi Usman, followed him. The two men faced the guards at the gate.

Colonel Zawde and Taddese Tageny (the governor) were furious. They hurried behind Wako Gutu and his friend to catch them before they exited. Colonel Zawde got in front of Wako Gutu at the gate. With his intimidating, penetrating eyes, and contracted eyebrows, Zawde asked Wako Gutu, "Where do you think you are going?"

Wako Gutu looked him straight in the eye and did not answer. He wanted to show that he was not intimidated by the military colonel. The people were kept at bay by guards, but they could see the intense exchange between the two men from a distance. They were simultaneously concerned for Wako and proud of him for standing up to this powerful government representative.

Colonel Zawde with his intimidating look moved closer to Wako Gutu and asked him again, "Why don't you leave our land?"

"Explain to me why I should leave my land," Wako said calmly. "And where would I go if I left my land?"

"This land is not your land," Colonel Zawde explained, perhaps sarcastically and angrily. "This land actually sued you. Your land is Dhadacha Warraq [referring to a place in Somalia]."

"My land sued me? Why would my land do that?" Wako responded. "My great-grandparents lived here. How come this land didn't sue you? Certainly you don't belong here. You are eating from this land, and now you are eating us. Why didn't the land sue you?"

Colonel Zawde was angry by now. "Did you expect the land would sue us? That won't happen. The question is," said the colonel, "are you going to leave this land or not? I need a short answer!"

"Before I answer that, let me ask you this: have you ever seen a termite mound built in the middle of a road?" Wako said.

"Yes," Zawde said.

"Have you noticed that the termite mound is destroyed every day by cars and people? And that every morning the mound returns to its original position because the termites were repairing and building at night?"

"Yes, I have seen it." Then, losing his patience, Zawde said, "What is your point?"

"The mound never stays destroyed," Wako said. "Why do you think that is?"

Wanting to speed up this interrogation and not realizing what Wako was intending, Zawde responded, "Because the termites are underground. The car only destroys what is above the ground. It cannot destroy what lays below the ground."

Zawde was falling into Wako's trap exactly the way he'd planned it. Wako kept his composure and replied, "Not bad! You knew the answer. Things that have roots in the underground cannot easily be destroyed. You knew it."

(Researchers have found that, when in danger, termites react in an orderly fashion and protect one another. They are guardians of the soil and their brethren in much the same way that the Arsi Oromos are guardians of their land.)

"This land that you are asking me to evacuate?" Wako said. "My umbilical cord was buried here. My grandparents and great-grandparents are buried here. My father, Gutu Usu, was buried here in Bitatta. [Bitatta is six miles from Nagele city.] You can ask me to leave your house, but you can't ask me to leave my land!" With that, Wako turned around and walked out of the camp.

Through this interaction, Wako Gutu proved himself a natural leader. He demonstrated bravery and determination to stand up for his people in the face of tyranny. As a result, the Arsi Oromos selected him to lead the mission to seek arms support from the Somali government so they could defend themselves, their families, and their properties from the brutal Ethiopian government. Along with Wako, the Arsi elders recruited Kadir Wario, Hussein Harcumma, and Muhammad Balade. Soon after the meeting with Zawde and Taddese, the four men hired a Somali road guide named Ali Dhur and then took off on foot on the road to Somalia.

*

Meanwhile desperate Arsi families began evacuating, taking with them only their children, the few farm animals of their own that they could find, and whatever they could carry.

The hundreds of displaced families headed north toward Madda Walabu, Bale, all at once. Before they could reach their destination, they had to cross the Ganale River. It was the rainy season, and the Ganale was full with no bridge to cross over. As the Arsi families left town, their route was very visible to the government, which saw an opportunity to attack the vulnerable civilians. The government in Nagele dispatched its police force to make sure the Arsi left and ordered the confiscation of their properties. In addition, the government encouraged the Borana and Guji tribes to chase the Arsi across the Ganale River. The army commander told them, "If you find any Arsi south of the Ganale River, kill them, women and children included. If you find their properties and belongings, take them. It is legal for you." Some groups within the Borana and Guji wanted to take advantage of the situation. These people were driven by personal gain more than their hate for Arsi Oromos.

The vulnerable civilians faced bullets and death by drowning in the Ganale River. Many chose to drown rather than beg the Ethiopian police and mercenaries for their lives. Countless men, women, and children—as well as their property—disappeared into the river. In some cases, children were eaten alive by crocodiles in front of their parents.

When Arsi Oromos from Madda Walabu heard about what had been done to their brothers, they responded immediately. A few had access to boats that they used for business; they turned these boats into rescue vessels. One of the rescuers was Malim Muhammad Maane Aaga, who used his boat to help families cross the Ganale.

Wako Lugo, Dayyu Hadama, and a few others played a significant role in protecting the families from the armed police and militias as they crossed the Ganale River. Wako Lugo was a wealthy man. He perpetuated his wealth through relationships he developed over the years. He purchased and sold livestock throughout the region at a lucrative margin. Since returning to Bale, he had married and divorced many wives in search of more children, and by this time, he had close to twenty children.

Wako Lugo became the de facto host for the displaced Arsi families. Most of the families who moved to Madda Walabu became his guests. The displaced Arsi Oromos swarmed to Wako Lugo's house for two reasons. First, these families had left behind all their belongings. They escaped with only their lives. Wako could help get them on their feet again. Wako distributed his cattle to the displaced families so each had at least a cow to milk for their children. Second, the families needed security and safety. They felt safe at Wako Lugo's house because he was the chief of his people. Wako owned rifles and had volunteers who could guard his family if needed. A few families decided to stay at his residence permanently. Among them were the families of Haji Gobana, Adam Jilo, and Haji Abdulqadir Haji Ali Wale.

The year was 1962, and my uncle was six years old. He vividly remembers making two friends from the families that stayed at his house: Ahmed Haji Gobana and Mohamed Adam Jilo. Both were close in age to Hangasu, perhaps one to two years older. They played soccer together after Madrasa (Quran studies). Their relationship grew with time. Eventually, the family of Haji Gobana opened a grocery shop in Bidire. Hangasu and Ahmed used to sleep over at the shop. This was a common practice; there is usually a room behind the shop where "guards" sleep. If something strange happened, like an attempted break-in, the kids would simply scream.

Here, my uncle and Ahmed experimented with smoking cigarettes. They were alone each night. Everything in the shop was available to them. Hangasu recalled, "We just wanted to try it because adults always smoked cigarettes or chewed tobacco.

When I first smoked, I coughed a lot. We had the whole night to ourselves; what else would we do? In the morning, we brushed our teeth very well so that our parents didn't notice." They continued this practice at night until smoking became a habit. Hangasu added, "Nobody in my family knew I was smoking."

Mohamed Adam Jilo became Hangasu's lifelong friend. My uncle recalled, "When Mohamed first came to Bidire, his family stayed at our house. Mohamed used to be afraid of the dark. So when we used to roam around in the city at night where there was no electricity, he used to hold my shirt and follow me around."

Mohamed's father, Adam Jilo, was a skinny, dark-skinned, well-spoken, and cunning middle-aged man. Adam Jilo was sharp in logical argument and in poetry. Proverbs rolled off his tongue naturally. Wako Lugo used to say, "Adam Jilo's wisdom resides on his tongue; Wako Gutu's wisdom resides in his heart." Wako Gutu was wise, but he wasn't as articulate as Adam Jilo. This competition over who was most valued in the community later became apparent as the two men took divergent paths to pursue Oromo freedom.

Meanwhile, the Arsi elders sent forty more men to Somalia to follow in the footsteps of Wako Gutu. Their mission was to bring back any weapons Wako convinced the Somali government to provide. The leader of these forty men was Chamari Gutu, an older brother of Wako Gutu. Chamari represented the Arsi Oromo in Nagele when Wako Lugo decided to return to Bale right after Italy's expulsion from Ethiopia.

Wako Gutu entered Somalia in Bula Hawo, a city where the Somali military was based, after a journey of a month and a half. Bula Hawo was the Somali military camp closest to Ethiopia's southern border.

Wako and his men went straight to the camp. The army commander in Bula Hawo asked Wako about the purpose of his journey. Wako replied, "The Ethiopian government displaced us out of our land. We left our families in danger. You are our brothers. I ask you to support us with arms so that we can go back and defend ourselves."

The army commander told them that such a request would have to be run up the chain. He asked them to wait. Wako and his crew stayed five days in the Bula Hawo military camp.

On day five, a military helicopter took Wako and his friends to Mogadishu, the capital of Somalia. Mogadishu was different from Ethiopian cities like Finfinne. Hangasu lived in both cities for an extended period in the 1970s and 1980s. Later in life, my uncle told me what Mogadishu and Finfinne looked like during that time.

"Mogadishu was smaller in both size and population than Finfinne," Hangasu said. "However, Mogadishu was much cleaner. In Finfinne, people frequently peed on the side of the road. Mogadishu was a desert. Its ground was covered by sand with no hint of soil. Mogadishu is located right by the Indian Ocean. Finfinne was green and wet due to frequent rain. It is located on a well-watered plateau surrounded by hills and mountains."

In Mogadishu, Wako and his crew were picked up by the head of police, Colonel Umar Muhammad. The police head had conducted his own investigation into the nature of Wako's mission to Somalia. After his investigation, Muhammad turned Wako and his crew over to Somalia's defense minister, General Dawud Abdulle.

General Dawud also conducted his own investigation. He questioned Wako and his crew together and separately to figure out the truthfulness of their appeal. After he gathered the information he needed and cross-referenced it with the previous interrogation by the police chief and the Bula Hawo commander, he called Wako Gutu to talk to him privately.

"Ethiopia is an ancient, powerful country," General Dawud said. "Forget about your small community uprising; we as a country don't dream of fighting Ethiopia. We simply don't have the resources to fight. I will provide you with a house and what you need. Stay here with us and wait for an opportune time."

It was a reasonable and logical recommendation from the defense minister. Haile Selassie was considered the leader of pan-Africanism and was perhaps the most senior African statesman with international recognition. Challenging him was not in Somalia's best interest.

Wako didn't like this recommendation one bit. Wako wanted to create his own opportunity and not wait around until one presented itself.

For General Dawud, it was not the first time he had encountered oppressed groups from Ethiopia who wanted arms support from the Somali government. Led by Haji Hassan Gababa, the Garri tribe that lived in the southernmost tip of Ethiopia and northern Kenya had gone to Somalia for the same purpose a few years before Wako. Another Arsi Oromo from the eastern part of Bale, led by Haji Isaaq Dadhi, had gone just one year before Wako. The Somali government had told them the same thing it told Wako Gutu: "You are a small group; you can't fight the Ethiopian government. Even Somalia as a government can't fight Ethiopia."

These groups had accepted General Dawud's recommendation. But not Wako. Wako said, "You are correct; the Ethiopian government is powerful. But we are not concerned about its power. We came to you in the hope that you may help us with some guns, or at least ammunition for our rifles. If you just support us with ammunition, with the help of God, I have confidence in my people's ability to kick out the Amhara oppressors."

"Besides, we didn't leave our land in search of a better life in Somalia," he continued. "An enemy attacked us. Our elders, women, children, and belongings are still exposed to that enemy. I will not rest until I go back and defend my family and my people. You say the Ethiopian government is too powerful for you to fight; give me some ammunition for our rifles, and I will show you what I can accomplish with that."

General Dawud listened very carefully to Wako's words and observed his body language. Wako delivered his message with full conviction, as if he could see a future when he and his people would liberate his region from the Amhara rule.

Wako continued his appeal with an analogy. He told General Dawud, "You [Somalis] are our brothers. God helped you, and you gained your independence. Our situations are like a single person who had his two legs in the mud; by gaining your independence, you were able to remove one of your legs from the mud. Would this person leave his other leg in the mud? We are like your other leg. You are not fully independent until we are also independent. Please *help* us so that I can defend and free my people."

General Dawud was touched by Wako's conviction and sense of urgency. The Somali government had a full view of the internal issues in Ethiopia at this point. The general observed that different groups from different areas of the country were swarming to Somalia for help. None of them knew about each other or coordinated their efforts. They all had the same enemy: the Ethiopian government. From the Somali government's viewpoint, the oppression was real. These different groups couldn't have orchestrated the stories of the atrocities they'd faced. General Dawud saw an opportunity.

"I understand your situation fully," General Dawud said. "However, you should know that we are a very young country. At this stage of our nation, like a young tree, we are very vulnerable, and we need to be extra careful not to piss off another nation. But your conviction has impacted me. Return to the Bula Hawo camp where you first arrived. In terms of support, I will do what I can. I will talk to my superiors." With that exchange, General Dawud returned Wako and his crew to Colonel Umar Muhammad.

Wako shared his conversation with his comrades. They were hopeful that the Somali government would provide some support. A few days later, Colonel Umar sent most of the group members back to Bula Hawo, keeping Wako Gutu and Kadir Wariyo in Mogadishu. The men were puzzled; they didn't understand the government's intention in separating them. They were anxious about what was going to happen next.

To their surprise, General Dawud came to pick up Wako and Kadir. They flew together to Bula Hawo. In the Bula Hawo camp, all the Bale fighters from Ethiopia were gathered. The

Somali government wanted to carry out an experiment to create problems for Ethiopia. These Bale fighters had the motivation and the people's power. All the Somali government had to do was give them a few rifles and ammunition. If all went well, they would destabilize Ethiopia. If the Bale fighters were crushed, the Somali government would have lost nothing other than a few outdated rifles.

General Dawud asked each group of rebels to appoint a single leader. There were three groups of fighters that sought arms support from the Somaila government: a group from Ehtiopian-Kenyan border (Garri tribe), a group from eastern Bale, Ginnir area (Arsi tribe) and a group from Bale-Borana border (Arsi tribe). Wako Gutu and his team were part of the Bale-Borana border group. When General Dawud saw that the people were hesitant, he offered to appoint a leader for them. The general gave each group one box of ten dhombir rifles and one Thompson rifle. To Wako's group, he gave four boxes of rifles and two Thompson rifles. Neither type of rifle was automatic.

It was not clear why the general gave more rifles to Wako's group. Maybe it was because of his conviction and determination. Maybe it was due to his urgency and focus. Perhaps General Dawud had studied how Wako's family could be influential in sustaining resistance against the Ethiopian government. Wako came from a long line of men who had made their names in Bale as a symbol of resistance against the Ethiopian rule. Lugo Usu, who'd killed the settler; Waayyu Teesso, who became instrumental in spreading Islam by extending protection to new Muslims from the community's persecution; Muhammad-Gada-Qaallu, who orchestrated the resistance army in Welmal River against the re-establishment of Haile Selassie after the Italians were defeated; and, of course, Wako Lugo, who'd earned respect by beating up the Italian governor and serving his people in the Sidamo and Bale zones; and Chamari Gutu, who was the leader of Rahitu Arsi in the Sidamo zone. From his distribution of the rifles, it seemed like Dawud was betting on Wako's group.

General Dawud asked his men to distribute ammunition for each group. He addressed and challenged all the groups, saying, "What we just gave you is not enough. Not even close. I don't expect you to crush and drive out the Amhara oppressors from your land. Rather, you may use this support to defend yourselves and your families.

"I only have one request; show me a result next time you come. A uniform, a hat, a belt you took from a member of the Ethiopian military or police. If you show me that evidence, I promise I can find more support for you." The general then turned to Wako's group and told them, "Wako will be your leader. May God help you." It seemed that he was betting on Wako to deliver the result.

Wako and his group were relieved to get the support they needed. However, there were only four people. They'd received forty Dhombir and two Thompson rifles. How were they going to carry these weapons back? A few days later, a group of thirty-five Arsi Oromo men, led by Wako's brother Chamari, arrived in the Bula Hawo camp. This group's mission was to reinforce Wako's appeal by showing their number and the imminent danger their community was in and to bring back any support received from Somalia.

For Wako, it felt like everything came together just right. He grew more confident that his cause was the right cause. He couldn't wait to return to Ethiopia and put these weapons to work.

CHAPTER NINE:
THE BALE REVOLT BEGINS

THE YEAR 1963 WAS A PIVOTAL YEAR in the Bale Oromo's movement. Approximately forty Arsi Oromos returned to Ethiopia under the leadership of Wako Gutu. They had never been trained in conventional military or guerilla warfare. They'd gone to Somalia because they'd been driven out of their homes. Their children had been killed, and their properties confiscated by the government. The oppression was unbearable. Now they returned to face their arch enemy, the Ethiopian government. They demanded to live on their ancestral land with dignity.

On their way to Bale, the group discussed how to operate in the country. They discussed a name for their newly formed guerilla organization. They settled on *Hizbi*, an Arabic term meaning "the people." The name implied that this was the People's Resistance Army or the people's struggle against oppression. However, this name was not widely used because it was not catchy enough.

The guerilla army was divided into groups. One group, led by Muhammad Balade, was sent to the Sidamo region of Ethiopia. Wako Gutu took the second group to the Bale region. Each small guerilla group was able to move quickly, minimizing their chances of being spotted by the Ethiopian army. Each group reached their destination without being caught.

My uncle, 7 years old at the time, remembered seeing Wako Gutu for the first time. "Our family was in a place called Sammu in Madda Walabu. My uncle Wako Gutu stopped by our house. He slaughtered one ox and fed his soldiers. He was tall and strong. I still remember he wore shorts and a short sleeve shirt. He kissed me on my cheeks."

Wako Lugo and a few other elders advised the newly established guerilla army not to engage with the Ethiopian army. "This uprising requires more than forty armed men," Wako Lugo said. "The Ethiopian army is powerful. We cannot compete with their army. Instead, these forty men should hide their guns and integrate into the community. The government cannot declare war on us as long as we pay its taxes. We need to continue paying taxes, and in the meantime, let's keep sending more men to Somalia to acquire more arms until a significant number of people are armed from the Ganale River in the south to Goba and Gadab in the northeast. If we can be patient, I can see a path to defeating the Ethiopian army."

However, Wako Gutu and his small army were reluctant to follow this advice. Wako Gutu was young and driven and couldn't wait to take revenge on the government that had displaced them from their homes.

Meanwhile, the Ethiopian Fourth Division Army, based in Nagele, heard about the Arsi Oromo when they left for Somalia. In anticipation of the trouble they might cause, the army sent scouts to different areas. The scouts figured out that a few armed Arsi men led by Wako Gutu and Kadir Wariyo had entered Madda Walabu and were spotted near the Ganale River. The Fourth Division dispatched an army of approximately one hundred, led by a man called Shi Alaqa Buzuna and aided by a few hundred native auxiliaries, to quickly capture and destroy the small group of resistors.

Shi Alaqa Buzuna and his army approached the guerilla army with full confidence that they would destroy them. He said, "Since when *gaallaa* [a derogatory term for Oromos] refuse our order, we will capture them and slaughter them one by one. Do they think their guns will kill us?" His arrogance and contempt for the Arsi Oromo was staggering.

In April 1963, the battle of Malka-Anna occured. The Arsi set their Dhombir rifles to task. The Ethiopian army was caught off guard; they never imagined the level of resistance and fight these civilians-turned-guerillas had developed over the course of only a few months. The Ethiopian army began retreating. The guerilla army followed. Because their guns were not automatic, no bullet went to waste. They wanted to conserve their ammunition for the next battle, so they made every bullet count.

By early afternoon, the guerilla army had a clear victory at the battle of Malka-Anna: forty-three dead Ethiopian soldiers and more than one hundred wounded, according to the Bale fighters. The Bale fighters also seized eight automatic machine guns and thirteen rifles as well as uniforms, helmets, and food from the defeated soldiers. The guerilla fighters lost only two men.

The Bale fighters were fascinated by the guns and helmets they had seized. The guns were distributed to the many people willing to join the struggle after this clear victory. The helmets, though, the Bale fighters didn't want to wear, so they turned them into water containers and cooking pots. They kept a few to show General Dawud Abdulle. Because they had accomplished this victory with Dhombir rifles, the guerilla army called itself Dhombir, which caught on as their name. Therefore, the Bale Revolt (1963–1970) was referred to in Bale as *Weeyra Dhombir* or *Weeyra Wako*—that is, the Dhombir War or the Wako War.

Looking back, it seemed like General Dawud Abdulle had made a good bet. The Bale fighters led by Wako Gutu successfully entered Ethiopia and confronted the Imperial army. The other two rebel groups were met with resistance on their way home and retreated to Somalia.

*

A great victory in hand, Wako Gutu turned his attention to his family. While Wako Gutu was in Somalia, the Ethiopian police had arrested Kadde Gobana Tosi—Wako Gutu's wife—and her newborn baby, Abdul-Qadir Wako (nicknamed Shanqo) in Nagele. Wako heard of this heinous act and sent nine of his men to Nagele to extract his wife and the child from jail. The men entered Nagele, leaving their rifles in the suburb. They approached influential Werji businessmen to help them accomplish their mission.

In Nagele, Werjis were considered family with Arsi. Wako Lugo had married Fato (Hangasu's mother), and that made them in-laws. Werjis were every bit a part of the struggle. The Werjis were merchants, not pastoralists like the Arsi. As such, they kept good relationships with every ethnic group in Ethiopia, including the Amharas; it made business sense to do so. This relationship came to benefit the Arsi Oromos as well.

Kadir Wariyo approached several members of the Werji ethnic group to help him free Wako Gutu's family. The Werjis played a smart card; they bribed the police chief. At the appointed time, in the darkness of a city where the streets were pitch-black, the prison police went to grab dinner and intentionally left the prison door open. Maalim Muhammad Maane went in and picked up Wako's wife and son. They escaped the city immediately. Wako had scored two victories.

Meanwhile, another son of Arsi, Aliyyi Chirri, encouraged by Wako's accomplishment, raided the police station in Oborso city (in Madda Walabu) and drove the police out of the city. Those who escaped entered Bidire. Here, too, Wako Gutu's guerilla army attacked the police station and drove out the entire police force. The guerillas had gained three consecutive victories. They had also led a prison break. In response, the Ethiopian Fourth Division, led by Shi Alaqa Buzuna and previously headquartered in Finfinne, was permanently moved to Bidire and stationed there.

By this time, in mid-1963, Madda Walabu was in chaos. The Bale fighters had created enough agitation against the government that the government was ready to suppress the rebellion by force. Hangasu's family evacuated Bidire and temporarily settled in the countryside in one of the jungle prairies of Madda Walabu. The new home was temporary because the family was on the run from the government. Fato (Hangasu's mother) was born and grew up in the city; this was the first time she had lived in the countryside. Life in the countryside was rough, even under the best of circumstances. During wartime, it was doubly difficult. Food was limited, and the luxury of cooking a meal was gone. Now people simply consumed milk and meat. Shelter was no longer stable; it was constantly exposed to rain and heat. There was very little privacy. Nevertheless, Fato handled the new situation very well.

*

One month after the battle of Malka-Annaa, the Ethiopian army received reinforcements from the Sidamo and Bale zones. This time, the Ethiopian army was well prepared. They identified Wako Gutu's location: Jilo Welmal. Jilo Welmal was a river, so it was central for all life, people and animals alike.

The Ethiopian army picked midday for their attack—the busiest part of the day for the pastoralists. At this time of day, all their animals are near the water, either coming to drink, drinking, or having finished drinking and moving on to grazing. All of these activities require constant supervision and must be done in an orderly fashion. Everybody in the community was busy making sure their cattle were fed and watered. Knowing that the government would be coming after them, the Wako guerilla army had assigned a couple of men to constantly scout the environment for any approaching army. Unfortunately, these men dropped the ball; they slept. In doing so, they exposed the guerilla army and their families.

The Ethiopian army had prepared three hundred to four hundred soldiers for a surprise battle. They knew that Wako had, at most, forty men with guns. They bet that this would be their turn to give a big blow to these backward Bale fighters—to destroy them, their families, and their livestock all at once. The Ethiopian army was equipped with the latest automatic and semiautomatic machine guns; the guerillas had one semiautomatic and the rest were manual rifles. The guerilla army was completely outgunned.

Early midmorning, out of nowhere, the people saw the Ethiopian army advancing on them while their cattle, camels, and goats were drinking from the Jilo Welmal. Wako Gutu was the most experienced person in the guerilla army. He was mostly self-taught but had an incredible intuition for warfare from an early age. Wako called all his men and ordered them to get ready. He told everyone not to shoot at the Ethiopian army. He knew full well his men were outnumbered and outgunned, so he quickly devised a plan to outmaneuver the mighty army. He had two rules: do not shoot until I give you permission, and do not take their guns.

Neither of these rules made sense to his fellow fighters, but Wako's rules were purposeful. The first rule was designed to ensure every bullet was put to good use, killing the enemy without wasting bullets on merely wounding the Ethiopian soldiers. His men's rifles were short range; he had to make sure the enemy was close enough. The second rule was intended to protect his men and to prevent them from exposing themselves by rushing to pick up the better guns from the Ethiopian army's dead. He told his people, "If we win, the guns will come to you."

The first line of the Ethiopian army advanced. The guerilla army took its position. The Ethiopian army kept advancing. Still, Wako gave no order. Some questioned if he had any plan after all. Some speculated their leader was planning to surrender.

When the Ethiopian army got very close and Wako was certain that every one of his men could kill the enemy, he shouted, *"Ilma Haati deetteef, amma tokkosuun geette!"* meaning "For the braves, the time to shoot is now!" This was the Arsi way of inspiring and instilling confidence. The guerilla army took out the first line of the Ethiopian army, then the second. The third line retreated. By this time, both sides had taken a lot of damage. Wako's army also retreated, reduced from about forty men to fewer than ten.

Suddenly, the Ethiopian army received reinforcements. Wako told his men to take the wounded and retreat. Wako wanted to stay behind and fight. As a leader of the resistance army, he blamed himself for the outcome. Most of his army retreated immediately at Wako's orders; only a few (Wako Korma, Sheikh Ahmed Wako Gada, and Hassan Kotte) refused. Wako eventually convinced Sheikh Ahmed and Kotte to leave, but Wako Korma refused, telling him, "You, too, only have one life, like all of us!"

The two Wakos continued to fight the Ethiopian reinforcements. Wako Gutu had two guns: one automatic machine gun with two mags in his pockets and his beloved old rifle, called "Yayyo." Perhaps the gun had been a childhood toy. In any case, Wako Gutu used his Yayyo for long range and the automatic weapon for short range. Suddenly they heard a whistle. The Ethiopian army retreated and returned to Bidire. During the battle, more than seventy people died. Thousands of cattle were slaughtered.

While on their way to Bidire, the Ethiopian army, defeated and angry, massacred everyone in Buri village, more than twelve people—women, children, and elderly among them. They were all one family, the Bowwe family. Just like that, the Ethiopian army inflicted pain and fear on the innocent population.

*

In Ethiopia, the emperor was considered, "King of Kings, Conquering Lion of the Tribe of Judah, Elect of God." His avid supporters worshiped him. People would whisper his name in the middle of nowhere, as if he could hear them. He instilled fear throughout the country.

The news of the uprising in Bale reached Emperor Haile Selassie. The police and army forces had been defeated multiple times by ordinary peasants who were unhappy about their treatment at the hands of the local government. The emperor wanted to end this annoyance as soon as possible by annihilating the Bale fighters and particularly their rebel leader. For this task, the emperor selected the administrator of Adaba district, Baqqala Aragu. The emperor personally ordered Baqqala to bring him Wako Gutu's head, dead or alive. The emperor added, "*Our* resources are at your disposal." Should Baqqala achieve his goal, the emperor promised him an immediate and significant promotion.

Baqqala was excited about the assignment. First, he got to be face-to-face with the emperor—a dream of any government employee in the country. In addition, he had received the promise of a promotion.

Baqqala felt the task would be quick and easy. When he studied the Bale fighters' weapons, there was no comparison. The Bale fighters carried outdated, bolt-action rifles. These were ordinary nomads and subsistence farmers, not trained soldiers. Baqqala made the best preparation he could. He gathered soldiers from every kind of military group—including the Imperial Guard—and mixed them with locals. He planned simultaneous attacks in different cities and villages where the Bale fighters might be present. Baqqala's order was to show no mercy to the enemy—to kill them and destroy their property indiscriminately.

By this time early in 1964, the people of Madda Walabu, Dallo, and Haranna Buluq had joined the Bale fighters in large numbers. Their cause spread throughout the region like wildfire. The Bale fighters acquired more weapons as they took control of police stations and won further battles against the Ethiopian army. The Bale fighters spread weapons among those interested in joining the struggle. They believed they could defeat the oppressive government that treated them like second-class citizens on their own land. Many in the region, and throughout the country for that matter, had never imagined that this government could be challenged. Wako Gutu and the Bale fighters proved everyone wrong; they showed that the government could, in fact, be defeated. Therefore, the people believed they should bond together to defeat their enemies. After all, the government was killing them indiscriminately, whether they'd joined the Bale army or not.

Baqqala dispatched the first army to the village of Nansabo in Haranna Buluq. He led this army to attack the closest Bale fighter group (led by Sheikh Ahmad Wako Gada) near Nansabo. The fighting went on for two days. Baqqala found that the Bale fighters were not as easy to defeat as he'd expected. By the end of the second day, the Bale fighters had killed approximately one hundred Ethiopian soldiers, including Baqqala Aragu himself. The Bale fighters seized sixty-eight M1 rifles, twenty-seven other rifles of various kinds along with their ammunition, two automatic machine guns, and a pistol. The Bale fighters won the battle, then loaded the haul of weapons onto the backs of donkeys and returned to the base camp. Meanwhile, Baqqala's army returned to Adaba and Dodola defeated and humiliated.

Until then, the Ethiopian government had never taken the Bale fighters seriously at a federal level. The government had treated them as a minor regional annoyance, but the problem of the Bale fighters had continued to grow for the emperor. Now the government gathered its force in three locations encircling Bale: Dodola (in the Ganale district), Goba (the capital of Bale), and Nagele (in the Sidamo region). The government launched constant attacks from these three bases, killing people and destroying property. The Bale fighters avoided head-on battle with the government army. Instead, they would hit and run.

*

More people joined the struggle than the guerillas had weapons available. The Dhombir leaders decided to send people to Somalia again to ask for more weapons. When the Bale fighters had received the first forty rifles, General Dawud made one request: to bring back evidence that the Bale fighters had put the guns to work against the Ethiopian government.

The Somali government was well aware of what had happened in Ethiopia over the last year, so when the Dhombir leaders arrived in Somalia, there were no questions asked. The government provided guns and ammunition generously. More than six hundred people went to Somalia for the second round; they returned to Ethiopia fully equipped. This time the freedom fighters brought back not only rifles and ammunition; they also brought bombs, bazookas, and many other weapons.

As soon as the Bale fighters returned from Somalia, they were assigned to strategic areas near where the Ethiopian army had been stationed. The government army stationed in Dodola was particularly angry at the Bale fighters because of the humiliation they had caused in killing Baqqala Aragu. They came up with a motto to motivate their troops: *"Haranna baddaa dagalaa; hin baasu gumaa Baqqalaa Gaallaan shantama,"* meaning "Haranna is full of forest; fifty Gaallas are not enough to pay us back for one Baqqalaa's life." This meant that "a life for a life" didn't apply here; they had to kill *fifty* Oromos to take revenge for one Baqqala.

Kadir Wako Shaqe was assigned to the Haranna forest. The Dodola-based army launched its attack on Oromo fighters in Haranna to take revenge for Baqqala Aragu's death. Kadir prepared his men and waited for the army. The forest was advantageous for Kadir; he had grown up there. He knew where to hide, where to engage in battle, and at what time of day.

As the Ethiopian army entered the forest, Kadir Wako Shaqe ambushed them. He shouted, *"Haranna jedhantu tanna. Kadir jedhantu ana. dhihana keetu kana,"* meaning "This is the Haranna forest you heard about. I am the Kadir people talked about. Here is how I would welcome you." Kadir and his comrades continued shooting until the army retreated. As they ran back to Dodola, the government's army killed women and children and burned homes along the way, taking out their anger on the innocent population again.

In this way, the entire lowland of Bale joined the revolt within a period of two to three years. In the Ginnir area (in northeastern Bale), Haji Isaaq Dadhi, in collaboration with Hussein Bune, Mahmud Bune, Abdullahi Badhaso, Ismi Abba Washa, and others, successfully attacked the Ethiopian army with the arms support he had received from Somalia, just as Wako's group had. In the Sidamo region, forces led by Aliyo Gababa and Roba Hassan Gababa successfully attacked the Ethiopian army in southern Ethiopia and northern Kenya. All of the fighters maintained constant communication. Each group went to Somalia multiple times to acquire more weapons.

The blow to the Ethiopian government came when influential Bale leaders, who had (at least on the surface) worked with the government, joined the struggle. Haji Isaaq Dadhi Tarre (the brother of Sultan Nuho) was a senior intelligence officer in the Bale and Sidamo zones before he joined the armed struggle against the government in Ginnir (in the Wabe River area).

Wako Lugo had held the people's representative role in Nagele (Sidamo) and Dallo (Bale) before he joined his cousin Wako Gutu in the armed struggle in the Dallo and Madda Walabu area. In 1964, Wako Lugo went to Somalia with many other influential elders of Dallo and Madda Walabu and brought back weapons to sustain the armed struggle.

In addition, Wako Lugo played a pivotal role in spurring the uprising. He traveled across Bale to recruit high potential tribe leaders and young men to join the revolt. Many of his recruits became iconic leaders during the Bale Revolt and beyond. Simultaneously, he assumed a diplomatic role in organizing and managing civilian affairs. Throughout the conflict, the Ethiopian government believed the region was ungovernable. However, Wako Lugo and his council of elders made sure disputes were resolved fairly and in a timely manner. The council made sure the fighters were well fed and their families were taken care of. They also gathered intelligence on the government's planned operation through their network in the city.

In 1966, the government put the Bale and Sidamo zones under martial rule. The army was stationed in Nagele in the south and Robe in the north. Their goal was to attack the Bale fighters from all sides and cut off their supply routes. Within one year, the government troops had silenced the resistance in Sidamo, but Bale was not so easy. Bale continued the resistance for another three years.

During the 1960s, Bale was a dream for the guerilla troops and a nightmare for the Ethiopian army. First, there were no roads to allow the Ethiopian troops to move around quickly and efficiently across the vast and remote region (Bale and Sidamo, now Borana, make up almost half of the Oromia regional state). In addition, the region was sparsely populated. The government took note of the geographic disadvantage and its ground troops' limited options.

*

A poignant memory that my uncle had was with his father, Wako Lugo. The two had just returned from a trip to another of his father's houses outside of Bidire. On their way back to Bidire, they stopped at Makko Hassan's house, my paternal grandmother. She was the widow of my paternal grandfather, Dire Irressa, who was assassinated by the Ethiopian government in Goba along with Muhammad-Gada-Qaallu. Dire and Wako Lugo had been friends, so Wako wanted to say hello. Dire had wanted to have many children, but he had only one son, Adam, my dad.

Hangasu recalled, "As we entered the house and said hello to the family, Makko started making coffee. This was the tradition; guests must be fed with something. I started conversing with Adam, and my dad was having a conversation with Makko. All of a sudden, we heard a loud sound. My dad raced out of the house and said, 'That is a military fighter jet.' That was a very scary sound."

Because it was flying so low, Wako deduced the jet had come to attack Bidire. "My dad told me to stay there while he picked up his gun and rushed to the city," Hangasu said. Wako's goal was to shoot down the jet. Before he made it to the city, the jet had already struck a place called Hara-Gurraatti. The airstrike killed one person and 150 cattle.

The cattle belonged to a young man named Mohamed Gelma. Mohamed was 15 or 16 years old and a wealthy youth. Tragedies like this devastated people. His family's entire wealth was destroyed at once. Although Mohamed had an abundance of cattle, it was not important to him. He had foresight and valued education more than the cattle he'd inherited from his family, which was unusual for a man his age at that time and in that part of the world.

Mohamed lived in Oborso to attend school. At that time, Oborso was the capital of Madda Walabu, which would later move back to Bidire. Hangasu said, "I remember once, the governor of Madda Walabu came to Bidire. The governor was accompanied by a young boy. The boy followed the governor everywhere he went as a delegate of the government. People asked why the governor took such a young boy with him. People close to the governor explained that the governor didn't know how to write, and so he'd hired this boy, Mohamed Gelma, as his secretary. It was a huge advance at that time for a local kid to be able to read and write in Amharic."

Mohamed currently lives in Finfinne in a beautiful villa with his family, working for a European-based non-governmental organization (NGO). Looking back, Hangasu said Mohamed made the best choice in focusing on his education.

*

Makka Bariso was a survivor of Ethiopian airstrikes. She was the wife of Adam Jilo, the skinny, dark-skinned, cunning, middle-aged man with an eloquent tongue described earlier. Later in life, Makka Bariso came to the United States as a refugee and lived in Minneapolis, Minnesota. People called her *akko Makka*—grandma Makka. She had been through many difficult times; people wanted to hear stories of events she witnessed. She is pleasant to talk to and always smiling, except on March 21, 2014, when she shared the following story:

"It was a midmorning in rural Madda Walabu. Men sat outside of the house and talked. Women cooked food. We heard a fighter jet approaching our location. We were all scared. My husband told our son, Mohamed, to bring the machine gun from the house."

Mohamed was a 12-year-old. With the romanticizing of heroes, he wanted a piece of the glory. He went into the house, brought out the gun, aimed it in the direction of the fighter jet, and fired. Doing so provided a target for the fighter jet. Zeroing in on the site from which it was fired upon, one minute later the fighter jet came back, passed them, and then U-turned to destroy everything in that vicinity.

Makka told me what happened:

> The jet dropped bullets like hail. We all ran away in different directions. I ran with my children. The land was open, there were no trees to hide under. Running out of options, I lay my children down, and I dropped on top of them to cover them from the bullets.

> I took *shahada* [testimony of faith: There is no deity worthy of worship except God]. I asked, 'Oh God, kill me before my children. I can only think about my children.' I was also pregnant at the time. Two bullets missed my right rib by a few inches. The jet came back again, dropping more bullets. This time the bullets pierced the ground to my left, creating a huge dust cloud. My husband's mule was right next to us. The mule was scared and jumped around, stuck in one place since it was tied up.

The strike continued. I kept repeating the testimony of faith and my prayer to kill me before my children. A few yards away, I heard crying. It was the voice of Ahado. Ahado was the wife of Adam Jilo's brother. Ahado had given birth to a baby girl three days prior. [She was a young lady, married only the year before. It's safe to say she was under the age of twenty.] The bullets stopped. I ran to Ahado. She was wearing a white dress and was leaning against a tree. There was blood all over her body and the surrounding area. She was cut in half by the bullets. I didn't know what to think. There was no time to think. The infant was crying at her side. When she saw me, she said, 'Who is going to raise my *gurratti*?' [meaning "my black one," referring to her infant girl]. I picked up the infant. Ahado's breast was tender, full of milk. She said, 'Please give me [my daughter], I want to breastfeed her one last time.' I broke into tears and screamed!

My husband and the rest of the men heard me and came running. When Ahado saw my husband, Adam Jilo, she said, 'Please, please, please kill me!' Shocked by what he saw, Adam Jilo fell down, unconscious. He was carried away to another location. Soon everybody left from where she was because it was extremely difficult, watching her suffer. People dragged me away from there also.

A short moment later, my husband asked me discreetly to go check and see if she was still alive or dead. I went. She was still alive; she was breathing. I went back to my husband and asked him, 'She is still alive. Why don't you ask people to recite *Yaasin* [Quran] on her?' He responded, 'What is *Yaasin* going to do for someone dying of bullet shots?'

I went back again to see her. This time she is no longer breathing. She died. Her eyes were closed. Her bottom half was away from the rest of her body. I picked it up and put it right next to her, where it used to be. I took off her shoes. I took off her bracelets; her wrists were full of bracelets. I took off her necklace. Now more women joined me, assisting her for burial. I went back and announced she was dead. We buried her there and evacuated that area that evening. I can count at least five women who died that day.

These are only two stories of many in the region. The emperor's airstrikes inflicted irreparable damage on the lives of innocent civilians and their property. The goal was to terrorize the population and destroy their morale and livelihood.

CHAPTER TEN:
WAKO LUGO'S PROPERTY AND
WAKO GUTU'S APPOINTMENT

THE REBELLION EXTENDED TOO LONG. The Ethiopian government continued to bombard the people from the air and ground. The Bale fighters ran out of ammunition. Thousands of guerilla fighters were sent to Somalia under the leadership of Toore Boru to obtain additional ammunition and arms. The fighters were supposed to get guns from the Somali government and return to the battlefields as soon as possible. A few months passed, and nobody returned with guns as expected. It could mean only one thing: The Somali government had refused to provide arms support. The entire native population was vulnerable, and the resistance was in jeopardy.

The year was 1967. Somalia had elected a new president, Abdirashid Ali Sharmarke. Military aid was suspended because the Somali government was focusing on its own internal affairs.

The Bale Rebellion leaders and elders in Dallo and Madda Walabu decided to go to Somalia and make a statement that they needed the arms now more than ever. All the military and political leaders headed to Somalia. They left behind only one military leader, Dubro Wako. Dubro was a brave, well-recognized, and battlefield-tested leader. He was also the son-in-law of Wako Gutu. The Ethiopian government was well aware of the situation. The government civilian officers and military leaders turned this opportunity into a get-rich-quick game.

Hangasu recalled the events of 1967: "I was 11 years old. My family moved to a place called Muumme Farado. Farado is farther south and east in Madda Walabu. Here my family and other families were safe from the enemy. The guerilla army kept the government south of the Ganale River. Normally they would never cross over to Bale because they knew what the Bale fighters would do to them. However, since all notable fighters had left the country, the Ethiopian army saw an opportunity. Our family was on extra alert." Hangasu said about a dozen displaced families were living together at this location.

"One evening just before the sun set, we heard that the Amhara soldiers had crossed the Ganale River through Malka Idda," Hangasu continued. "Immediately, panic struck the families. There were no armed men to protect them. Dubro was the only hope for the families. Unfortunately, Dubro got sick a few weeks before this day, and he wasn't in shape to even stand up, let alone protect the families. It was all women and children."

Sunset was typically the time cattle and other animals came home after grazing all day. The animals would be led into the barns that protected them from wild animals. Cows and camels were milked at this time for dinner. On that particular night, "after the cows and camels were milked, it was decided to let cattle and camels go into the jungle. Their barns and fences were no longer safe," Hangasu said.

The government army already knew these families' location. The families needed to leave. Lacking anybody to coordinate the move, the families were confused about what to do. There was no central command or recognized leader to guide them. The effort to get the families moving and to let the animals out of the barns took a long time. Despite the delays, the families moved one or two miles from their original location deeper into the jungle. By then, the children were tired, and the cattle and camels had no interest in this night journey. Tired and unsure of what to do, the families decided to stay there for the night.

My uncle remembered what happened when the government army stormed his family's village: "That night, around 10 p.m. or so, we heard gunshots. Almost immediately armed men were spotted in the family camp, running around terrorizing women and children. I heard people screaming, *Amaara! Amaara! Amaara!* We all ran for our lives. We left everything behind.

"My mother grabbed my hand and my sister's and took off. I refused to run with her. I withdrew my hand. She asked me what I was doing. I told her I had a hand grenade, and I will go back to burn the Amharas. I added, 'I know how to use it because my brother showed me how.' My mother was shocked but curiously said, 'Where is the hand grenade?' I took it out of my pocket and showed her.

"She snatched the grenade out of my hand, threw it in the jungle, and gripped my hand, this time extra tight, and ran away in the jungle. I was angry at my mother for doing that at the time. Trying to find this one bomb in the middle of the jungle in the pitch-dark night was close to impossible. So I followed my mother, but I was angry the whole night."

Luckily, the government didn't pursue them. Their objective was to accumulate wealth by stealing from the families; they seized more than five hundred cattle and camels. That evening was remembered throughout Bale as the night Wako Lugo's property was confiscated. Other families had some cattle taken, but probably more than 90 percent of what was confiscated had belonged to Wako Lugo. "That night, and for the next few days, we kept running away to exhaustion until we reached a place called Kafanney. Kafanney was always a hot place; on top of that, it was a dry season. There was no water nearby."

These families lived off of their cattle, camels, and goats. They relied on milk and meat from these animals. Camels were used for milk; they can be milked three to four times a day and produce enough for many families and their guests. Camels are also used to transport goods and water. Literally overnight, these families lost *everything* they had ever owned. Wako Lugo's family had been devastated; they went from rich to destitute. There was no milk for the children. There was no meat.

My maternal grandmother, Fato, now in her late 80s, recalled one event. "The night our cattle were taken, I took my two children, Zamzam and Hangasu, and ran away. The next day we met up with some of my family members. Some were still missing, but we kept going toward Kafanney. After all day of traveling, we were tired. We rested. We all ran out of food and drink. I saved up a small container of milk from the previous night. I kept it all day long because I didn't know when we would have something to drink or eat again. I especially saved it for Hangasu because he was young. I hid it from everyone and gave it to Hangasu to take a sip. Hangasu refused it.

"When I asked him why, he proposed something else. I still remember. He said, 'Make tea out of it so that everybody can drink it.' I was shocked about how he came up with that. At the same time, I was proud of him. I cried out of happiness. I knew he would grow to be a humanitarian."

Hangasu remembered that year was the hardest on him and his family. "One day after a long trip, we came across a drying lake. There was still some water, but it was dirty and contaminated by cattle feces and urine. We were told to drink because there was no alternative. I couldn't drink it. I refused to drink it. My mom took the water and poured it over my head and body to help me cool off from the sun's heat.

"The news of what happened to my family spread. As we got into populated areas, people recognized us as Wako Lugo's family. My dad was a legend when it came to generosity. Everybody remembered him for his generosity. The community responded in kind and took care of us by giving us food and sharing their cattle with us. It took us one week to reunite with all our family members. Once my extended families were reunited, the community started fundraising to support my family."

The Arsi Oromos have a culture of emergency self-help called *Hirphaa*. It is like fundraising to help families in need. Every member of the community must contribute. Every household in that community contributed five or six cattle.

"My father came back at the end of that dry season from Somalia. People gathered again to collect more cows and camels for our family. The news of property confiscation spread through the region. People from the south side as far as Nagele and to the north side in Bale as far as Barbare extended invitations to my dad. They sent word to him to come and visit. I remember him traveling to the north side of Bale in Haranna, Barbare, etcetera. He was given more than seventy cows, camels, load of honey, and coffee! My dad distributed these cattle among his family members."

The community response was overwhelmingly positive in support of Wako and his family. The family's general situation improved slightly, but it was far from the way they used to live. They owned fewer cattle and farm animals. They drank less milk and ate meat less frequently, if at all. Regardless of what happened, Hangasu reflected, "If you do right by your people, they will do right by you when you need them. My dad's generosity paid off. To see people's love for my dad was priceless.

"I observed my dad during that time, I did not see any signs of depression or constant worry for the loss. His only complaint that I heard was that he was not able to help people the way he used to. 'My hand is short,' he said." That is, Wako had nothing to give others.

The officials and troops who had seized Wako's cattle and property distributed the animals among themselves. The troops took the cattle and camels to different cities and villages to sell them as quickly as possible to get money so they could drink and party. The troops flooded the towns with an oversupply of cattle and camels. The story was that some bar owners got cattle for free in exchange for alcoholic drinks or prostitutes.

*

The Bale freedom fighters finally returned from Somalia with more weapons. They were able to convince the new Somali government to support their cause.

The Ethiopian government intensified its air and ground attacks, especially as more militants returned from Somalia with arms. Successive Ethiopian generals were tasked with extinguishing the uprising, but they were unable to do so.

The Bale guerillas constantly heard that they were fighting against this Ethiopian general or colonel. When the guerillas visited Somalia, the government there provided a three-month military training to some of the leaders and gave them military titles—everything from ordinary soldiers to colonels. When they returned to Bale, the elders wanted to formalize their organizational structure. There were too many colonels but nobody with the title of "general" within the guerilla army.

By this time, Wako Gutu had established himself as the de facto leader. The guerillas recognized his distinction, integrity, honesty, and ability to connect with people at a visceral level. The people said, "We need a general from amongst ourselves, and his name is Wako Gutu." This proposal was unanimously approved. From that day forward, his name became General Wako Gutu, the face of the Bale Oromo people's struggle for freedom. By promoting him to the rank of general, the resistance army was elevating itself to go toe to toe with Ethiopian generals, psychologically and militarily. The smallness of their means didn't hold them back; they had full faith in themselves to defeat the giant, tyrannical government.

At their inaugural meeting, General Wako Gutu addressed his men. He clarified and emphasized the objectives of the struggle. Theirs was a loosely organized army with no proper management of food, clothing, training, or drills for the soldiers. Everybody was on their own. From time to time, community members were able to contribute food, but it was not enough. Wako Gutu was worried his soldiers would be forced to disturb the community and take people's belongings by force. He proactively addressed the military in particular. Among other things, he said, "We stand for freedom; we fight for freedom. Guard yourselves from taking the community's property. Let's put all our anger and frustration to the tyrant government." The message was well received. The elders who were worried about the troops were glad to hear the message.

Adam Jilo was appointed second-in-command on the same day. He was given the title colonel of colonels. Adam Jilo was comical and eloquent in speech. Part of his eloquence was his ability to use body language to communicate deep messages. Adam Jilo's speeches were usually long and had multiple meanings. To fully capture his message, one had to listen and watch him attentively. Otherwise, one might miss his point. This was in contrast to General Wako Gutu. His messages were clear and brief. He said what he meant, and what you heard was what you got.

After Wako finished his address on the day of the inauguration, Adam Jilo stood up. Many soldiers loved Adam Jilo because he was always entertaining and youthful at heart. The young soldiers loved him because he said what they wanted to hear. He was not strict. He stepped forward and stood facing the army, right in front of General Wako Gutu. People in the back could only hear what he said, those in the front could hear him and see him, which was important to understand his multilayered messages.

"As our general mentioned, we stand for freedom; we fight for freedom," Adam Jilo said. This much was clear. He continued, "Guard yourselves from taking community's property." Except he delivered this message while wiping his face and rubbing his right leg on the ground. For his loyal troops, the message meant, "Go ahead and take what you need to survive. Break the laws and norms if necessary, as long as you continue to fight the enemy." For the elders who were sitting in the back, Adam Jilo's speech was no different from General Wako Gutu's.

When one of Adam Jilo's loyal supporters was asked why he supported him, he said, "We were involved in this war. We had no support from a central place. We left behind our cattle and businesses for this cause. How could we survive? Beg? What Adam Jilo meant made sense to us."

CHAPTER ELEVEN:
A FIGHT FOR THEIR HOMELAND

BY LATE 1968, THE ETHIOPIAN ground and air force had silenced the uprising in and around Bale. The resistance army was trapped in Dallo and Madda Walabu between the Ganale River in the south and the Welmal River in the north. The Ethiopian army's objective was to finish off these Bale fighters once and for all.

The timing couldn't have been worse for Wako Gutu's army. They were out of ammunition, and Somali help was drying up. Six months prior, Adam Jilo was sent to Somalia to get arms support. If anyone could convince the Somali government, it would have been him with his eloquence and strategy. As hopeful as they were about Adam Jilo's ability, nobody expected much out of this trip. Nonetheless they wanted to try; giving up was not an option.

In anticipation for the most consequential battle in the Bale Revolt, all the leaders, elders, and families were gathered in a place called Arrojji, in the center of Madda Walabu. Wako and the team knew that if they lost this battle, they would lose it all.

Losing Arrojji would be symbolically huge. It would go beyond losing a battle or even the war; it would mean losing Madda Walabu. That loss would mean the Oromo people all around Ethiopia would give in or be subjugated. No one would challenge the tyrannical Ethiopian government again because even the brave sons of Arsi from Madda Walabu could not defeat the mighty army.

The Ethiopian army changed their tactics. Whereas before they would attack and return to their base in Nagele or Masno, this time they decided to advance and engage in battle by going deeper into the rebel-held area. Day by day, the government continued advancing from both the north and the south without any retreat. They dug holes and stayed there. Their goal was to capture and/or annihilate the Bale fighters once and for all. Reinforcements were constantly dispatched from the Bale (north) and Borana zones (south) to encircle the Bale fighters. "They surrounded our families from all directions," Hangasu said.

The government also conducted airstrikes every day. Because the land was sparsely populated, it was difficult to kill many people. Instead, the airstrikes were focused on destroying cattle. This strategy was effective because the Bale fighters relied on these cattle for their livelihood. If the government could weaken their economy, they could weaken the Bale fighters in the process.

The people of Madda Walabu devised their own strategy to counter the government's airstrikes. They learned that the airstrikes were targeting two things: smoke and animals at water places. The pastoralist used fire from wood chips for cooking and light. Smoke is the natural consequence of insufficient wood burning. Water was a key place for community gathering because while animals drank, families socialized. It was also the best place to catch up on the latest news. With the intensified air attacks, the people were forced to adapt. They decided to remove the two targets that the government was using: smoke and animals. They shifted their activities to the evenings. They cooked at night. They fed their animals at night. Because the jets came only during the day, this gave the Bale fighters a small relief from the airstrikes.

The Ethiopian army kept advancing, zeroing in on the rebel-held territories. Meanwhile, the Bale fighters retreated because they were out of ammunition and were conserving everything they had for the last moment—to defend their families until their last breath. Those who didn't have rifles sharpened their knives. The destruction seemed imminent.

According to Hangasu, there were meetings after meetings in big groups and small groups. "One afternoon after a meeting, everybody was dismissed. I only remember my dad and General Wako Gutu, but there were only two or three other people left. I just sat in the meeting. I am sure nobody noticed me as I was sitting right next to my dad. The meeting was a classified top-leadership discussion. I don't remember what was discussed, but I said something that captured the attention of people in the room. Since that day, General Wako always allowed me to sit in the leadership meetings where even high-ranking military officers and elders weren't allowed. When my dad asked me to leave, General Wako says, 'Stay, I remember what you said in Arrojji.' I might have provided some insight."

The community gathering was turned into invocations of God. Many animals were slaughtered to keep the army well fed. They recited the Quran constantly and asked God to aid them because they fought for their freedom. They had no regrets that they were involved in this war because they didn't have a choice. The government had pushed them into it. The Bale fighters knew they would die anyway; they wanted to die fighting for what they believed in, to make sure their children didn't inherit the same destiny as theirs. Morale was low, but their spirit was strong because they were hopeful of God's help.

Exactly one day and two nights before the battle of Arrojji, Colonel Adam Jilo returned from Somalia. He brought two gifts for the Bale fighters. The first gift was that he was able to convince the Somali government to provide arms support just one more time. The government gave him advanced lethal booby traps and machine guns. The booby traps came with short strings with the option of extending them. The Bale fighters immediately got to work setting up the booby traps along the route the Ethiopian army was using for their approach. Morale had never been higher. Booby trap technicians such as Aliyyi Umar Aaga and Abdullahi Roba used a local "extension cord" called a *gaale*—a long, strong, yet flexible branch of a tree.

Traditionally, booby traps were set up across the road (or very close to the roadside) and hidden from the enemy. The enemy's action would trigger the explosion. But the Ethiopian army already knew these tricks. Booby traps were a common weapon in these wars. The government army had come up with sophisticated methods to avoid them. When they advanced to new territory that was previously held by the insurgents, they used the cattle they seized from the Bale fighters to set off the booby traps. If any booby traps had been set up, the cattle would die, not the army. The government army also used native auxiliaries called *Nachi Lebash* (literally "white [cloth] wearer"). *Nachi Lebash* walked in front of the army to neutralize booby traps and clear the way. These *Nachi Lebash* were locals who worked for the government in exchange for filling their belly. The Ethiopian army used them to transport items, to gather information, and to act as road guides.

Now, the Bale fighters wanted to detonate the booby traps on demand so nothing would be left to chance. The booby traps were set up slightly away from the road so they wouldn't be accidentally triggered by the enemy. To entice the government army, the Bale fighters and their families evacuated the hill they originally controlled. Normally it would have been a mistake to give up control of higher ground because elevated locations made it easy to see the enemy's movement, providing an advantage. By taking control of this hill, the Ethiopian army became more powerful—or at least they thought they would become so. The insurgents basically dangled themselves in front of the Ethiopian army, baiting the army to come and finish them off.

The Ethiopian army took the bait. They began taking over the hill. They sent the cattle, then the *Nachi Lebash* and followed them. When they realized there were no explosives on the road, the military quickly advanced. The Bale fighters watched them with patience. As the army advanced and the majority of them had entered the range, the Bale fighters began detonating the booby traps, one after the other. Explosions came from all directions. The army couldn't move forward or retreat. They cried for their lives. The few who tried to escape were pushed back in by the Bale fighters.

Nobody knew the number of casualties on the Ethiopian side. For sure hundreds, as eyewitness Dhombir veterans describe it. When the army commander, Colonel Daffara, arrived, he was told the troops had literally become crazy (from the chaos of the battle). Daffara was reported to have identified the crazy troops and executed them. He ordered the rest of his men to take control of the water at any cost. However, the Bale fighters had already cut the troops' water supply line except for one pond.

Gutu's army resisted the government army and eventually released the pond, but not before they contaminated the pond water with donkey carcasses. The water tasted and smelled horrible. Daffara's army was dying of thirst. They drank from the water, kneeling down to drink just like animals. Some got extremely sick. They were heard crying, "Wako, Wako, Wako..." It was not clear whether they were calling for help or calling him out of contempt.

At the end of that day, survivors were airlifted out by military helicopters. The guerilla fighters always seemed to be one step ahead of the mighty Ethiopian army in this battle. It was the most humiliating defeat for the Ethiopian army. Colonel Daffara returned to his base in Sidamo with his tail between his legs. According to Dhombir veterans, that was the last infantry unit dispatched against the people of Bale. The Ethiopian government escalated the struggle to only airstrikes. They dispatched airplanes to strike twice a day, in the morning and afternoon.

The second gift that Adam Jilo brought was two Oromo students. The first was Jarra Abba Gada, and the second was Abdul Hafiz. Both were from the Harar region of Ethiopia. They wanted to witness the much talked about Bale Oromo People's struggle for freedom. Jarra acted as a journalist, taking photos during this battle. Abdul Hafiz took notes. The presence of these two Oromo students was significant because later in the 1970s, Jarra Abba Gada went back to his hometown in Harar and founded his own Oromo Liberation army, using the experience and inspiration he'd gained from the Bale Rebellion. This is how the Oromo people's struggle spread throughout Ethiopia.

When the dust settled, the top leaders of the Arrojji battle were Abdullahi Magan, Ibrahim Qaallu, and Abdullahi Ibrahim. While they had a definite victory over the mighty Ethiopian army, the Bale fighters also lost one of their best. Abdullahi Magan, a distinguished hero, was martyred in this battle. But the Bale Oromo defended themselves and their homeland for another day.

That was the last Ethiopian military ground attack on the Bale fighters.

The Bale fighters fought courageously, but their families also played a critical role. The Bale fighters were not soldiers in the technical sense. They lived at home with their families. They didn't go to battlefields. Their lands *were* the battlefields. Their women and children were casualties of the war. Lack of proper organization and management exposed the families to daily bombardment. Wako Lugo had initially advocated for separating the army from the general population so battles didn't have to take place in the neighborhoods. This idea was not accepted, partly because after the first battle with the Ethiopian army at Malka-Annaa, things had snowballed; one battle led to another. The fighters kept reacting to the government attacks without time for strategic thinking. Eventually neighborhood battles were accepted as the norm.

On another airstrike day in Madda Walabu, Hangasu and his people were at the intersection of the Ganale and Welmal rivers, which join and flow toward Somalia. "We were [many families] trying to cross the river," Hangasu said. "We had a caravan of camels carrying our provisions. As we were attempting to cross the river, the camel at the head of the caravan refused to cross*

"As adults tried to convince—or more likely force—the camels to cross the river, all of a sudden, the Ethiopian fighter jet struck our caravan. We were showered with bullets. Dust was all over the place, and it was hard to see everybody.

"My dad [Wako Lugo] picked up his machine gun and ran after the jet to shoot it down. I ran after him. Other people used barriers, like a tree or a rock, while shooting. My dad was walking and shooting. I admired my dad for his bravery. Bullets from the jets were all around us almost like a shower. I have no idea how we survived. In the middle of all of this, my mom [Fato Sheikh Ahmed] followed me. She came and grabbed my hand to take me back out of this danger zone. I refused to go with her because I wanted to be with my dad. My dad told her to leave me alone and get out of there. I still remember the tears that covered her face and the pain I was inflicting on her."

Fato was born in and grew up in a city. At this time, she lived in the deepest jungle of Madda Walabu, bombarded daily with airstrikes. She still managed to run to the battlefield to rescue her son, who wanted to be just like his father—a freedom fighter.

---

* In a caravan, camels "obey" direction from the lead camel. If the lead camel stops, they will all stop. In this case, the lead camel was disturbed by the river in front of it and immediately after by the loud sound from the jet.

CHAPTER TWELVE:
JAGAMA KELLO AND THE
PEACE DEAL

ACK IN FINFINNE, EMPEROR Haile Selassie was frustrated. He wanted a permanent solution to Bale's rebellion. He realized that the more fire he threw at Bale, the more it blew back in his face. He sent one general after another to silence the uprising, all to no avail. He sent Fitawrary Worku Inku Selassie, followed by Colonel Mengesha Gebre-kidan, followed by General Kabeda Yakub. They weakened the Bale fighters. They destroyed the pastoralist economy by killing their farm animals. But they were unable to stop the rebellion. The emperor knew military action wouldn't solve his problem in Bale; he was a tyrant but shrewd in political and military maneuvers.

This time Haile Selassie wanted to try peace. He selected General Jagama Kello for this mission. Jagama was an ethnic Oromo. He was also loyal to the emperor. Jagama was among the few military generals who'd restored the emperor to the throne after the 1960 coup attempt. Jagama was considered a national hero because he was part of the army that fought and defeated the Italians in 1941. The emperor tasked Jagama with bringing the Bale uprising to a close through peace. Jagama embraced the mission: If he did it right, he would both please his emperor and save his fellow Oromos from destruction.

Jagama initiated a peace talk with the leadership of the Bale fighters. He simultaneously began encircling the Bale fighters from all directions, cutting their supply line from Somalia.

In early 1969, Jagama traveled to Nagele, where the Fourth Division Army was stationed to control the uprising. He sent three military men, led by Basha Hussein Yahya, armed and in full military uniform. This was Jagama's first experiment to learn what kind of people these Bale fighters were.

Basha had been born and grew up in Nagele. He joined the Ethiopian army at a young age. His mother, Asha Butta, was Wako Lugo's cousin. Asha was in the business of buying and selling arms. The government found out because her neighbor, Ibrahim Madob, snitched on her. One night he called her out, making it look like he had an arms deal for her, but after leaving with him, she never returned home. It is believed that Madob turned her over to the authorities and that Shi Alaqa Buzuna (the Ethiopian army commander in Nagele) had her killed. To this day, nobody knows the location of her grave or if she has a grave at all. Stories like this happened all too often in southeast Ethiopia.

Basha Hussein Yahya was the translator for the peace talks. He spoke both the Oromo language and Amharic fluently. Jagama's message was, "We want to talk to you. We want peace. The government is ready to pardon you if you surrender and turn in your weapons. Please send one of your leaders to discuss the details."

Wako Lugo, Wako Gutu, Muhammad Balade, Hussein Haji Somo, and many Bale fighters listened to the message. They fed the three government messengers while discussing what to do.

After some discussion, the elders told the three messengers to return to Jagama and tell him, "We heard your message; we will consult our people." The messengers went back to Nagele. The Bale fighters had a lukewarm reaction to the message because they didn't trust the government. They also knew the power of the whole Ethiopian government was focused on them because the Bale fighters in other parts of Bale (such as Ginnir, El-karre, and Barbare) and Sidamo had given up. The Wako Gutu group in Madda Walabu wanted to buy time to find a better solution.

When the messengers returned to the Fourth Division camp in Nagele, Jagama couldn't have been happier. The experiment had worked. "These people are not *shifta*," he said. *Shifta* was an Amharic term for bandits. It was what the Ethiopian government used to call the Bale freedom fighters. Now that view had shifted for Jagama. Jagama had sent three men in military uniform to provoke the Bale fighters because he was curious what they would do to a messenger wearing their enemy's uniform walking freely in their territory. The Bale fighters took care of the messengers and sent back a diplomatic message.

Jagama became hopeful that the peaceful approach could work. He sent another message, this time specifically asking to speak with Wako Gutu or Wako Lugo face-to-face. The Bale fighters decided that Wako Gutu should not meet with the Ethiopian government. He was the head and face of the movement. If anything went wrong, it would further weaken the resistance.

Wako Lugo, on the other hand, was the best choice. He had worked with the government before as the people's representative in Nagele, Dallo, and Madda Walabu. He knew how to handle the government. Therefore, the responsibility of dealing with the government was given to him. Because he was sick at the time, the negotiation was delayed a few months. Jagama was impatient. He wasn't sure if the Bale fighters were dragging their feet for the negotiation or if they were planning something else. Still, he understood why the Bale fighters did not trust the government.

Back in Finfinne, Haile Selassie began developing additional options to make sure the negotiations would work.

One option was to build a bridge on the Ganale River to make sure his army could cross over to Bale (Madda Walabu). At that time, his army was trapped in Nagele. A bridge would make the ground military a viable option. For this task, he enlisted the support of the British government, which provided the funding and civil engineers for technical support. This bridge was completed in 1969.

At the inauguration of this bridge, Haile Selassie wanted to meet with Wako Lugo and other Bale Rebellion leaders. When Jagama was told Wako Lugo was still ill, he asked Wako Lugo to send his children to meet with the emperor. Three people were selected to attend the inauguration: Hussein Wako Lugo, Sheikh Musa Bati, and Hussein Quri Bullicha. That was the first substantive exchange of people.

On Ethiopia's eastern border with Somalia, there was a new development. On October 21, 1969, General Siad Barre became president of Somalia following the coup d'état that killed the previous president, Abdirashid Ali Sharmarke. Abdirashid had tentatively supported the Bale fighters over the previous two years. This change of government in Somalia had a significant impact on the Bale Oromo fighters. Somali support for the Bale fighters became uncertain.

Haile Selassie saw an opportunity and exploited the situation to expand his options for negotiation. He could use the new Somali government against the Bale Oromo fighters.

He met the new military ruler of Somalia, General Siad Barre. He promised to recognize Siad Barre if he ended Somali support of the Bale fighters in Bale and Ogaden (a region in Ethiopia that is highly disputed by Somalia and Ethiopia).

For General Siad Barre, Haile Selassie's congratulations would help legitimize his presidency because Haile Selassie was considered Africa's eldest statesman. Selassie had a strong influence in the Organization of African Union (OAU). Siad Barre accepted the offer and immediately stopped all support of Bale fighters in Ethiopia.

According to Hassan Sheikh Bashir Dado, who was 14 and living in Somalia at the time, the transition from Abdirashid Ali

Sharmarke to Siad Barre was the hardest period for the Bale freedom fighters. Hassan was born in Nagele (Mi'esa village) in 1955, and his father took him to Somalia in 1968.

"When the Somalian government support halted, the thousands of Oromo people from Bale who were previously provided with accommodations all of a sudden lost it," Hassan said. "Quickly, people ran out of food. My father was slightly well-off because he got married to a Somali woman, and he owned his own home. However, almost 100 percent of the families were exposed to hunger. I have witnessed people going from door to door begging for food. The Somalis were overwhelmed by the mass community that turned hungry almost overnight. They told their children that Arsi Oromos will eat you. So, run away if you see them."

These were people who had come to Somalia to liberate their country. They may not have been rich, but most had a good living back in their country. Now they had become beggars to survive in a foreign land. If the Siad Barre government stopped meeting the basic needs for these people, there was no way the government would provide arms support. The Bale fighters were stuck, hungry, in Somalia.

Back in Madda Walabu, the Bale fighters saw no option but to negotiate with the government. Wako Lugo sent three of his children (Kadir, Hussein, and Hangasu) to meet with Jagama in Nagele. "I remember meeting General Jagama Kello," Hangasu said. "He took a picture with me. I was told we were pardoned. My brothers and I stayed at Basha Hussein Yahya's house in Nagele. A few days later, my dad came to Nagele with sixteen other people to meet with General Jagama Kello."

Wako Lugo's arrival was a big milestone for Jagama. General Wako Gutu was the overall leader of the Bale Rebellion, while Wako Lugo was the leader of the elders on political and administrative matters.

My uncle recalled of that meeting when he was 13 years old, "General Jagama seemed like a reasonable person. I remember the conversation he had with my dad. He said, 'Many generals were sent to you before me. They killed you, your children, and your cattle. For doing that they got promoted and decorated with more stars. I also want to get promoted, but I also want to save you because we are the same people. Please work with me.'"

*

Jagama Kello was born in Shawa, Ethiopia. He rose through the military ranks as a result of his bravery and loyalty to Emperor Haile Selassie. He was an introvert yet was also confident and dignified in interacting with people. Hangasu said, "You could be with Jagama all day long, and he only says a few words." Jagama was results oriented. The emperor gave Jagama unique latitude to make decisions without consulting him every step of the way. The emperor rarely gave such latitude to other generals. He trusted Jagama. Jagama deeply believed in a united Ethiopia.

Jagama met with Wako Lugo and the Bale delegation. He made an offer: "His Majesty Janoy will pardon you. Janoy wants peace. You need peace. As part of this deal, you must lay down your arms."

"We would accept the deal if we are allowed to self-govern our region," Wako Lugo said. "We were abused by the emperor's deputies. We were told by this government we didn't belong in this country. That was the reason we got into this war. We need an Oromo to govern our region."

Jagama agreed to bring the request to Emperor Haile Selassie. Jegema and Wako Lugo had an understanding. The negotiation moved forward. Jagama wanted to quickly spread word of this accomplishment to the whole region of Bale to make sure Bale fighters heard the big news: Peace is on the horizon, and Jagama had sat down with rebel leaders and reached an agreement for a cease fire.

Before he could do that, he had to take Wako Lugo and his comrades to the emperor so they could be pardoned. Hangasu said, "I don't remember everybody, but I remember my dad, Hassan Wako Gutu [son of General Wako Gutu], Hussein Haji

Somo, and Muhammad Balade [a total of seventeen people] were airlifted with General Jagama to meet with Emperor Haile Selassie."

Jagama introduced the Bale delegation to the emperor, who then pardoned them.

Jagama took pictures with the Bale delegation so the news that Wako Lugo and his comrades had met with the emperor and been pardoned could be included in pamphlets that would then be distributed throughout Bale.

The pamphlets essentially went viral. They said that Wako Gutu's second-in-command, Wako Lugo, had been pardoned by the emperor. The delegation quickly returned to Nagele, then to Bale, where the rest of the freedom fighters were located.

From the Bale fighters' perspective, General Jagama had so far not disappointed, but they still didn't trust the government. With Somalia cutting its ties with the Bale fighters, continuing to fight would only destroy whatever was left of their families. The Bale fighters divided themselves into two groups. One group was sent to Somalia in case this negotiation didn't work out to regroup and resume the armed struggle. The other group surrendered to make peace with the government. The peace deal wouldn't be sealed without General Wako Gutu, the leader of the movement.

Wako Lugo took Wako Gutu and the rest of the elders to Jagama. A total of forty-eight people, including General Wako Gutu, were flown to the emperor's palace for pardon in 1970. Hangasu was one of the forty-eight people. He was 14 years old.

Jagama finally brought the uprising to an end. He was anxious to make the peace agreement official. He brought the Bale Rebellion leaders to the palace; the only thing outstanding was for them to receive the emperor's pardon.

In his autobiography, General Jagama Kello said, "When I brought the Bale leaders to the palace, General Kabeda Yakub was waiting for me there." General Kabeda had been in charge of silencing the Bale Rebellion until he was replaced by General

Jagama. General Kabeda was the head of the Fourth Division, headquartered in Finfinne.

"General Kabeda took a good look at General Wako and got angry. He entered the palace; I was still outside waiting for permission to enter. A few minutes later, the emperor summoned me, and I entered the palace. General Kabeda complained to his Majesty Haile Selassie that 'Wako should not be pardoned. This man destroyed the countless lives of our uniform men. He must be prisoned. Pardoning him would encourage others like him to cause more destruction in this country.' His Majesty told him that Jagama gave me his word that won't happen.' His Majesty now looked at me and said, 'that was what the Head of Infantry recommended and that was what I told him. What do you say?"

"I said, '*Girmawe Jahnoy* [that was the proper title the emperor wanted to be addressed as], Your majesty thinks much further than us.' Flattered but curious, 'How so,' asked the Emperor." Jagama continued explaining himself, "As you know, we sent multiple messages to Wako Gutu conveying the message that the emperor wants to pardon him and his people. These Bale fighters are still suspicious. First Wako Lugo came to test us. You pardoned him and his friends. Only after this confirmation, Wako Gutu decided to come. The Bale Rebellion is not over. They still left behind other military leaders in the jungle. The Bale situation is fragile, if it gets worse, even the words of the King of Kings won't stop it. The pardon declaration must be implemented as planned, *with your permission.*"

Jagama was nervous to his bones. If the emperor changed his mind in favor of General Kabeda's proposal, everything he had worked for over the last two years would be wasted. That was exactly what Kabeda wanted. Kabeda was jealous of Jagama because he had brought the Bale Rebellion to a conclusion through peace, something Kabeda hadn't achieved by force.

Finally, Haile Selassie broke his silence. He looked at Kabeda and said, "Look, didn't *we* tell you?" (That was the royal *we*. The emperor was talking about himself.) He delivered that message with his penetrating eyes on Kabeda. "Wako is still suspicious of *us*," Haile Selassie said. "*We* must stand by our words. We were looking for him for a long time." Jagama was relieved at last, and the emperor told him to bring in Wako and his group.

Hangasu remembers entering the palace: "Haile Selassie was sitting on his chair. Everybody else was standing. He had two dogs that sat around him. As we entered the carpeted room and stood in front of him, he looked at General Wako for a few minutes as if he was trying to intimidate him."

Haile Selassie addressed Wako Gutu. "Picking up a few rifles and killing people does not make you a king. *I am the only king in this country!* Wako! Why did you burn your country? Please explain it to *us*."

Jagama captured the exchange in his autobiography. Wako Gutu said, "I was forced to leave my country [by your people]. Why would I be asked to leave my country? I am an Ethiopian, not a Somalian. But I was told to go back to Somalia. In this process, my people were killed. Our properties, cattle, were seized. Hundreds were drowned in the Ganale River and were chased by the government police, army, and Guji and Borana. I moved my family to Bale. They didn't leave me alone in Bale; the governor in Sidamo ordered the Bale authorities that I be arrested because he said, 'I rebelled against the government.' So the government in Bale confiscated my properties, cattle. My family was separated from each other and scattered all over the place due to this government terror. Thus, I went to Somalia and acquired forty rifles. With those rifles I re-united my family and took back some of my properties previously confiscated by the government. Because of this, they called me *shifta* and continue to terrorize my people to this day."

According to Hangasu, at this point, Wako Lugo took over. "We were forced into this war because your governors and settlers were thieves and corrupt. We had to pay them bribes so that they would accept government taxes from us. There were no channels for bringing up grievances because your provincial authorities were all corrupt and arrogant. We had no choice but to fight back."

After intently listening to both Wako Gutu and Wako Lugo, Emperor Haile Selassie said in an understanding voice, "So, in essence we forced you to rebel. You are all pardoned. In the future, if you face bad administration, you directly bring your issue to *us* through Jagama."

A few days later, Jagama was assigned to Bale as a civilian governor to ease administrative grievances. Lamma Gobana, another Oromo, was assigned as Madda Walabu district administrator. The goal was to reform the Bale provincial government to allow Oromos to govern their region. These new administrative appointments were a huge step forward for the people Bale. It came as a direct result of their struggle for self-governance and autonomy.

*

Jagama was not the only Oromo general who had risen within the Ethiopian military establishment. General Tadesse Birru was another famous officer from the Oromo ethnic group. Just like Jagama, Tadesse also fought the Italy invasion to defend Ethiopia. Tadesse was also instrumental in reestablishing Emperor Haile Selassie on the throne after the 1960 coup attempt.

General Tadesse Birru was also assigned to provide military training and protection to Nelson Mandela of South Africa during his stay in Finfinne in 1962. General Tadesse Birru was credited for saving Mandela when an attempt was made on his life the same year in Finfinne. Therefore, General Tadesse Birru was every bit like General Jagama Kello in assimilating and embracing Ethiopianism.

Tadesse was a loyal general. So much so that some Amhara elites like Prime Minister Aklilu Habtewold, assumed that General Tadesse Birru was an ethnic Amhara. On multiple occasions, the prime minister asked to General Tadesse Birru to limit the number of *Gaalla* (a derogatory name given to Oromos back then) in the educational system. These encounters with the prime minister completely shocked and changed General Tadesse Birru's view toward the Ethiopian government and pushed him to join the Macha-Tulama Association.

The Macha-Tulama Association was established in 1963 in Finfinne by Oromo professionals. The organization's stated goals were to organize and educate civilians in literacy, health, and development. However, the real objective was to organize and mobilize Oromo nationalism. The stated goals gave the organization a sort of cover from the emperor's scrutiny early on.

Tadesse became a prominent figure within the organization. This angered the emperor and his officials. The prime minister used a bombing in Finfinne and a rebellion started by Oromos in the Bale province as a pretext to ban the Macha-Tulama Association. General Tadesse Birru was arrested and sentenced to life in prison. His organization was disbanded in 1966. General Tadesse Birru fought the Ethiopian system once he realized its ill intentions and actions against the Oromo people and became the state enemy. General Jagama Kello remained in the system and supported the system to the end.

*

Finally, the Bale Arsi Oromo struggle for freedom came to an end. They never had a fancy name. They'd tried *hizbi,* meaning 'the struggle of the people.' They'd tried *Dhombir*, the name of the first rifle they raised against the government. They didn't have a comprehensive strategy or vision for the struggle. They had no plan for taking arms against the government, yet they were forced to fight the government to restore their liberty and dignity. Still, they shook up the mighty Ethiopian army and sustained their guerilla war for almost eight years. According to some estimates, more than thirty thousand Bale people lost their lives. Almost all their livestock was destroyed, estimated in the millions. People who were considered wealthy before the uprising were, by all measures, poor by the time the war ended. Thousands of people were stranded in Somalia and became refugees as a result of the war.

The Bale Revolt caused significant damage to the Ethiopian government as well. According to Hangasu, material and property damage was more than $75 million USD. Thousands of government soldiers were killed.

While in Finfinne, Wako Gutu was surprised and disheartened to see and hear Oromos in uniform, particularly in the air force. He remembered all the airstrikes. This meant the government had used one Oromo group against the other, just as they had done in Nagele with the Guji and Borana tribes. These officers were told they were fighting the invading Somali army; most of them had no clue they were killing their own people.

The Borana Oromo leaders such as Molu Sora and Ali Galgalo later joined Wako's army and fought along with him reversing the early bitter start between their tribes. In fact, Ali Galgalo was martyred along with Wako's close comrade, Abdullahi Usman, while fighting the Ethiopian government. Similarily, the Guji Oromos joined the second wave of Oromo movement dubbed Sowra in large numbers under the leadership of Haji Muhammad Quxxa Danbi and Xula Dube.

The Bale Arsi Oromos inspired Oromos across the country. They demonstrated bravery and determination. The smallness of their means didn't stop them from standing up to the mighty emperor for their own rights. They defended their homeland. They showed the country that the emperor could be challenged.

The motto of their leader, General Wako Gutu, was, "*Gabrummaa Hiddaan Buqqifna; Dadhabnu Ilmaan Itti Guddifna.*" This means "We will uproot the slavery from its source; if we are unable, we will raise a generation that will do so." This motto inspired Oromos and many Ethiopians.

CHAPTER THIRTEEN:
THE ACADEMY

I N 1970, AFTER THE WAR ENDED, the emperor wanted to deepen the relationship with the Bale people and their leaders and make sure this type of rebellion never happened again. The emperor asked Bale leaders if he could take thirty children from the region to educate them in Finfinne with the goal of hiring them in the government when they became adults. Eventually some would serve Bale on behalf of the government in civilian and military capacities.

The people still distrusted the government and refused to send their kids. More importantly, many people in Bale feared that the government would attempt to convert their children to Christianity. They would rather lose the opportunity to educate their children than possibly lose their children's upbringing in their religion.

Only Wako Lugo and Wako Gutu volunteered to send one child each. Wako Lugo sent Hangasu, and Wako Gutu sent Hassan. "Hassan and I were airlifted from Nagele by Colonel Mulatu," my uncle said. "I was almost fourteen years old. I

remember the tears on my mom's face as I boarded the plane."
Wako Lugo and Wako Gutu had no choice but to cooperate with
the emperor. If they chose not to send their children as
everybody else did, it would be a clear message to the emperor
that these leaders were planning something else or still holding
him in contempt. It wouldn't be good for the people of Bale. As
the leaders, they had the responsibility to maintain a working
relationship with the government to ensure the safety of the
general population, and they did so by giving up their own sons.

In addition, Wako Lugo had already worked with the
Italians and the Ethiopian authorities. He understood that part
of the reason the government sent administrators from another
place to govern their region was because their children hadn't
been educated. He also saw this as an opportunity to solve the
bad administration issues they'd experienced year after year.

This was one of the pivotal points in my uncle's life. He grew
up literally on the battlefield. Now he is 14 years old, separated
from his family and living with his former enemy. He has no
idea what the future holds for him. In time, he would realize
that the experiences he gained in Finfinne were highly valuable
in his pursuit of liberty for the Oromo people.

My uncle and Hassan were put in school right away. First,
they attended Akaki Basaqa Elementary and Shemelis Habte
Middle School. They were put on an accelerated path and
constantly moved from grade to grade. As Hangasu recalled,
"We lived inside the Fourth Division Army Camp in Finfinne.
We were told it was for our own safety." In 1970 when Hangasu
and Hassan arrived in Finfinne, the elite public and military
opinion was very negative toward the Bale Rebellion. The
government could only ensure their safety inside the military
camp.

"One evening I went to a restaurant for dinner and to watch
soccer," Hangasu said. "I ended up staying longer than usual. I
returned to the camp around 9 p.m. The guard at the Fourth
Division gate stopped me. He asked me where I had been, and
I told him I was watching a soccer game. He asked me, 'Do you
have any idea how much danger you were in?' I didn't know
what to say. He said, 'If you knew how much danger you were

in walking around by yourself at night, you would not have done it. People lost friends and family members because of what your family did. I don't want to see you walk around at night anymore!'" Just like that, Hangasu was reminded that every day he was in danger. He needed to be more careful.

"During holidays when school was closed, I would visit my family in the Bale and Sidamo region," Hangasu said. "My mom and sister lived in Bidire."

My mom, Zamzam, recalled, "Your uncle used to bring something for all of our relatives and neighbors. There were a few close friends of our mom in Bidire, and he would bring them gifts as well. He brought different kinds of clothes for us. He thinks differently—he would remember things men of his time didn't think about. He brought us sponges for cleaning dishes, different cooking utensils—things that would make our lives easy."

My uncle recalled more from this period. "One Monday morning, General Jagama told Hassan and I to get ready. The emperor wanted to see us. We dressed up and got in General Jagama's car. We entered the palace. Everybody had to bow, so we bowed and entered the emperor's room. Two dogs came and sniffed us and went right back and sat by him. Last time I was here with my father and forty-six other people from Bale, I stood much farther away. This was my first time seeing the emperor in close proximity. He was a tiny man, short and skinny. He was wearing military attire with multiple stars and string decorations across his chest. He sat on a comfortable chair. He had big afro hair, big beard. There were two guards standing in each corner, left and right. He spoke slowly in Amharic with his hands locked by bringing his fingers together [hand steepling]. I later realized that he kept his hands together because otherwise his hands would shake.

"The emperor said, 'You will be given the title of *Mato Alaqa* immediately, and after you complete the training, you will be given *Shi Alaqa*. You will serve your country. You will be taken to the military academy.'"

Mato Alaqa means "one who commands a hundred men;" *Shi Alaqa* means "one who commands a thousand men." The proper answer to the emperor was to say, "Yes, Your Majesty Janoy," followed by a giant bow.

Hangasu said, "I knew we didn't earn this title. So I responded, 'No, we want to continue our school.' The emperor looked at me and said, 'You don't want to serve your country?' I said, 'Yes, I want to serve, but we are too young to serve in the army, and we want to continue our education first.' Jagama was embarrassed by me responding directly to the emperor without using his proper title. He whispered to me to say, 'Your Highness, with your permission.'"

They were told to return the next morning. After they left the room, Jagama agreed that Hangasu and Hassan were not ready for military training or assignment. He only wished Hangasu had spoken properly with the king.

"On Tuesday morning, we returned to the palace with Jagama. At the same time, the emperor also summoned General Tadesse Malke, who was in charge of the military academy. The emperor asked General Tadesse, 'Why don't you accept these kids to the academy?' General Tadesse had no idea what the emperor was talking about. Nobody had briefed him. Not knowing what was going on, his primary response was to show his submission to the will of the emperor. He told the emperor, 'No reason. No reason for not accepting.' Tadesse asked to be briefed by Jagama.

"After Jagama explained the situation, General Tadesse agreed with me and General Jagama that kids either have to complete tenth grade and/or be twenty-seven years of age to enter the advanced military academy," Hangasu said. "I was sixteen and in seventh grade at the time. General Tadesse added, 'These kids are at least six years away from getting accepted at my academy. They need basic military training before they start advanced training.'"

According to my uncle, Haile Selassie condescendingly said, "Ugh, I don't understand this six years you are talking about. These kids already know all the prerequisites you mentioned." The emperor was impatient to have Hangasu and Hassan out in the field. Perhaps he was monitoring what was going on within the country and the surrounding countries. He wanted to send them to Sidamo (Nagele) and Bale to secure the southeast. With no resolution at this meeting, Hangasu and Hassan went back to their schooling.

"That afternoon while we were in school, General Jagama and General Derase Dubbale, the head of Ethiopian Infantry Division, came with a military vehicle. General Derase said, 'You guys refused the command of Janoy? We received a letter from Janoy. Refusing the command of Janoy is not good. It is not good for you and not good for your families!' He seemed to know what he was talking about. We didn't have much choice anyway, so we went with them."

Apparently, the emperor ordered Hangasu and Hassan to start the academy no matter what. Regardless of the rules and procedures, the words of the emperor prevailed at the end of the day.

"They took us to Holeta Military Academy," Hangasu said. "The head of the academy said he didn't have a basic training program for newcomers. He transferred us to the Fiche Military Academy for nine months of basic training."

Hangasu seemed to have benefited from the military training. He believes, if at all possible, everybody should go through military training. The lessons and experiences acquired apply to life in general. "We were trained in military tactics, shooting, maneuvers, using equipment and maps, dealing with nature like water, trees, bridges, hills, provisions, etc.

"We would wake up every morning at 4 a.m. Trumpet will be blown. We had to wake up, dress in uniform, and eat breakfast in three minutes! We would run forty kilometers every day. We wore long shoes with long laces, khaki pants and shirt, and a hat. We had a class where we learned theory, and then we would go practice. It was harsh training conditions.

"You have to be spotless—perfect clothing, shoes tied at all times. I liked it though," Hangasu said. "My friends get a penalty every day. I never got punished except once. One time my shoelace was not properly tied, and I had to do push-ups.

"I learned so many life lessons in that eight-month period than in all my life before that. We were put in harsh conditions, we learned how to survive. The endurance training you get there would help you to tolerate bad conditions in life, not just bodily challenges, but also mental challenges. I learned to be alert all the time and to be conscious of my surroundings. I also learned self-confidence and discipline. Having your habits under control, without indulgence. I believe everybody should go through such training of some sort. Because one that is trained is not like one who is not. One month before our graduation, there was chaos within the army. They sped up the training, and I graduated with one star!"

This idea of promoting people like Hangasu through military ranks was unpopular. Many military leaders opposed the idea. The popular slogan was, "Ethiopia is for the one who killed her, not for the one who died for her!" These leaders said, "These guys' [Hangasu's and Hassan's] families destroyed us. We lost countless friends and comrades because of them. How could they be promoted to be our leaders?"

Hangasu said, "They called us names like 'sons of *shiftas.*' Jagama took us back to Finfinne for our own safety. The military title and promotion were put on hold to ease the situation."

There was a protest from low-level officers in the Fourth Division Army stationed at Nagele. The grievance stemmed from the abuse of high-level army officers. These officers kept water for themselves and their families instead of sharing it with the rest of the army at the base. To make matters worse, the wives of these officers used the water to clean their clothes. The ordinary army officers and their families were thirsty, while the wives of higher-level officers changed their beautiful white *natela* (a traditional white Ethiopian scarf with stripes on the edges) frequently. The ordinary army officers asked for a share of water for their families, but their request fell on deaf ears. These officers organized and arrested all the high-ranking army officers inside the camp and imprisoned them. They elected one of their own to be in charge.

The Fourth Division Army leaders in Finfinne received the bad news. They escalated the issue to the country's defense minister. General Derase Dubale, the head of Ethiopian Infantry, and a few high-ranking officers went to Nagele to resolve the issue. When he arrived in Nagele, the officers who had taken over the camp explained their grievances.

General Derase scolded the officers on how they had handled the matter. He emphasized that they should have resolved the matter through the military chain of command and that their behavior was not acceptable. He requested the high-level army officers be released. Instead, the officers who had taken over the camp arrested General Derase and the officials who had come with him.

This news reached Haile Selassie. He thought hard about what to do next. He selected General Abera Woldemariam from the air force for this mission. General Abera was very popular and much liked by the military. By selecting General Abera, Haile Selassie knew he could win the heart of the ordinary army. General Abera came from a military family. His father and brother were in the military. His grandfather was a Borana Oromo who had immigrated to Ethiopia from Kenya. General Abera himself was born in Maqi, Ethiopia.

When General Abera arrived in Nagele, he explained to those in charge that he was there to listen to their concerns at the command of the emperor, Janoy. "Tell me all of your problems. You have the ear of the emperor who solves your issues." The officers voiced the issues clearly. The general gained their trust by listening to their needs and because of his preexisting credibility with the army.

General Abera promised to resolve the issues as soon as he returned to Finfinne with permission of the emperor. The general also asked for a favor from the protesting army. He wanted General Derase Dubale and his crew to be freed and returned with him to the capital. The army freed General Derase and his officials. They returned to the capital to deliver Abera's end of the bargain.

By this time, other military brigades had aired similar grievances. The military began communicating within its base and to the other divisions. The Second Division, based in Asmara, and the Third Division, based in Harar, began their own protests. The only military division that didn't participate was the First Division—the Imperial Guard. The group had recently been reformed after the failed coup attempt in 1960. While this was going on, university students also continued to protest.

Grievances from the military and students got out of control. The emperor had more than he could handle. General Abera couldn't deliver on his promises; by this time the issue was much bigger than simply the Fourth Division in Nagele. Haile Selassie's power began dwindling, and his fall became apparent.

CHAPTER FOURTEEN:
THE DERG

I N 1973, ALMOST EVERYBODY IN ETHIOPIA was unhappy about one thing or another. Business was disrupted in major cities because taxi drivers were protesting the high gas prices that resulted from the Organization of the Petroleum Exporting Countries (OPEC) embargo. Peasants were protesting for the right to own their own land. Students protested for better governance, for the rights of peasants to own land, and for government reform. The military complained about the need for salary increases and improved service conditions. Eventually the military's complaints overshadowed those of the other groups because the military was the only organization that existed in the country. Ethiopia had no other political or social organization because the country had been led by feudal, totalitarian governments since ancient times.

The military established the Derg, a temporary transitional committee, to manage the aftermath of the events they knew were to come. The Derg consisted of 120 secret members, all low-level army officers. No officer above the rank of major was included. The members were diverse; they came from the armed forces and police. Members' views were as diverse as the members themselves.

"I was asked to join the Derg by recruiters at Fourth Division, but I refused on the basis that I didn't know what was going on or what to contribute," recalled my uncle. "I also didn't know any of those guys, and my friends weren't in it. I didn't want to entangle myself in things I didn't understand."

The Derg came up with a slogan to motivate the army and country. The slogan was *"Ethiopia Tikdem!"* meaning "Ethiopia first!" Quickly thereafter, they modified the slogan to *"Yale Minim Dem, Ethiopia Tikdem!"* meaning "Without any bloodshed, Ethiopia first!" Perhaps through naiveté or lack of political maturity, the newly formed committee wanted to bring about the needed change in the country without spilling any blood.

"On the morning of September 12, 1974, I was working in the file room at Fourth Division camp, organizing military officers' documents," Hangasu said. "The military base was very quiet. All of a sudden, I heard a noise and chanting from outside. I ran to see what was going on. I couldn't believe my eyes. The camp was overrun by the general population. The crowd filled both sides of the road as far as I could see. The crowd repeated, '*Leebaw! Leebaw! Leebaw!*,' meaning, 'The thief! The thief! The thief!' I asked the person standing next to me what was going on. He told me Emperor Haile Selassie had been deposed and arrested. The man said, 'Look, that is him,' pointing to the tiny, slow-moving Volkswagen.

"The car was parked right in front of Atnafu's office (a colonel at fourth Division and later vice chair of Derg). Two uniformed men took him [Emperor Haile Selassie] out of the Volkswagen. He was wearing a black suit, and he had a giant wristwatch. Atnafu's office was fenced, but one can see through the fence. The crowd entered the gate, and everybody was standing at this fence looking at the former emperor. I stood with everyone else at the fence and looked at the man. Journalists were at the fence with everyone else with big cameras, taking pictures. Haile Selassie seemed irritated with the people watching him. He walked around with his usual two hands held together finger to finger. He said to the crowd, 'What are you looking at? I am a person just like you.'"

"I am a person just like you?" This was the guy who claimed he was king of kings! God-elect. Some even ascribed divinity to him. "Were these the same people who prostrated for him every Friday when he used to drive by to the suburb of Debra-Zeit for a weekend stay?" Hangasu wondered. That was an unforgettable scene for Hangasu — the sight of people who used to prostrate to Haile Selassie now calling him thief on one hand and the sight of him saying he was just a person like everyone else on the other. It was a different day in Ethiopia. The feudal system Ethiopia had been built on was gone. Nobody knew what was ahead. It was both refreshing and scary at the same time.

At age 18, my uncle decided to stay in Finfinne and navigate the changes that were happening around him. He went to Finfinne to attend the academy at the request of his family, but now the decision to stay was his. His cousin, Hassan, decided to return to his home district in Madda Walabu after the emperor was deposed. I asked my uncle why he decided to stay. He said, "Here I was right at the epicenter of change. I thought it was an opportunity to see how the transition would play out. It was a risky decision, but I'm glad I did because I gained extensive experience about Ethiopia's politics."

The same day Emperor Haile Selassie was deposed, General Aman Andom was appointed Derg chairman. Mengistu Haile Mariam and Atnafu Abate were appointed vice chairman of the Derg.

General Aman Andom was a famous Ethiopian hero who had led the Third Division. He retired because he wasn't the emperor's favorite. He was originally from Eritrea. By selecting him as chairman, the Derg hoped the Eritrean separation agenda wouldn't come up during this difficult time of transition. The Derg wanted him to keep the country together. They thought General Aman could do it because he was an Ethiopian military hero who believed in one Ethiopia.

Mengistu Haile Mariam was a colonel from the Third Division in Harar. He was good at logical arguments and had no respect for high-ranking officers in the military. In fact, he was selected from the Third Division to go to the capital and join the Derg because his commanding general in Harar wanted to get rid of him. He was a troublemaker and always clashed with his superiors and senior officers.

Atnafu Abate was a colonel in the Fourth Division. By night, he was a law student at the University of Addis Ababa. Atnafu was partly responsible for starting the student movement at the university. "Atnafu was a formal and religious man. I saw him all the time in the Fourth Division. Before he was appointed to the vice chair position, he lived in the Fourth Division at a house. Haile Selassie was kept under house arrest at the same house after he was deposed. Atnafu moved to the palace," Hangasu recalled.

Two months later, on November 23, 1974, General Aman Andom was accused of harboring an Eritrean separatist agenda. A kangaroo court led by Colonel Mengistu Haile Mariam decided, in General Aman's absence, that he should be killed. A team was sent to arrest him at his residence. He refused to surrender and exchanged gunfire with the military. When they couldn't capture him, they ordered a tank to bulldoze his house, which killed him.

The same day, General Taferi Benti was appointed chairman of the Derg. If General Aman Andom had been selected to calm the Eritrean dissidents, General Taferi Benti was selected to calm the Oromos. Many Oromo students and professionals held positions during the transition.

Mengistu and Atnafu remained vice chairmen, but it was clear that Mengistu was running the show. Mengistu Haile Mariam was born in Walayta, a district in southern Ethiopia. His father was a soldier in the Ethiopian army.

Mengistu consolidated power by purging his opposition through the bloody Red Terror campaign that followed Haile Selassie's deposition. Under his leadership, the Derg ruled Ethiopia through Marxist-Leninist inspired policies from 1974 to 1991.

Hangasu lived in the Fourth Division military camp during the transition. He recalls meeting Mengistu Haile Mariam five or six times. Mengistu was not yet the chairman of the Derg; he was one of a few vice chairs. Like many young officers in the camp, my uncle was selected to guard Mengistu; the key criteria to be selected for the guard role was discipline. Officers who often smoked or drank were excluded.

"I smoked during that time, but nobody knew I did because I had it under *control*," Hangasu said. "The young people came from different regions; none of them knew each other. This was key because these guards didn't know one another and therefore were less likely to trust each other and conspire against the government.

"Mengistu usually came home at night. He always had two things in his hands: a pack of cigarettes and a notebook. As soon as he entered the house, he would go straight to his room, take a shower, and change into pajamas—a process that took a half an hour or so. Then he would come to the living room to spend time with his family or to talk to us. He looked for feedback; he repeatedly asked the following questions: 'What do people think of what we are doing? What do people want [to hear]? What do you think about what we are doing?' We simply said, 'It is all well.' The last thing we wanted to do was to say the wrong thing and get in trouble."

My uncle observed two very different sides of Mengistu. In public he was tough and stubborn; people feared him. At home he was humble. He played with his family and talked to his guards. He had two daughters at the time—Anchinesh ("You Are") Mengistu and Yanchinow ("Yours") Mengistu.

"It was interesting to watch the difference between Mengistu and Atnafu," Hangasu noted. "Atnafu was a formal guy. He was the traditional Ethiopian monarch, even though he was advocating for change. His style remained as that of the old monarch. For example, it is a military tradition to give salutations to senior officers and head of state. Every morning when Atnafu left the camp, the guards at the gate would give him salutations. They would do the same when he returned. Sometimes during this, he would come and go several times.

The guards must salute him every time. If they didn't, Atnafu would have them disciplined. Atnafu was actually reported to have punished a soldier for not giving proper salutations in the past.

"Mengistu was totally opposite. He never cared for these salutations. He saw it as a waste of time and an unnecessary thing. One morning I saw Mengistu leaving the camp, and the guard gave him salutations as usual. A few hours later, he returned to the camp. The guard gave salutations again. This time around Mengistu told his driver to stop the car. He asked the guard, what is the meaning of salutation? He answered that it meant greetings. 'One greeting is enough for one day. From now on, no more than one salutation per day,' he declared. Soldiers loved him for that. He had this rebel mind-set. He hated the system and his superiors when he was in the military. He also preferred driving his own car. He would roam the city in his own car, and most people didn't even recognize him."

During the transition period, a few Oromos gained influential positions. Baro Tumsa was a senior advisor to the Derg. Dr. Haile Fida was the chairman of the All Ethiopian Socialist Movement (MEISON). When the Derg regime declared "Land for the tiller," the Oromo people were among the major beneficiaries because, under previous Ethiopian regimes, they had been stripped of the right to own land. The land was owned by the king and the church only. Now, for the first time, peasants could own up to ten hectares of land and produce for themselves. This was a huge departure from the stance of previous regimes.

For their part, the Derg regime also wanted to make connections with the Bale fighters. In fact, during the transition, the military had taken control of the country and eliminated all formidable leaders. Thus, the military controlled everything but had no credibility in the eyes of the public. To build public credibility, the Derg needed endorsements from mature, credible heroes with national name recognition.

The Derg sent a delegation to Bale to find General Wako Gutu. The Derg saw General Wako Gutu as a national hero—someone who'd fought the feudal system. His endorsement for the new government would go a long way in winning over certain factions in the country. However, General Wako Gutu had already fled to Somalia to resume fighting. At the same time, the Derg sent another delegation to find Ali Mira, a famous leader of the Afar people. He had escaped to Djibouti by the time the delegation began looking for him.

After the unsuccessful search for endorsements, the government tried stabilizing the country by talking to different groups. The government sent twenty elders and government representatives from Bale to meet with the Bale Rebellion leaders. Their message was that the people of Bale had fought the feudal system and the Derg wanted to see change just like the Bale fighters did. The Derg wanted to engage the Oromo and build a peaceful relationship to stabilize the country. Hangasu led the effort along with his Oromo colleagues. He met with Oromo elders in Ginir and Dallo to deliver the message.

The meeting was arranged in advance. The Bale fighters now called themselves *Sowra*. *Sowra* was derived from an Arabic term *thawr*, which means "bull." The idea was that this new organization would renew the struggle against the new Ethiopian regime. The Bale fighters never trusted the government, but they agreed to meet with the delegation because the delegation was full of reputable people.

Haj Adam Saddo was considered the wise elder of Bale. He was famous for his candid communication, including speaking truth to power. Haj Adam Saddo was the major link between the Mecha-Tulema Association (an Oromo professional organization banned in 1966 by Haile Selassie) and the people of Bale. He was a man of great stature in Bale. By this time, Hangasu had also made a name for himself. He was a son of Wako Lugo, he had received the opportunity for education, and he cared for the Oromo cause; people were at ease meeting with him.

The delegation finally met with the elders and leaders of Sowra in Ginnir at a location called Gabaa Koolla. Representing the Sowra were Mahmud Bune, Abdullahi Haj Aliyyi (Gees Diir), AbduSabur Aliyye, Sheikh Muhammad Fato, Shafi Aliyye, and Hassan Chiriqsa (Juure).

According to Hangasu, he and the Bale elders delivered the message that "The Sowra are not *shiftas*. You were freedom fighters. The entire country is open for you. You can attend and shop anywhere in the country. You don't have to turn in your weapons; instead keep them and use them for defending your country. Our [government] causes and your causes are the same. Let's work together."

The Sowra leaders were suspicious. Why would the government that had oppressed, abused, killed, and bombed them all of a sudden be nice to them? The fact that Haile Selassie's government had collapsed and a new group was leading the country didn't make much difference to them. Their mistrust of the Ethiopian government ran deep.

CHAPTER FIFTEEN:
THE OROMO LIBERATION FRONT

THE OROMO LIBERATION FRONT (OLF) was established in 1974 in Finfinne. From the start, the organization's true mission was unclear. Some believed it was to pursue total independence from Ethiopia's oppressive rule and establish an independent Oromo country, Oromia. Others believed that the mission was to seek freedom and equality for the Oromo people within Ethiopia. The organization was put together in a very short period of time during the transition.

When Emperor Haile Selassie was deposed, it created a power vacuum. There was no concept of political parties in Ethiopia's history. The emperor was the beginning and end of political power. As soon as he was removed, political parties sprang up. Some parties were founded by Ethiopians abroad, while others were formed from ethnic networks. OLF was one of the political parties formed.

Oromo students and professionals wanted to take advantage of the change happening in the country. Some knew each other through work, others through school. They met in secret to discuss the fate of their people and decided to form an Oromo political organization. Secrecy was important because the military monitored activities in the country, especially in the capital city.

The new military government wanted to gain the support of the masses. To differentiate itself from the previous government and gain the acceptance of the various people in the country, the government endorsed cultural and language initiatives for all of Ethiopia's ethnic groups. The Oromo people were the largest ethnic group in the country.

The Oromo students and professionals saw this initiative as an opportunity to launch their political party. They planned an Oromo Cultural Week. Oromo artists were called from every region of the country to attend the grand Oromo cultural show. The event was held at Ras Hotel in Finfinne. "It was an amazing show!" my uncle recalled. "It created a lot of buzz in the media. Under this cover story, Oromos from different regions met and exchanged ideas. OLF was established."

*

Hangasu recalled one evening. "I had an appointment with Ayyub Haj Adam Buse, my best friend, at Selam Manyita Hotel, room number 2, at 8 p.m. I knocked and opened the door—who I found there was a total surprise! My uncle, Adam Jilo Webo. I didn't expect him, and he didn't expect me! Equally surprised, he asked me, 'Who told you I am here?' I replied that I had an appointment with someone else in this room. Now it was my turn. 'How did you get here?' He said, 'I have no idea.' He added that everybody had left for Somalia except me."

After the two exchanged several questions about their unlikely encounter, Hangasu observed another strange thing. "I had never seen Uncle Adam Jilo chew khat [a popular stimulant made of a flowering evergreen shrub used in social situations in East Africa and the Arabian Peninsula] before or after that day.

I offered to buy him dinner, but he told me he had already eaten. I quickly went shopping and bought more khat and soda. We caught up. He'd come from Bale. We spent the whole night hashing out plans. I had visibility with the government. I knew the plans. I knew what they were looking for and what they were missing.

My uncle told Adam Jilo Webo, "The Derg government is in need of respected national figures. Aman Andow was killed. Nobody knows the military leaders, no name recognition. Ali Mira escaped to Djibouti. General Wako Gutu escaped to Somalia. Here is the plan: I will say this is General Wako Gutu." Hangasu meant he would make sure the government would take Adam Jilo seriously by explaining that he was as important as Wako Gutu. Hangasu assured Adam Jilo by saying, "I have confidence you will present the ideas we discussed even better than me. Just remember, there is no famous person from Bale, and for that matter from the entire country, that stood with the new government. I will connect you with key people in the government. You need to say, 'I was sent by the people of Bale.'"

Adam Jilo thought about it and said, "Hangasu, are you crazy? Nobody knows me." Hangasu assured him not to worry and that he would take care of making him famous. "All you have to say is 'I was sent by the people of Bale.' And that we want peace. Tell them there is a war on us from Somalia. Ask for their help to participate and stand with our people. I know you have the ability to convince them." Adam accepted the plan enthusiastically. After all, he had never liked the Somalian government and didn't mind fighting them if needed.

"My day schedule was full and tightly controlled," Hangasu said. "I couldn't go to places with him. Instead, I connected him with Getachew Waqjira in the morning. Getachew was the head of Intelligence for Bale. I talked to Getachew and told him to take care of Adam and make all the necessary connections. This plan would ensure the Somalia's ambition of annexing part of the Oromia region wouldn't succeed, and it would reinforce the strength of Oromo youths' power in the Derg. The plan would also ensure the Bale people would be protected. Getachew accepted and took Adam Jilo with him."

Getachew took Adam to Baro Tumsa. Baro Tumsa was one of the founders of OLF. Baro was also a senior advisor to the Derg. The next day Getachew and Baro took Adam to the Derg leadership—Mengistu Haile Mariam. They discussed the plan. Getachew later told Hangasu, "Oh my God, the old man [Adam Jilo] can talk *forever*! I got thirsty listening to him and finished three glasses of water!" Apparently, Adam Jilo impressed Mengistu Haile Mariam. Mengistu was reported to have said, "If Ethiopia had three people like Adam Jilo, Ethiopia won't be messed with by anyone!" Mengistu gave Adam Jilo 150 guns and other resources to defend himself and his men from the Somali government. Adam Jilo was then transported back to Bale by airplane as a sign of courtesy.

"Having a Bale representative like Adam Jilo was advantageous from two perspectives," said Hangasu. "First, the Derg government had removed the top feudal/Adahari from their posts. However, by and large, the feudal Haile Selassie system was still in place. This system was built on Amhara supremacy and very hierarchical. The Derg system supported regional self-governance. I wanted to take advantage of this. Second, it was difficult to argue with these old officials with experience and long titles. Nobody would listen to us; we were too young. But Adam Jilo could go toe to toe with these people."

Right after Hangasu and his friends made this connection, Siyoum Serte Madin was appointed the governor of Bale. The Oromo students didn't like him because the Haile Selassie machinery was still running the system. Siyoum had experience, but he believed in Amhara supremacy and couldn't imagine Oromos could be equal partners. Siyoum headed for the capital of Bale, Goba, accompanied by twenty buses to demonstrate to the people of Bale how resourceful the governor was.

The Oromo youth in Finfinne, including Magarsa Bari, Getachew Waqjira, and Hangasu Wako Lugo, objected to this decision. Hangasu took Adam Jilo to talk to Colonel Legesse, who had appointed the governor. Given the mounting complaints from the Oromo youth and Adam Jilo about the man, Colonel Legesse reversed his decision. Legesse sacked the new governor before he even reached Goba. He sent a telegram to Goba informing the authorities there that "the decision was reversed. He is no longer the governor of Bale." Upon reaching Goba and hearing what had happened, the governor-to-be committed suicide by shooting himself in the head with his own handgun to save himself from embarrassment.

The Oromo youth now moved to find the appropriate person to be governor of Bale. They selected Haile Mariam Lenco because he was part of the Imperial Guard (*Kibur Zebenya*). He would listen to different ideas and was not part of the deep feudal network trying to maintain the status quo. The young people believed Haile Mariam Lenco would give them the cover they needed to advocate for the Oromo people's cause, particularly that of the Bale people. The Derg government approved their request and appointed Haile Mariam Lenco as governor, Magarsa Bari as deputy governor, Getachew Waqjira as senior intelligence officer, and Adam Jilo as Bale's elder. Hangasu was nineteen or twenty years old at the time and was too young to be appointed. He was asked to work closely with Magarsa and Getachew. He was also tasked with connecting the Oromo youth with more of the Bale elders.

In his early twenties, my uncle was confident—maybe too confident at times—and hot-tempered. He believed that liberty and dignity for the Oromo people was urgent and that he had a role to play in achieving it. Therefore, when he observed an injustice, he would take it upon himself to correct it. He often did this without thinking about the consequences.

Hangasu had a great partner in the deputy governor of Bale, Magarsa Bari. The two worked together closely. Magarsa was in charge of strategy, and Hangasu was in charge of executing the tactics on the ground due to his familiarity with the province, his name recognition in Bale (as a son of Wako Lugo), and his ability to quickly connect with ordinary Oromo people of all ages.

My uncle recalled, "Once while we were in Robe, Bale, I heard from the people that more than a dozen Oromos were jailed without any justification. I was angry. I went straight to the police station. There was a major meeting in progress in one of the conference rooms. I knocked and opened the door. There were three groups in the meeting: Derg members, Bale administrative leaders, and police."

My uncle stood at the door and asked the police chief, "Why did you jail these people?" Hangasu knew that the police chief was a product of the old feudal system built on the belief in Amhara superiority. Magarsa and Hangasu were trying to change the system, but the old system was too deeply ingrained to change quickly.

The police chief calmly responded, "They were jailed because they were *adahari*" (*adahari* means a feudal member of Haile Selassie's regime). Hangasu said, "Do you know that there is a blind person among these people you labeled *adahari*? Do you know that there are merchants and farmers among them?"

The police chief responded, "Well, they have an *adahari* ideology then."

"You and me are more *adahari* than these people," Hangasu said. At this point, the police chief had had enough and ordered Hangasu to be arrested. "Next thing I knew, I was in jail," he said.

A few hours later, Magarsa heard the news and ordered the police chief to release Hangasu immediately. "The next morning I met with Magarsa," Hangasu said. "He took me for a walk. He asked why I was jailed, and I told him what had happened. Magarsa said, '*Nama of eegetti, Ummata eega*,' meaning 'You can protect the people only if you protect yourself first.'"

Hangasu responded, "I can't let them get away with the injustices they are committing against our people. I don't care if they kill me. I know I am doing the right thing."

Magarsa said, "*Don't you ever think you are one person!* You can only benefit the country and your people if you take care of yourself first. If you are gone, it takes us a very long time to replace you. We can't afford to take that kind of risk now."

CHAPTER SIXTEEN:
BETWEEN ETHIOPIA AND SOMALIA

L OOKING BACK TO 1969 AND 1970, when the Bale Rebellion concluded, thousands of Oromos were in Somalia. They had gone there in search of more weapons. From 1970 to 1975, while Oromos in Ethiopia made some progress toward regional self-governance and the ability to exercise cultural and language freedom, Oromos in Somalia suffered greatly at the hands of the Somali government. In 1969, Siad Barre, the president of Somalia, promised to halt support for the Bale fighters. In exchange, Haile Selassie recognized him as the new leader of Somalia, even though Siad Barre came to power through a coup d'état that had overthrown the democratically elected president, Abdirashid Ali Sharmarke.

According to Hassan Sheikh Bashir Dado, who was born in Nagele, Ethiopia, and moved to Somalia with his father in 1968 at the age of 13, the transition from Abdirashid Ali Sharmarke's government to Siad Barre's government was the worst time for the Bale Oromo fighters in Somalia. He said, "In 1969, the

Somali government didn't just stop the arms support to our people in Ethiopia; they stopped any and all support to the people in the camp who originally came to acquire arms and training. The Somali government halted the rations they had provided, and as a result, people had no food. I still remember our people going door to door in Somalia to beg for food in the hope of some generosity from the Somali public. This tragedy reached a point where Somali mothers told their children to run away if they saw Arsi Oromos because they would eat you."

The Oromos in Somalia had been reduced from freedom fighters to refugees. The refugees knocked on every door they knew for help. It wasn't just the hunger that bothered the refugees; it was also loss of morale. Here they were, having left behind their families and properties to acquire arms to protect their land. That door closed when the Somali government stopped its support. The refugees were depressed. They scattered throughout towns and cities to survive.

After persistent knocking at the government's doors, Siad Barre's government finally agreed to provide a ration. The government wanted an accurate count of the refugees. Adam Jilo was tasked with the job of creating the list and took an interesting approach to creating it. Rather than going from town to town to survey the people to get an accurate number, he sat down and created the list himself. This was Adam Jilo's way of getting back at the Somali government. He had come to Somalia to get arms, but he didn't see any alignment of goals between the Somali government and the Oromo people. The project of preparing the list gave him an opportunity to antagonize the Somali government.

Adam Jilo listed the names of all the people he ever knew, regardless of whether they were in Somalia. He used traditional Oromo names and avoided the Muslim names used by the Somalis. He did this in part to demonstrate that the Oromo were distinct from Somalis—to show that the Oromo people have their own language, culture, and country. He told the people their new names. He even added his mule, Mamite Adam Jilo, to the list.

At this time, the refugees lived in a city called Johar. In 1970, the refugees were moved to a city called Luuq. Each person received twenty shillings, six cans of food, and one bottle of oil per month. Mamite Adam Jilo got the same amount as everybody else. In addition, the Somali government offered free education and military training for anyone who was interested. The refugees were not interested in education—they didn't value it. For many, education and a good life were not the reasons they had left their homes and families behind. They wanted weapons so they could go back to Ethiopia as soon as possible. Few were inclined to pursue military training. Those who did were taught guerilla tactics such as hit-and-run.

The move from Johar to Luuq was on balance positive for the refugees; at least they were no longer hungry. However, the move was still difficult. Even though they had food, it didn't make their lives better. They were not used to the food in the camps. These were people who milked their cattle, camels, or goats and drank fresh milk in their country. They could slaughter cattle or goats to eat fresh meat. Butter and honey were abundant. For them, living off of canned food and oil was brutal. Many got sick and died. The rest were homesick. They had heard the war ended and people were pardoned, so there was no reason for them to stay in Somalia, but they didn't want to go back empty-handed.

The Somali government moved the refugees again, from Luuq to a rural area called Shimbirole. The idea was to give the refugees work. By keeping them busy with farming, the Somali government wanted them to forget about the war while producing grain to support the Somali economy.

"Shimbirole was a harsh place. It was muddy and rural. Elephants could be seen during the day. We used to collect water out of a pit made by elephant's foot. This place was full of mosquitoes as well. Many people were infected by malaria right away," Hassan recalled.

Once the harsh conditions in Shimbirole became apparent, the refugees were moved again, this time to a city called Qoryole. "Qoryole was much better," Hassan said. "The food was great. We had rice, pasta, and macaroni." Apparently, the

Italians had left part of their food culture behind in Somalia after the colonization ended.

In Qoryole, "the refugees were divided into four groups based on ethnicity and where they came from in Bale, Ethiopia," Hassan said. "The first group was called Birimo. They were the Karalle and Ajjuran tribe who immigrated to Ethiopian more than a hundred years prior due to famine. They enjoyed the same rights and responsibility under the Arsi Gada system as other Arsi clans. The second group was called Sugunto. They were the Gurra tribe. Their story was the same as the story of Karalle and Ajjuran above. The third group was called Terso. They were Arsi Oromos from Dallo and the Madda Walabu area. The fourth group was called Karto, and they were Arsi Oromos from the Ginnir area."

The Somali government built a square camp. Each group occupied one side of the square. The center of the camp was used as a military training ground. Apart from a handful of women, the camp was occupied entirely by men. Somali military personnel provided training every morning and frequently conducted emergency drills, sometimes in the middle of the night.

In the early 1970s, once the refugees had settled in Qoryole, President Siad Barre summoned the leaders of the four groups: Mahmud Rube of Birimo, Mahmad Addow of *Sugunto*, Adam Jilo of Terso, and Hussein Bune of Karto.

Hassan Sheikh Bashir remembered the moment when Siad Barre told the Bale fighters that the Somali government would no longer supply them with weapons. "The time is not good for you or for us to engage in war," Siad Barre said. "Instead, we offer you access to school, the opportunity to be trained as cadres, and free land for farming."

It was a generous offer, given the situation, but the leaders of the four groups were disappointed with it. They had no interest in education or farming. Their only goal was to acquire arms. Each of the leaders was instructed to convince his group about the new mission. However, their message fell on deaf ears. The people simply ignored the message from the Somali government. Adam Jilo didn't have patience for that. He sold his house and his mule and escaped back to Ethiopia. A few days later, it was announced on the radio that Adam Jilo, the second in command for Wako Gutu, had surrendered to the Ethiopian government. Many people attempted to follow in his footsteps and return to Ethiopia, but the Somali government arrested them and returned them to Qoryole.

Next the Siad Barre government began implementing the new policies. "Farm tractors were everywhere, cutting down the trees and plowing the virgin land. The people in the camp watched the trucks with amazement," Hassan said. "And then every person in the camp was given a hand digger and told to start digging. Day one, everybody refused to pick up the digger, let alone dig, on the basis that 'this was not why we came to Somalia.' The Somali military men in charge of the initiative were surprised at this refusal. They reported this to their superiors. On day two, more military men showed up to force the people to dig. They refused again, even with the armed men standing behind them." It was clear the government would have to change its tactics or abandon the initiative.

According to Hassan, on day three, the senior commander of the Somali army, Colonel Salaad, summoned the leaders of the four groups to the camp again. This time Colonel Salaad spoke to the leaders' interest. He told them, "We will send you to Korea for military training. You have to pick up the hand digger and dig the land tomorrow morning. Your people will follow what you do."

The next morning all four leaders picked up their digger and started digging without telling anybody in the camp why they were doing so. People watched their leaders dig with utter surprise and confusion. The following morning Colonel Salaad reached out to the next level of leaders in the camp with the same promise that they would be sent to Korea for military training. They too started digging. Eventually everybody started digging, even in the absence of a promise. This top-down approach worked beautifully for the Somali government; the farming initiative took off. After the people in the camp complied with the farming initiative, their monthly allowance increased from twenty to sixty shillings, and the government bought what the new farmers produced at market value. It ended up being a win-win.

As promised, the senior leaders of the four groups were sent to North Korea for three months of military training. "When they returned from North Korea, they brought back two things: a book about Kim II-Sung and a foldable AK-47 machine gun," Hassan said. "Multiple rounds of people were sent to North Korea. Those who attended the foreign training in North Korea received an additional bump in salary. Instead of 60 shillings, these men received 260 shillings per month. They also gained military titles and identifications, and essentially were considered part of the Somalian army." Hassan received comprehensive training in Somalia, including guerilla tactics, conventional warfare, and nursing. "We practiced injection on oranges as a proxy for human thigh muscles," he said.

*

When the Dhombir War concluded in 1970, Wako Gutu made peace with Haile Selassie's government to spare his people from further bombardment. Wako was forced to accept the peace treaty because the Somali government had withdrawn its arms support. This created a leadership vacuum in Somalia within the group of freedom fighters. While Wako was in Ethiopia, the Somali government appointed Mahmud Rube as the chairman for the Bale fighters. Mahmude Rube was from the Ajjuran tribe of Somalia; this tribe had immigrated to Ethiopia and integrated with the Arsi Oromo of Madda Walabu.

Some factions within the Somali government viewed the absence of Wako Gutu and other Arsi Oromo leaders as an opportunity to fill the void of leadership and put forth their own agenda. These factions believed in the Greater Somalia ambition—one in which all five Somali regions would be combined and led under one Somali flag. The five regions were the current Somalia, Somali Land, the eastern Ogaden region of Ethiopia, Northern Kenya, and Djibouti.

In the absence of the Arsi Oromo leaders in Somalia, the small group of Somali-Ethiopians and factions within the Somali government discussed new names. They settled on the name *Somale-Abbo*. *Somale-Abbo* means "Somali people who say *abbo*." *Abbo* means "you." Somalis would say *warya*; Oromos would say *abbo*. According to this definition, there were two types of Somalis: *Somale-warya*, the real Somalis, and *Somale-abbo*, another type of Somali. Implicitly, factions within the Somali government believed that the *Somale-abbo* group must be liberated and united with the rest of Somalia.

The Oromos explicitly reject the idea of *Somale-abbo*. However, there were Somali-Ethiopian groups within the Bale movement. These groups saw an opportunity to gain leadership roles within the movement. Some of them even agreed with the Somali government's vision to annex part of the Oromo region for Somalia. They had a seat at the table with the Somali government. Mahmud Rube took part in the new naming discussion. Rube was a well-respected leader from the Ajjuran tribe, which was originally from Somalia. People close to Mahmud Rube said he believed in the original mission of the Bale movement and not the Somali government's agenda. However, Rube didn't oppose what the Somali government proposed.

*

When Emperor Haile Selassie was deposed on September 12, 1974, the Somali government saw an opportunity. In 1969, Haile had made a deal with Siad Barre's new government. In exchange for Haile Selassie's recognition of his government, Siad Barre would stop arming Ethiopian Bale fighters in Somalia. Siad Barre agreed. He kept his promise by cutting support from the Bale Oromo fighters. With the emperor gone, the Somali government no longer had to abide by the promise. The armed struggle could resume.

Around the end of 1974, Mahmud Rube, the new leader of the Bale Rebellion, set out to Ethiopia with a few hundred trained and armed men to resume the struggle in Ethiopia. When he reached Dallo, Mahmud Rube learned that General Wako Gutu was under surveillance in Bidire; he was not allowed to leave the city.

Mahmud Rube sent messengers to Wako Gutu telling him to get out of the city and join his men. One day Wako Gutu went to the mosque as he usually did for the five daily prayers. But instead of praying, he entered the mosque on one side, changed his clothes, and exited from the other door. He then immediately left the city. A couple of days later, he joined Mahmud Rube and the soldiers in the Bale jungle. Mahmud Rube turned over everything he had brought from Somalia to General Gutu: soldiers, weapons, and provisions. Mahmud Rube knew that for the struggle to continue, Wako must lead. As far as soldiers and the public were concerned, Wako was back in his leadership role.

While General Wako Gutu focused on the military operation, Wako Lugo focused on organizing the population to support the struggle. Hassan Sheikh Bashir, a young man who was trained to be a nurse, was embedded in this military mission. Because he could read and write, Bashir was assigned to work with Wako Lugo. "I travelled with Wako Lugo. I stayed at his house for extended periods of time. I watched how he interacted with the Arsi Oromo community," Hassan Sheikh Bashir said. "Wako Lugo was the undisputed leader of Arsi in Dallo and Madda Walabu. He was probably 6'0" but had a strong and built body. His eyebrows looked like those of a lion. He was a man of few words. He was feared and respected at the same time."

Wako Lugo was most known for his generosity, which he used to build support for the struggle. "At his house, he would never allow anybody to serve him," Hassan Sheikh Bashir said. "He had a unique tradition I'd never seen anywhere else. Nobody eats alone in his house. His wives know to bring their food to one house, usually the house of the eldest wife. As the chief of people, he receives and hosts guests on a regular basis.

All of his guests and family members would come to the main house when food was ready. His wives would bring the food, tea, and/or coffee and walk away to enjoy their food. Wako Lugo would taste the food himself. After he approved, he would distribute the food and pour tea or coffee for every guest, young or old." Meat was expensive. Most people couldn't afford to eat it on a regular basis, but at Wako Lugo's house there was always meat. According to Bashir, "He slaughtered cattle for guests on a regular basis. He loved meat himself, and more importantly, he loved sharing it with his guests and visitors."

When General Wako Gutu returned to Somalia in 1975, the Somali government asked him to give his organization a new name. They informed him of the possible names with the emphasis on the name Somale-Abbo. General Wako Gutu asked for the decision to be delayed because he didn't want to make any decision until Mahmud Rube had returned to Somalia. Rube was in charge of the organization's affairs while Wako Gutu was in Ethiopia, so Gutu couldn't make a decision this big without consulting Rube.

As soon as Mahmud Rube returned to Somalia, the Somali government summoned the elders and leaders in secret to decide the name. The meeting was by invitation only. Arsi Oromo youth were excluded because it was assumed that they wouldn't accept the proposal.

General Wako Gutu was in the meeting but had only a couple of other elders with him. The majority of participants in the meeting were Somali-Ethiopians carefully recruited by the Somali government. Rube suggested the name Somale-Abbo because this had previously been discussed among the Somalis. General Wako Gutu disagreed but was quickly overruled by the others in attendance. Wako was disappointed, but he realized there was nothing he could do. This had been well plotted in advance.

Haji Isaaq Dadhi, a well-respected elder Oromo leader from Ginnir, Bale, was also at the meeting. He was recognized in both Ethiopia and Somalia as a wise and courageous man. He had left Ethiopia and entered Somalia in 1962 after killing a settler with whom he'd had a dispute. He then connected with Hussein

Bune in Ginnir to escalate attacks on the Ethiopian government in the Ginnir area.

When Haji Isaaq Dadhi understood the Somali government's intent and saw the weak position that the Arsi Oromos were in, he told a story:

"Once upon a time, there was a servant. She got sick and complained about her stomach. The king was informed that the servant had a stomachache and needed medical attention. The king ordered that the servant's forehead be burnt. The king wanted to make a mark on the servant's face so she would be known as his designated servant. The king's messengers and police came to implement the king's order. They informed the servant of what the king ordered. She said, 'What I needed was medicine for my stomach, but if the king thinks burning my forehead is better for my stomach, then please go ahead and do it. My king knows best.'"

Haji Isaaq understood that the Somalis were determined to put their mark on the Oromo struggle, and there was nothing he and General Wako Gutu could do about it.

General Wako had two choices. The first was to reject the Somale-Abbo name. He realized the consequences could be severe for him and his people. He was a wanted man in Ethiopia. Without support from the Somali government, he would either get stuck in Somalia or go back to Ethiopia and surrender. This was not an option for him. The second choice was to accept the name. This option would put him in a difficult spot with his own people because it would appear that he would be fighting on behalf of the Somali government, which was not the case. But he convinced himself that at least the struggle would continue. He also thought he could convince his people that he accepted this name to gain short-term support from the Somali government with the goal to gain long-term freedom from Ethiopian oppression.

General Wako agreed to continue the struggle under the *Somale-Abbo* name. Once the new name was accepted and announced, the Somali government demoted General Wako Gutu to the head of the military. He was the supreme leader of the movement no more. Mahmud Rube was promoted to supreme leader as chairman of Somale-Abbo, overseeing all political and military affairs of the movement.

Factions within the Somali government wanted to fully control the Bale Oromo movement to expand their ambition for Greater Somalia. This meant appointing people who shared their Somali ideology and renaming the movement. Even though the Somali government had agreed to halt arms support to the Oromos, they didn't want the movement to stop. The Somali government saw it as a temporary ceasefire. They wanted to use the time to prepare for future attacks on Ethiopia. If the Oromos decided to make peace with Ethiopia, Somalia's agenda wouldn't advance.

They thought the time had come to begin destabilizing Ethiopia. Unfortunately for the Somalis, the early transitional Derg government was friendly to the Oromos. The Bale movement leaders were viewed as freedom fighters who had stood up to the feudal empire, and the Ethiopian government wanted to build a relationship with them. The Oromos were given the freedom to roam the country unhindered, at least initially. This was worrisome for the Somali government on multiple fronts. If the Oromos could control their own destiny, they wouldn't need Somali support anymore. If they didn't need Somali support, they wouldn't be obligated to do any favors for Somalia.

For these reasons, the new name was devised with three goals. First, to weaken the Oromo movement by sowing disagreement between those who agreed with the new name and those who didn't. Second, to minimize the influence of Oromos in the struggle by elevating the Somali-Ethiopians, thereby creating conflict within the struggle. Third, to paint the Oromos as agents for Somalia by changing the organization's name and leadership and assigning it Somali army identification. Then when the Ethiopian government realized that these were not Oromo freedom fighters but rather Somali soldiers, the Oromos would lose the freedoms they were enjoying in Ethiopia and run to Somalia for help once again.

When it came time to implement its plan, the Somali government dispatched the army under its new leadership to several regions in southern and eastern Ethiopia. When these groups were caught by the Ethiopian military and their documents were confiscated, the Ethiopian government would realize that these were Somali army soldiers executing the Somali government's plans rather than Bale Oromo fighters striving for their freedom. The plan worked exactly as the Somali government had hoped.

CHAPTER SEVENTEEN:
HANGASU AND MAGARSA

WHILE THE SOMALI GOVERNMENT plotted to hijack the Oromo struggle in Somalia, Hangasu and Magarsa each had two jobs in Ethiopia. Their official job was to be the civilian administration of Bale. As far as the government was concerned, they did this day in and day out. But my uncle and his friend also had another job—a secret one. This job was to organize the Oromo people, including students, professionals, merchants, and farmers, wherever they were in Ethiopia. Hangasu and Magarsa also worked to protect the Bale Oromo fighters in rural Bale by providing cover from persecution or attacks by the Ethiopian government. It was a risky business. The two jobs, civil administration and organizing the Oromos, were contradictory. The Derg government didn't hesitate to kill anybody if there was the slightest suspicion of working against its interest. The Derg would view prioritizing the Oromo cause as working against the government.

Magarsa's and Hangasu's plan to maintain two jobs became more difficult with time. In 1976, multiple groups of Bale fighters, armed by the Somali government, entered Ethiopia. One of these groups was a Somale-Abbo army led by Hasan Goro. This army entered Ethiopia through its southern border and made it to Borana province. The Ethiopian army received intelligence that this group was coming and ambushed the soldiers, confiscating their equipment.

After searching through the Bale fighters' belongings, the Ethiopian army discovered the group's telegram and valuable documents. The documents were immediately sent to Goba (the capital city of Bale at the time). Until this happened, Magarsa and Hangasu had been assuring the government that the Bale fighters would do no harm and that they were struggling for the cause of the Oromo people. The government accepted that the Bale fighters had good reasons for not quickly trusting the government because the Ethiopian government had a long history of subjugating and oppressing the Oromo people.

"When the documents reached us in Bale, we were shocked!" Hangasu said. "They contained names of people, military titles, and identification numbers; some of the people were actual military officers of the Somalian government with the goal of reuniting Greater Somalia." After the discovery of this document, the Derg regime concluded these were Somali soldiers, not Oromos. My uncle recalled, "Magarsa and I had no response; we were caught off guard. The documents were immediately sent to Derg headquarters in Finfinne."

A couple weeks later, the Sowra army, consisting of thirty to forty men under the Somale-Abbo banner, entered Bale. The Sowra army confronted a similar number of Ethiopian army troops at a place called Baarre, Bale. The Sowra army defeated the Ethiopian infantry because they had a slight technological advantage. The Somali government had given them automatic guns for the first time. The soldiers couldn't wait to use them in the field.

The Sowra army troops had never used automatic rifles before and quickly learned how efficient they are. Upon realizing his group had won the battle, Tula Dube, the prominent Guji Oromo fighter, turned to his Kalashnikov and said, "*Ee Bada Kalashii kiyya*," meaning "Oh, my dear Kalashnikov" and kissed the smoking tip of his gun. He burned his lips! He is still remembered as the hero of Baarre who kissed the hot tip of a gun. He had a large lip blister to show for it.

When news of the Ethiopian army's defeat reached the capital city, Mengistu immediately summoned Magarsa. Magarsa was in Goba, Bale, at the time and left right away. Mengistu asked Magarsa. "How did this happen on your watch?" Mengistu wanted to know how Magarsa had allowed the Ethiopian army to be defeated.

Magarsa was offended and angry that he had to answer such a question. He told Mengistu that he should be asking his generals why they lost the battle. Magarsa reminded Mengistu that his role in Bale was as civilian administrator, not military oversight. Both Mengistu and Magarsa had the tendency to get easily irritated, and they argued back and forth for a while. In the end, others in attendance stopped the argument. Mengistu didn't have evidence, but he did have a hunch that Magarsa and his allies were engaged in more than just civil administration. The conversation deescalated, and Magarsa went back to his post in Bale. However, he knew sooner or later the government would figure out what he and his friends were doing. He started thinking of an exit strategy.

*

In 1977, Oromo professionals held key positions in the Derg government, but they realized they didn't have real influence. Mengistu Haile Mariam had a good grip on power, but his power was continually challenged by other political parties. This resulted in political parties eliminating one another. The Oromos were simply at the mercy of the government. They had no real authority. To have power, they needed to find a way to get weapons.

While working for the Derg government the Oromo professionals had their own informal organization (the OLF). Nuguse Negassa was responsible for making arms purchases on behalf of Ethiopia. That was his official role as the Derg agent. Nuguse was also one of the handful Oromo professionals who joined the OLF. He used his Derg position and access to information to help the Oromo cause by diverting the arms that was coming for Ethiopia to the OLF. Similar to the OLF, the Eritreans had a professional group that worked for the Derg but in secret actively advocated for an independent Eritrea. At that moment, Ethiopia was going to receive two ships full of arms from the United States. The OLF and the Eritrean People's Liberation Front (EPLF) planned to intercept and redirect the two ships, then divide the weapons between the two organizations. Nuguse's job was to track the two ships and redirect them.

At this time, the OLF didn't have its own soldiers. They wanted to leverage the Bale Fighters. Hangasu was tasked to meet with the Bale Rebellion leaders and persuade them to work with the OLF. Hangasu planned to assemble the top OLF leaders (Baro, Magarsa, and Nuguse) and the Bale Rebellion leaders in Shashamanne, Ethiopia. There the two parties would outline how to work together for the long term and more immediately how to intercept arms that Nuguse was working on securing.

Hangasu met with a group of Bale Rebellion leaders in Ginnir, Ethiopia. After explaining the situation, he asked for volunteers. Only one person, Hassan Juure, volunteered for the mission. Hassan Juure said to his colleagues, "What are you afraid of? Are you afraid the government will kill us? I will die anyway. I may as well die advancing the Oromo cause." The elders told him, *"Si qabanne,"* meaning "Hold on. We advise you not to do it." Juure was forced to withdraw his offer.

The Bale fighters met with Hangasu because they trusted him. But the Bale fighters didn't understand the OLF. How could one work for a government and still fight it? It was counterintuitive for the Bale fighters. They saw the world as black and white—you either supported the government or you fought against it.

Hangasu went to Madda Walabu to meet with another group of Bale Rebellion leaders. When he got there, most of the leaders had already left for Somalia. Only a few elders remained. The Bale fighters who remained didn't see much difference between the Derg government and Haile Selassie's regime. Hangasu, on the other hand, saw a noticeable difference between the two governments. He believed in working with this government to change things for his people. The Bale fighters' perspective was that one Amhara government had been replaced by another and nothing had changed for the Oromo people.

My uncle felt he had to do something to capture the voice of the people of Madda Walabu. He was from Madda Walabu, so he assumed he knew what the people wanted. Hangasu wrote a letter on behalf of the people of Madda Walabu to the Derg government. He then gave the letter to the locals to deliver to the Bale administrative officials based in Bidire.

In the letter he outlined the people's demands:

- We want self-determination. For that to happen, we need to be able to practice our religion freely; read, write, and speak in our language; and have access to university-level education in Bale.
- We need equality of religions. Christian faith leaders share power with the government by owning land and having extra privileges. How come the Muslim *Qadhi* (judge) can't even get a salary?
- Each region of Ethiopia has a university. How come Bale doesn't have one?
- We want to govern ourselves. We don't want the government to impose administrators from different areas of Ethiopia on us.

As Hangasu expected, the Bale administrative officials were thrilled when they read the letter. The letter aligned with their policies because it was written by one of their own. The locals who delivered the letter were told to tell others that they were free to return to the country and resume their business as usual.

My uncle was not able to bring the representatives of the Bale Rebellion to Shashamanne as he had originally hoped. He was now in Nagele and wanted to return to Finfinne. On June 27, 1977, Hangasu arrived in Awasa, Ethiopia on his way to Finfinne. "That evening I heard on the radio that Nuguse Negassa had been assassinated by an unknown group while returning from the celebration of Djibouti's independence," Hangasu said. "Nuguse was the leader of the Ethiopian delegation that had attended the celebration. I couldn't believe it."

Hangasu wondered if Nuguse's assassination was related to the plan to intercept the two boatloads of weapons. "But how?" he asked himself. Nuguse's mentor was positioned high within the country's security apparatus. Either way, my uncle figured it was no longer safe for him to stay in the government. He debated whether to go back to Nagele and disappear from the radar or to return to Finfinne and check in with his colleagues. He decided to go back to Finfinne and meet with his friends, including Magarsa. While in Finfinne, Hangasu attended Nuguse's burial.

After a few brief meetings, the OLF ordered all of its members to leave Finfinne because of safety concerns. OLF members were assigned to different regions: eastern Ethiopia (Bale, Arsi, and Harar) and Wollega. Hangasu was assigned to Bale.

*

In the summer of 1977 while preparing to exit Finfinne, Hangasu was conflicted about his destination. The OLF didn't have an army that Hangasu could join in Bale. The only Oromo armed group in Bale was the group led by General Wako Gutu— the Bale fighters. Hangasu knew that the Somali government had already applied the Somale-Abbo name to the group. The Bale fighters' philosophy about liberating the Oromo people may have differed from that of the OLF. Hangasu wanted clarity before he left Finfinne.

Hangasu said, "I asked Magarsa, the deputy chair of the OLF, 'How am I supposed to work with the Somale-Abbo in Bale? They have their own structure and objectives, which is different from ours.'"

Magarsa replied, "Hangasu, this is an unnecessary question. You know what I know."

Hangasu said, "Still, I need clarification on how to engage with them."

Rather than answering his question, Magarsa asked Hangasu one of his own. "Why did they [the Bale fighters] accept the name Somale-Abbo?"

Hangasu replied, "Because they wanted to get arms to fight the enemy."

Magarsa said, "Okay, do these arms use people, or do people use the arms?"

Hangasu said, "People use arms, not the other way around."

"Then," Magarsa concluded, "why does it matter whether they [the Somali government] call us Somale-Abbo or Somale-Harree as long as we get their weapons and use them to defeat our enemy?"

Harree means "donkey." Magarsa made it absolutely clear to Hangasu that it did not matter what the group called itself as long as it had the same mission. Magarsa believed that the ends justified the means.

Hangasu added, "Magarsa's understanding was the mainstream opinion at the time. Those in the field and those in the office understood each other." However, a few years later, this issue of Somale-Abbo would be politicized and become a stigma for those who'd accepted the name. The politicization and defamation would be done by the OLF leaders who would arrive later.

On February 3, 1977, Mengistu called a committee meeting. He excused himself and stepped out of the room. Then his bodyguards opened fire on the other Derg members, including

Chairman Tafari Benti. Mengistu essentially purged all of his formidable opponents at once. After he consolidated his power, he started the Red Terror campaign to uproot all his opponents. For the next two years (1977–1978), the streets of Finfinne were littered with the dead bodies of young people. The streets turned into mass graves.

Families were terrified to claim the bodies of their children and relatives. They could face the same fate if they challenged the government in any way. Some brave mothers claimed their sons anyway to give their children a proper burial. The Derg government charged these mothers twenty-seven Ethiopian birr for each bullet the government had "wasted" killing their children. It was a merciless campaign.

By this time, the Derg had already begun eliminating opposition based on the slightest rumor. No two people could be seen together in public because they would be suspected of conspiring against one of the other groups. Hangasu recalled that the names of the OLF leaders and members were on the Wanted List: "Every interaction with another person had life-and-death consequences. Nobody trusted anybody. It was the most dangerous time in modern Ethiopia's history. I would wear a long jacket, my left hand in the jacket pocket with my finger on the handgun's trigger. My right hand was free to shake hands if it turned out to be a good interaction; otherwise, the left hand in my pocket would be called to the occasion. It was a horrifying period. Either you get killed or you kill to avoid being killed. Everyone had to escape on his own. My friend gave me a fake ID and a driver to get me out of Finfinne.

"Luckily, most of our members were able to escape and make it to their assigned regions," Hangasu said. "A few decided to stay and live in hiding instead of joining the field. Once I made it to Bale, I stayed in Gadab (Adaba) with Haji Abdullahi Ganamo. Haji Abdullahi was a famous Bale Oromo warrior and hero. When I heard his stories from others and observed him closely, he reminded me of my father, Wako Lugo. Haji Abdullahi never took a position behind a rock, a tree, or a ditch during battle. He would walk straight to the enemy line and shoot without any fear of getting shot. My dad was just like that; he shoots the enemy while walking."

Today one might think these men were crazy to expose themselves to the enemy in such a way. In that period, doing so was a badge of distinction. Wako Lugo and Haji Abdullahi Ganamo knew they could die, but they preferred to die while fighting in the most dignified position for the liberty of their people.

By going to Bale, Hangasu essentially joined the Bale Rebellion army. His job was to establish the OLF in Bale, so he tried to stay in touch with the OLF organization. He quickly learned that the OLF was in trouble, not because of the enemy but because of its internal politics. Bad news kept developing amid OLF leadership. Within three months after leaving Finfinne, more than a dozen OLF leaders and founders had been assassinated.

Hangasu's closest friend and mentor, Magarsa Bari, was assassinated in Harar, Ethiopia, along with eight other OLF Central Committee members while they were on their way to Somalia. OLF claimed that the men were killed by the Western Somalia Liberation Front (WSLF) Army.

Reflecting on the incident, my uncle quickly dismissed that claim. "It doesn't add up," he said. "If that was true [that those leaders were killed by WSLF], how come OLF has maintained a good relationship with WSLF to this day?" He insists there had to be another explanation.

One month before the assassination of Magarsa and his comrades, Baro Tumsa, one of the pivotal founding members of the OLF, was also assassinated. A few weeks before that, another leader, Kinfe Haji Hindhesa, was killed in Arsi, Ethiopia. The OLF gave no satisfactory explanations. To this day, many Oromos wish that OLF leaders would explain what happened to those leaders. The Oromo people deserve better.

Hangasu didn't know what caused the trouble within the OLF. The fact that the OLF didn't exist in Bale became a blessing for him. He was safe among the Bale fighters. Many of the fighters either knew him or knew of him due to his father's reputation. He continued organizing Oromos in Gadab, Bale.

While Hangasu was in Gadab, the Derg government discovered the Bale fighters' whereabouts and dispatched sixty-eight truckloads of militia to deal with them. The Oromos in Gadab fought back hard and resisted the government militia. However, they quickly ran out of ammunition. Hangasu was sent to Madda Walabu to restock the ammunition and find reinforcements.

When Hangasu arrived in Madda Walabu, the situation was bad. The Sowra fighters were divided. The Somali-Ethiopian army of the Somale-Abbo had taken control of the arms supply because they had been empowered by the Somali government. The Somali-Ethiopian group also controlled major resources. For example, they collected taxes from the black markets they had established in rural areas; they controlled fees collected at the entrances and exits of cities; they controlled fees for commercial merchandise crossing the Ganale River. They also enjoyed the spoils of war collected among themselves. Prominent Arsi-Oromo leaders were in the back seat. Here the objectives of the Oromo and the Somalis caused conflict. The Somalis were enlisted in the Somali army; thus, they had a salary, stipend, and titles. They believed in Greater Somalia ambition, which meant annexing part of Ethiopia to Somalia. The Oromo had none of those benefits, but they still paid the cost of war.

The Oromo land was in the region of Ethiopia closest to Somalia. The Oromo cause was basically doomed: the Ethiopian government was after them, and the Somali government wanted the Oromo to simply obey their command. Hangasu could not believe that the Arsi in Madda Walabu had given up and let the Somalia-empowered factions run the show. He assembled the Arsi youth in Madda Walabu as well as Hassan Sheikh Bashir and Mohamed Adam Jilo. He also mobilized the many elders, including Hussein Jibri and Adam Gelchu. Hangasu summoned the Arsi and Somali in the area to settle the conflict between the Somali-Ethiopian and the Arsi Oromo through discussion in Madda Walabu.

The meeting turned into a heated debate because the Somalis refused to share their resources. During the meeting, one of the Somalis took a rifle from an Arsi. Hangasu took the rifle from the Somali and returned it to its rightful owner. This act of defiance elevated the tension between the two groups. Luckily, nobody was killed, but the meeting immediately ended with the two groups holding one another in contempt.

As a young man, my uncle was demanding and impatient when it came to fighting for Oromo freedom. The news of the meeting reached Wako Lugo. The Karalle and Ajjuran elders complained to him that Hangasu was creating too much of a problem for them. Wako Lugo summoned Hangasu to give him advice. "My dad scolded me in essence. He told me, 'I heard a lot of complaints about you. Tone down this Arsi/Oromo campaign. Nothing will prevail overnight. You need patience. Sometimes your strength can turn into a liability. Weak people with long-term vision could achieve what strong people with short-term vision couldn't. You might be old enough to have your children, but you won't have children to inherit your vision if you rush things. I strongly advise you to avoid the blood of others at all costs; it's not worth it. Everything you are currently fighting for will come at its own due time.'"

Wako Lugo wanted Hangasu to understand that freedom doesn't come overnight. My uncle understood his father's advice to be patient maybe after twenty years, but at the time, not so much. But he listened. Hangasu turned to organizing the Arsi Oromo, not to fight the Somalis, but to reestablish the Arsi Oromo army.

Hangasu's father was also hinting that Hangasu should get married, just like other young men his age. Usually in this region of the country, young men get married at 16 or 17, and certainly by 18. Hangasu was 22 at the time, much too old to be unmarried.

However, my uncle was in no rush to get married. "I never thought about marriage. I believe the liberty of the Oromo people is *first*. I needed to see the Oromo struggle through." As the son of an Arsi Oromo from Madda Walabu who had the opportunity to observe both the Ethiopian government and the vast Oromo network around the country, Hangasu thought he would liberate the Oromo people first and then maybe get married. Getting married and starting a family was not on his radar.

*

After the fall of Emperor Haile Selassie in 1974, factions within the Somali government wanted to recover disputed territories in Ogaden from Ethiopia. A guerilla group called the Western Somalia Liberation Front (WSLF) had been engaged in an armed struggle against the Ethiopian government since the 1960s. Using supplies and troops supplied by the Somali government, the WSLF intensified attacks on Ethiopian troops in the Ogaden region.

In August 1977, Somalia invaded the city of Jijiga, deep in the Harer region of Ethiopia. Up to this point, the United States had allied with Ethiopia, and the Soviet Union with Somalia. Ethiopia understood that the United States had no interest in providing arms support for a regional conflict. Desperate, Mengistu Haile Mariam of Ethiopia made an urgent appeal for military support to the Soviet Union, which immediately provided military support to Ethiopia, switching sides in the conflict. Cuba also sent combat units to fight alongside the Ethiopian army.

By November 1977, the war was over. Ethiopia had won. The Ethiopian victory meant that the Bale fighters could no longer operate within the Ethiopian border. They had two options left. They could surrender to the Ethiopian government and face the consequences, which meant certain death, or they could move to Somalia in the hope of getting more support from the Somali government.

*

Meanwhile, pressure mounted from my uncle's family for him to get married. My mom, his sister Zamzam, was a big advocate for Hangasu to marry. While he was away advancing the Oromo struggle, my mom was lonely. Hangasu was her only brother by the same mother, and he was never around. When he visited the family, he would leave the next day before she had the chance to finish catching up. At one point, my mom considered changing Hangasu's name to something else. He disappeared as quickly as he appeared. Because his name means lightning, she wished by changing his name he would stick around longer to spend time with her.

A woman's life in rural Ethiopia in the 1970s was harsh. For example, my mother had no rights to a share of her father's cattle because she was female. She was constantly challenged on keeping her brother's portion of the inheritance. My uncle said, "She understood that I had to go out there and do what I believed in, but she could not handle the loneliness. I refused her requests [to marry] many times. One day she sat me down and said, 'If you can't be around to help me, then have a son. I don't care if that son comes out of wedlock!'"

Hangasu was shocked by her determination. "What she said had a profound impact on me. I agreed to get married even though I still decided the marriage wouldn't get in the way of me pursuing the liberty of the Oromo people."

My mom assembled a team of three to find a wife for my uncle: her father, Wako Lugo; my dad, Adam Dire; and her trusted friend and relative, Ibro Taji.

My dad and Ibro identified a tall, beautiful, smart girl named Maryam. Maryam was 16 and came from one of the three highly recognized wealthy families in Madda Walabu. Compared with Maryam's father, Wako Lugo was not wealthy. The measure of wealth was the number of cattle someone owned; her father had more than one hundred cows that gave birth each year. He was a millionaire in his own right.

Oromo marriage rituals vary from region to region. According to the Arsi Oromo custom of the time in Madda Walabu, once the boy or his family identifies the potential bride, the courting ritual begins. In this case, Hangasu liked the description of Maryam that his two friends, Adam and Ibro, had given him. His father hinted that the bride's family approved. Hangasu asked to see the girl himself. Bride sightings had to be done discreetly, preferably without the girl noticing. That way the boy had the chance to back out without hurting the girl's feelings if he was not pleased with her appearance. There was no concept of a girlfriend.

Ibro and my dad planned a day for Hangasu to see Maryam when she was shepherding her father's cattle. Cattle are taken to a water source between 11 a.m. and early afternoon each day. Cattle must be watered in an orderly manner. Typically, cattle are thirsty and can't wait to get a drink. If everyone's cattle drank whenever they pleased, it would be chaos. To address this, the community produced a schedule that dictated whose cattle could drink when. Sometimes cattle drink on a first come, first served basis. Other times, there is a well understood order.

My uncle, my dad, and Ibro stationed themselves at the base of this water source, called *Bishaan Yabbi*, to see Maryam in action. After a few rounds of cattle had come and gone, finally the cattle of Maryam's father descended upon Bishaan Yabbi. Unlike the cattle that had gone before, his cattle had multiple shepherds—boys and girls—to manage the massive number of animals.

As the shepherds focused on ensuring the orderly watering of the cattle, Hangasu and his friends scanned the shepherds to figure out which one was Maryam. "That's the one!" exclaimed my dad. "Look at her! Isn't she incredible?" added Ibro. The three men got closer. "Without her knowing, we started helping them with the cattle as the cattle seemed out of control," said Hangasu. Perhaps he just wanted to get a closer look. Ibro was an energetic and humorous young man. As soon as they left the scene, he proclaimed, "Hangasu! Have you seen her beautiful hands and fingers? Goodness, she looked like a princess!"

Hangasu was pleased with what he saw and approved the process of courting Maryam.

According to Arsi Oromo custom, the groom's family would go to the bride's family in what they called *kadhaa*. *Kadhaa* literally means "begging for the bride," but culturally it means getting buy-in from the bride's family.

During the *kadhaa* ritual, the groom's family would send community elders with presents. The groom's family would also bring gifts for the bride's family. Traditional gifts include coffee, salt, sugar, butter, honey, clothing, and money when possible. Wako Lugo didn't follow much of the traditional protocol. When he married off his own daughters, he had the groom ask him for permission to marry his daughter, no formality needed. He believed these traditional protocols made it difficult for young people to get married. But now it was his turn to go ask for a bride on behalf of his son. Wako Lugo took my dad and Ibro Taji with him to visit Maryam's family for the *kadhaa* ritual.

Wako brought all the traditional gifts with him. Maryam's family agreed to the proposal without much consultation with Maryam, as was the tradition. Of course, Maryam was informed after the ritual. "My mom told me with enthusiasm, 'Your father gave you to a guy. He is from a good family. He is the son of Wako Lugo,'" Maryam recalled. "I didn't know who he was or what he looked like, but I was okay with it." That was what was expected. If she had said no, it would have been complicated. Her family could have forced her to marry Hangasu or could have reversed their decision on the proposal because Maryam refused. If she was quiet, that was considered an agreement. A modest Arsi Oromo girl would not say "yes," or "I love him." She would simply say nothing when a proposal was brought to her. That was what Maryam did.

My uncle and Maryam got married on May 5, 1978, in Madda Walabu, in the village of Oda Boojji near the Bishaan Yabbi water source where he first saw her. "This was the first time I saw Hangasu. He was well dressed and good-looking,"' Maryam recalled.

Even on his wedding day, Hangasu was focused on the battle. "On the day I got married, a battle took place at Ganale River between the insurgents and the Ethiopian army. Mustafa Wako Kuula and Jaldo Helgol were the Oromo fighters' leaders. My close friend, Ali Abdullahi, got killed by the Ethiopian army. I wanted to go there right away, but I was discouraged by everyone due to customs. Twenty Ethiopian militia were dead as a result of the encounter. The Bale fighters gained more than ten rifles. However, the Somalis divided up the rifles among themselves, including those who weren't in the battle," Hangasu recalled. His father and his friends told him to focus on his marriage, saying the Oromo cause would be fine without him for a few days. His heart was still in pursuit of Oromo liberty.

Twenty-eight days after his wedding, my uncle decided to get back in the struggle. He heard about a supply of arms at the Ethiopian-Somalia border. He recruited 160 young men and set out to pick up the arms. By the time he got there, the arms had already been intercepted by another Oromo rebel group. Refusing to go back empty-handed, he took his men and headed to Somalia instead.

CHAPTER EIGHTEEN:
HANGASU AND SOMALIA

THE JOURNEY TO SOMALIA TOOK US twenty-three days total on foot. The land was desert. We were thirsty and sleep deprived because we had to move fast while also hiding from the Ethiopian army that patrolled the region," Hangasu said. "Managing the affairs of 160 men was not easy. I recruited sixty young men on my own. Other leaders in the group included Hussein Roba Jaarra and Hussein Roba Gutu. The group also included my colleagues Mohamed Adam Jilo, Adam Gelchu, and Hussein Jibri. As a ration for the army, we took camels, goats, and some grain powder for making bread."

My uncle was most concerned about the young men he had recruited. "I stayed at the head of the men. I periodically returned to check on the youth. Youth were tougher than other elders; they had a lot of energy. But there were two things they couldn't handle well—sleep deprivation and thirst. When we had the opportunity to do so, I made sure they rested well and always got something to drink."

Little did Hangasu know that when he entered Somalia through the Yed border, Somali authorities were already waiting for him. The Somalis in Ethiopia had warned the Somali authorities via telegram that "an Ethiopian general was headed their way and that he harbored anti-Somali ideologies in favor of Oromo independence." As soon as Hangasu and the 160 men arrived at the border, the security men asked, "Where is Wako Lugo?"

"I was angry that these guys mentioned my dad's name," said Hangasu. "I told them, 'He is dead. What do you want from him?' They said, 'We want you.' Everybody else was given clearance to enter Somalia. They put me in a Land Rover and took me to Mogadishu, escorted by three Somalian intelligence officers." Unfortunately for Hangasu, General Wako Gutu had exited Somalia into Ethiopia through another border on the same day Hangasu entered Somalia. He had nobody who had clout with the Somali government to speak on his behalf.

The Somalis promptly put my uncle in prison. Hangasu thought to himself, "They brought me exactly where I wanted them to bring me." His plan was to expose the corrupt Somali military leaders in Ethiopia — these were Somali-Ethiopian who joined the Bale Movement and later developed ambition for annexing parts of Ethiopia (primarily from the Oromo region) for Somalia. To achieve that goal, they had to control the Oromo movement by controlling the supply of arms from Somalia and the spoils gained in Ethiopia. "I wanted to inform the high-ranking Somali leaders how their efforts had been wasted by the corrupt army commanders. They were simply enriching themselves, not advancing the cause, and even worse, they were severing relations with the Arsi Oromo public." He was sure the Somali authorities would listen and take actions immediately to dismiss those commanders. Instead, he was taken straight to prison. "My hope for a fair hearing quickly vanished," he said.

The first question they asked him was whether he had been organizing Oromos. Hangasu answered yes. The officer followed up by asking, "Aren't you Somale-Abbo?" Hangasu replied, "I am Arsi. Beyond that I am Oromo." The interrogating officer continued. "Isn't Wako Gutu your uncle?" He wanted to drive home the message that if Wako Gutu accepted the name Somale-Abbo, who was Hangasu to object? Hangasu replied, "Isn't Mahmud Rube your uncle?" The officer got angry. Mahmud Rube was the man the Somalian government selected to lead the Bale Movement when it demoted Wako Gutu. After they put Mahmude Rube as the chair of the Bale Movement the Somalian government succeeded in renaming the Oromo struggle as the Somale-Abbo struggle. Hangasu was implying that he understands what's going on and he won't give in to their coercion. Hangasu said, "The officer pulled out his handgun and pushed it against my forehead. I calmly and confidently said, 'Move this handgun away before I kill you with it!' He was still holding the gun to my forehead. I stood up and said, 'I learned how to handle guns way before you!' The interrogator's superior was watching the whole thing behind a glass window. He told the interrogator to stop and leave the room."

*

Hangasu refused to accept the Somale-Abbo name imposed by the Somali officers. The superior officer's name was Colonel Mahmud. He said, "Haile Selassie!" when referring to Hangasu. The officer wanted to provoke Hangasu.

Hangasu shrugged off the name and waited. Colonel Mahmud addressed him next: "Are you Amhara?" Hangasu repeated his previous statement. "I am Arsi; beyond that I am Oromo." Colonel Mahmud said, "OK, if you are Arsi then show me by reciting a portion of the Quran. Read Surat Al-Fatiha." According to Colonel Mahmud, the Somalis and Arsi were Muslims, and the Amhara were Christians. Reciting the Quran was his litmus test for religion. His categorization was factually wrong though. There were Amharas who were Muslims the same way there were Oromos/Arsi who were Christians.

"I recited Surat Al-Fatiha, the opening chapter of the Quran in Arabic. Before I even finished the recitation, Colonel Mahmud exclaimed, 'Oh, my God! This Amhara learned *our* language.' When I heard this, I was extremely angry. I cried; I couldn't control my tears. And then I quickly stood up, grabbed Colonel Mahmud by his shirt collar, choked him, and pushed him against the wall. All of the sudden, Colonel Mahmud laughed and said, 'I was just joking. You don't understand jokes?' I released him and went back to my chair."

Colonel Mahmud fixed his shirt, went to his office, and typed up a statement for Hangasu to sign. He read the letter and refused to sign it because it said he was Somale-Abbo. "I told him to remove the word *Somale-Abbo*, and I would sign it." They argued back and forth for a while. Hangasu would object, saying, "You don't decide my identity for me. I am Arsi. If you want me to sign this letter, erase the word *Somale-Abbo*." Finally, Mahmud removed the term and listed Hangasu's crimes as organizing Oromos and opposing Somale-Abbo. Hangasu didn't mind signing this because he had never denied standing for the Oromo cause.

My uncle was transferred to Galshira prison, a high-security facility in Mogadishu. He was housed with people who had received capital punishment. His cell was two levels underground in an area of the prison called *shela morto*, "death ditch" in Somali.

"I shared a tiny cell with two other people. It was so small that only two of us could sleep in parallel. The third person had to sleep perpendicular to us. We couldn't extend our legs. The prison was built on the Indian Ocean coast. It was super hot. Sweat was a big problem. There were bed bugs too. On top of that, the cell was completely dark the majority of the time. It had a small hole. Through this small hole, in addition to the food, we received two things daily: sunlight and a pack of cigarettes. Apart from that, there was a skinny hallway that led to the toilet."

Two months into Hangasu's prison time, one of his cellmates was executed. When a prisoner was to be executed, he was informed three days in advance. He would be dressed in white shorts and a white shirt and tied with a chain to prevent him from committing suicide. Three days later, he would be killed. Hangasu's cellmate had been charged with treason.

A few weeks later, the second cellmate was scheduled for execution. The same process was followed. On the day of his execution, the man broke. He had been charged in a corruption case involving a massive amount of money. He had previously refused to disclose his co-conspirators, but under the pressure of facing certain death, he named the other participants. A few hours later, four Somali generals who were involved in the case were arrested and brought to the prison.

For corruption charges in Somalia at that time, there were two categories of punishments depending on the amount of money involved. Crimes involving less than 100,000 shillings resulted in life in prison; crimes involving more than 100,000 shillings resulted in death. Luckily for the corrupt officials, when the money was divided between the five of them, the amount was less than 100,000 shillings each. Hangasu's cellmate was moved from death row to life in prison. "When the guy came back to the prison cell, he had changed completely," Hangasu said. "His face had become dark and ashy as if blood was sucked out of him. His hearing was gone. Most of his body parts were paralyzed; he couldn't feel his body anymore. I guess that is what facing death looked like."

During his time in the prison, my uncle had a hard time coming to terms with his situation. "It took me almost five months to think straight and reflect on what happened. I realized my mistakes. I had miscalculated. I should have stayed in Ethiopia and mobilized the people there, particularly after I challenged the Somalis in Ethiopia. On the other hand, I needed the Somalian government to achieve my vision, which was to create a self-sustaining insurgent team."

Hangasu planned to do this by dividing the team into three groups. One group would focus on education, learning to read and write. One group would focus on military training. The last group would focus on modern farming and cooking. Hangasu could have leveraged the Somali government's resources to support all of these goals. In his view, this was what it would take to get free of Somalia meddling in Oromo affairs, especially if his vision was widely accepted and spread throughout southeast Ethiopia. But Hangasu was young and eager to do things his way, and compromise was not a word in his dictionary.

Two other Oromos were in the same prison at that time—Adam Jilo Webo and Tahir Ansara. Adam Jilo had been captured by Somali operatives and brought to Somalia because he had cooperated with the Derg government. "Adam Jilo appealed to the prison authorities to move me to a regular prison cell from the underground location, and his appeal was accepted. This move was a huge improvement—good sunlight exposure and the opportunity to talk to my uncle." In Arsi Oromo culture, in addition to blood uncles, a peer of your father is considered your uncle, especially if that peer is from the same tribe. Hangasu still calls Adam Jilo "*Abbeera* Adam"—Uncle Adam.

"One evening while I was in my prison cell, the head of the prison knocked on my door. When I approached, he said, 'Your father is dead.' I didn't know what to think. I threw all the swear words I knew at him. I pushed and kicked the prison door. I couldn't open it. I couldn't get to him. While I knew my father was mortal and I am mortal, this came out of nowhere!"

There is a difference between Somali and Oromo culture when it comes to announcing death. In Somalia, death is no big deal. It is widely accepted that everybody dies. Whenever somebody hears of a relative's death, that person can pass the news to other relatives without hesitation. There is no protocol or ceremony or sensitivity.

Oromo culture is the opposite. Death is a major event and therefore can't be announced haphazardly. Typically, the next of kin in another location is informed by community elders. These elders would usually go through a friend or a neighbor to make sure the next of kin is at home and not doing hazardous work (to avoid accidents when the person finds out the bad news). News of the death is usually broken in the morning even if the community elders find out the night before. Perhaps that was what shocked Hangasu. He took it as if the officer was insulting him. It was hard for him to process the news because it didn't follow the Oromo way. Not knowing what was going through Hangasu's mind, the officer said, "What did I do wrong? I heard the news and passed it on."

"The next morning, Adam Jilo and Tahir Ansara came to visit me. The moment I saw them, I realized it was true. My father had in fact passed away." The morning visit from the elders made it clear to him. My uncle mourned his father's death in prison. The last time Hangasu had talked to his father, he had told him to be careful and patient.

Maryam decided to visit Hangasu in Somalia. She attended Wako Lugo's funeral. Plus, she'd heard about Hangasu's imprisonment in Somalia, and she decided to be with him and provide support. It was rare for a woman to trek through the desert to reach Somalia, but Maryam was a courageous young woman.

In 1979, Maryam followed a small group of army troops headed to Somalia to obtain rifles for the Sowra guerilla movement in southern Ethiopia. "There was a lot of fear in crossing the road because the Ethiopian army was all over the region. We had teams of scouts that traveled one to two days ahead of us to check for the Ethiopian army," Maryam recalled.

The Ethiopian army was trying to prevent people like her from leaving the country. More important, they wanted to stop people from returning to Ethiopia with Somali weapons. "The trip to Somalia took us double what it usually took because we would move forward for a few days, and all of a sudden, we had to return back or move sideways for a day or two because the scouts found Ethiopian troops where we headed. The scouts used telegrams to communicate with each other. The journey was tiring and full of fear of getting caught by the government." Maryam arrived in Somalia after one and a half months of trekking on foot from Madda Walabu to Mogadishu.

When Maryam reached Mogadishu, her husband was still in prison. For three months she lobbied the Arsi Oromo elders for her husband's release, but nobody had the clout to influence the Somali authorities until General Wako Gutu returned to Somalia. Almost one year later, General Wako Gutu returned to

Somalia and appealed to General Siad Barre for Hangasu's release. "I was released from prison after eleven months and sixteen days," Hangasu said. "General Wako Gutu, Hassan Sheikh Bashir, and Mohamed Adam Jilo picked me up from the prison." Hangasu had spent nearly one year in prison for opposing the Somali agenda in Oromo land and organizing the Oromo to reclaim ownership of their own movement. But his time in prison didn't deter him from advocating for the Oromo cause. He would continue to fight for this again and again.

Maryam had hoped that her husband would tone down his Oromo advocacy and get along with everybody after his year in prison. However, my uncle was more determined than ever to oppose the Somale-Abbo name and mission.

*

The day he was freed from prison, Hangasu started gathering his friends and colleagues to make a plan for defeating the Somale-Abbo mission. He enlisted Hassan Sheikh Bashir to write a brief manifesto in red ink in the Oromo language and Somali language. The core message was: We are Oromo. Our mission is to liberate our country from the Ethiopian tyranny. Somale-Abbo won't represent us. We don't accept Mahmud Rube's leadership. We don't accept Hussein Bune's leadership.

They made several copies of the manifesto and sent them to Somali President General Siad Barre and his ministers at 9 a.m. By 2 p.m., Hangasu and his team received confirmation that their manifesto had reached the officials. The team also posted the pamphlet in public in three major cities: Beled-weyne, Qoryole, and Mogadishu.

According to Hangasu, "That evening, right after sunset, Muhammad Ali Samatar, the defense minister and vice president of Somalia, picked up General Wako Gutu from his house. Muhammad told General Wako, 'Wako, fear God! Stop what you are doing. Somalia had never experienced this kind of rebellion before. The government response will be severe. Not even I can stop it.' Of course, Wako had no clue what Muhammad Ali Samatar was talking about. Muhammad told Gutu, 'We will remove Mahmud Rube from Somale-Abbo leadership role tomorrow, but never repeat this campaign ever.'" Wako reflected overnight about who had the courage and was crazy enough to pull this off. By morning, Wako had a pretty good idea who it had been.

Wako paid a visit to Hangasu's house the next day. "What did you do last night?" he asked.

"What?"

"Mohammad Ali Samatar told me of the pamphlets you distributed, Hangasu."

Hangasu denied it. "I don't know about any pamphlets."

Wako looked at him skeptically. "You did it. I can think of nobody who would do this except you."

"We can't just sit back and be marginalized! I had to do something," Hangasu admitted.

"Don't do it again. You put us all in danger."

To Hangasu's surprise, an emergency meeting was held the next day for the Bale Oromo movement leadership. Mahmud Rube was removed from the chairman position and replaced by General Wako Gutu. Hussein Bune was removed as the secretary of defense and replaced by Siraj Haji Isaaq Dadhi. Hangasu and his team of young men had gotten half of what they wanted: Mahmud Rube was gone, and General Wako Gutu was back to his leadership role. Now Hangasu and his team wanted General Wako Gutu to denounce the name *Somale-Abbo* as his first symbolic action.

General Wako Gutu refused Hangasu's proposal to change the name because he still believed the Oromo could achieve their goal of liberation by working with the Somali government.

According to General Wako Gutu, keeping the *Somale-Abbo* name was the only way to guarantee they'd continue to receive the Somali government's support. He wished Hangasu would stop agitating the situation. Disappointed by Wako's decision,

Hangasu and the young men left the meeting. Of them, only Mohamed Adam stayed with General Wako Gutu.

Still in celebration mode after getting the leadership change they'd hoped for, Hangasu visited his uncle, Adam Jilo, at Galshira prison. Hangasu told him what happened and how he had scored a victory against the Somale-Abbo agenda.

After listening to the whole story, Adam Jilo asked Hangasu one question: "What did you stand on when you did all of these things?" He meant, on what ground? When Hangasu hesitated, Adam Jilo asked, "Who was backing you up from the Somali government?"

Hangasu responded, "Nobody." Adam Jilo concluded, "My nephew, you were defeated."

"Did you hear me?" Hangasu said. "We changed the leadership of the Somale-Abbo and restored our leadership. Now Wako and Siraj are in charge, and Mahmud Rube is gone."

"Let me tell you a story," Adam Jilo said. "A boy got in a fight with an adult man. The boy punched the adult man in public and made him bleed from his nose. The boy immediately ran home and told his father about his victory. He told his father that he got in a fight with the man and that he punched him until his nose bled. The father asked the boy, 'What did you stand on when you punched the man?' Not knowing what his father meant, the boy said, 'I stood on the ground.' The father said, 'You had no grounds on which to assault the man. I have to pay for your mistakes.'

Adam Jilo continued, "I was very excited when you first told me what had happened. I thought you had at least the backing of one influential Somalian government official. Now all that effort is for nothing. You have no cover; you are exposed. That's why I said you were defeated."

At the tender age of 24, my uncle understood only a little of the wisdom Adam Jilo had just imparted.

As Adam Jilo predicted, a few months later, General Wako was removed from the chairman's position again and replaced by Mohamed Haji Gobana as dictated by the Somali government. The government saw an opportunity to put in place a person who was Oromo but who had stronger Somali tendencies and greater sympathy to their agenda to advance Greater Somalia. They picked Mohamed Haji Gobana to fill that role.

Hangasu saw the move as another hijacking of the Oromo struggle by the Somali government. He gathered the youth at his house once again and prepared a pamphlet to condemn the appointment of Mohamed Haji Gobana.

"There was a multistory building. The first floor of this building was a restaurant and coffee and tea shop. People gathered there all the time. I went to the top level of this building's veranda and dropped the pamphlets," Hangasu said.

The pamphlet said, "We don't accept Mohamed Haji Gobana's appointment. He won't represent us. Somale-Abbo won't represent us." Fights broke out in front of the building. The youth on the ground turned into a protest and started beating those who were allied with the Somale-Abbo mission. Mohamed Haji Gobana locked himself inside his office, which was located across from the tall building.

Police and military quickly appeared and arrested the youth. Hangasu and the youth involved in the protest spent four months in Johar prison. Hangasu understood the reasons for his imprisonment. This time he didn't regret it one bit. My uncle was released a few days before his first son was born. Maryam named the newborn Abdu-Salaam—the servant of the Peaceful God—hoping for some peace in her family life.

CHAPTER NINETEEN:
HANGASU AND THE OLF

THE OROMO LIBERATION FRONT (OLF) moved its operation to Somalia in 1980. Beginning in the 1960s and continuing through the 1980s, the center of gravity for the Oromo people's struggle was in the east, mainly eastern Ethiopia (Bale and Harar) and Somalia. The OLF was late to the game and wanted to make a name for itself.

Sometime in early 1980, the OLF dispatched four "leaders" to Somalia to meet Hangasu. They told people that they came from Germany, but in fact they came from Khartoum, Sudan. My uncle was the only OLF member with both influence in Somalia and connections to the Bale Rebellion.

According to the OLF, Hangasu's job was to introduce the OLF visitors to the leaders of the Bale Oromo movement in Somalia. Their stated goal was to intensify the Oromo struggle in Ethiopia by joining their two Oromo organizations for the liberation of Oromia. This was music to his ears. Finally, somebody was ready to push the struggle forward. He fully accepted the assignment.

Hangasu immediately got to work. He introduced the new OLF team to his youth group. Because Borana Oromo still followed the traditional Oromo Gada system, Hangasu introduced the OLF visitors to Abba Gadaa, the traditional Borana Oromo leader. He also introduced them to General Wako Gutu and Mahmud Rube, the leaders of the Bale Oromo struggle. The OLF team met with each of these leaders separately.

Interestingly, both General Wako and Mahmud Rube told Hangasu that the newly arrived OLF leaders weren't there to push the struggle forward. Apparently, what the OLF told Hangasu, Mahmud, and Wako was different. But Hangasu was angry about Wako and Mahmud's feedback. He thought to himself, "These elders don't understand!" He blamed Wako and Mahmud for their lack of vision. Hangasu continued establishing the OLF in Somalia.

What Hangasu didn't realize was that he was dealing with two organizations with completely different missions. He was caught in the middle with his own goals, which were different from those of either organization. Hangasu's goal was to connect the Oromo professionals (OLF leaders) with the guerilla army (General Wako's people). Hangasu thought that uniting the political visionaries of the urban area with the military grit of the rural guerillas would give the Oromo people the chance to challenge the Ethiopian system that had marginalized the Oromo people for more than a century.

The OLF's explicit mission in 1980 was to establish and advance the Oromo struggle by any means necessary. Unlike the pastoralist Bale guerilla army led by General Wako, the OLF leaders were articulate. Most of the OLF leaders had received mainstream education in Ethiopia. A few had advanced degrees in science, business, and social sciences. They had studied and understood the psyche of the Oromo masses. Hangasu later believed that the OLF's real mission was to destroy the Bale Oromo rebellion that had come before it in order to establish the OLF as the *only* Oromo organization committed to liberating the Oromo people. The OLF's struggle was one for dominance in the hearts and minds of the Oromo people. This meant that their guns were aimed at other Oromo organizations, *including* General Wako Gutu's organization.

Wako Gutu's mission was much less elaborate. He believed that the Ethiopian rulers only spoke the language of bullets. Therefore, he committed to mobilizing his people to fight the Ethiopian rulers until he gained freedom for his people. Wako Gutu would partner with anyone who was willing to make this vision a reality. Around the mid-1980s, he was ready to head to Ethiopia with five hundred trained men and their Somali government–provided weapons.

OLF operatives in Somalia had gathered information that General Wako Gutu was preparing to launch attacks in Ethiopia. The OLF leaders in Somalia staged a counterplot to dismantle his plan. The OLF's goal was to crush General Wako Gutu and turn the Somali government against him. This would give the OLF room to maneuver and build their support with the Oromo population in Somalia. Unknowingly, Hangasu became the instrument for the counterplot.

The OLF planned to turn the Somali government against Wako Gutu by aborting his mission to enter Ethiopia for a war. General Wako Gutu and his organization relied entirely on the Somali government to meet their basic needs, including food, shelter, medicine, and arms. If the Somali government cut its support, Wako and his people would be vulnerable, which could cause Wako Gutu to abort his plans to enter Ethiopia for a war.

Three OLF leaders met Hangasu at the Ruba Hotel. They told him, "We heard General Wako is preparing to leave with five hundred men. Don't let him take the Somale-Abbo weapons."

"Why not?" Hangasu asked.

The leader of OLF responded, "We have two ships loaded with arms docked at Berbera Port: *our* weapons, *our* uniform from top to bottom, hats with OLF insignia, shirts, pants, and shoes with OLF printed on the sole. The days of relying on the Somalian government's support are behind us. From now on, we rely on *ourselves*. We cannot allow the Somalian government to undermine our struggle."

This message resonated with Hangasu. He felt exhilarated. This was what he had wanted all along. "Hearing that message was like a dream," he recalled. He was eager to gather a group to hear the message directly from the OLF leaders. He brought Hassan Sheikh Bashir, Mohamed Adam Jilo, Haji Umar Malka, and Haji Ibrahim to hear the message for themselves directly from the proverbial horse's mouth. The only question Hangasu and his group had left was the only question the OLF operatives were desperate to hear from them.

Hangasu asked it: "What can we do?"

The OLF operatives replied, "First things first: we have to stop General Wako from leaving with the Somale-Abbo weapons. You figure out how. Here is the money to make it happen." Hangasu and his group got to work right away.

Hangasu and his men quickly assembled a small group to convince all the military commanders who reported to General Wako Gutu to refuse the mission to Ethiopia. After all, the general couldn't pursue the mission without his commanders!

Hangasu sent the newly recruited small group of commanders to the Luuq military camp, where General Wako Gutu's army was stationed, to convince the army not to leave for Ethiopia. The commanders succeeded because nobody liked the Somale-Abbo name that had been imposed on them. Every Oromo fighter wanted the dignity to fight with his own name. They finally saw an opportunity to struggle on their own terms. Their hopes were flying high.

One week later, General Wako Gutu was ready to leave. He had no clue about what had happened at the Luuq camp. He arrived with a Somali general named Gani. General Gani blew the whistle as usual, signaling the soldiers to line up. Nothing happened. He blew the whistle again. Again, nothing happened.

General Wako and General Gani were confused. These were trained men who stood and lined up for drills at 3 a.m. General Gani blew his whistle a third time. This time a few elders showed up, looking down as a sign of embarrassment. They had a lot of respect for General Wako Gutu. They could feel his disappointment.

General Wako asked, "Where is the army?"

The elders responded, "The army is sick."

General Wako asked again, "*Everybody* is sick?"

They responded, "Yes."

With that, General Wako left the camp feeling betrayed and disappointed and did not fully understand what was going on. General Gani was angry. As a result, he cut off all the supplies, rations, and medicine he'd been providing to the Oromo army in the camp.

Hangasu's first goal had been accomplished. General Wako Gutu's mission ended before it could start. Now Hangasu believed he would be able to supply General Wako and his army with the Oromo arms and supplies prepared by OLF.

Hangasu took his group and met again with the three OLF operatives at Ruba Hotel.

"The mission was successful," he said. "We stopped General Wako. His army is now with us. What we need immediately is food and medicine for the army because the Somalian government cut off all its support. By the way, how soon can we supply the arms to troops at Luuq camp?"

After carefully listening to the outcome of their first mission, the OLF operatives said, "Mr. Hangasu, you are mistaken. What you are asking is what your uncles Wako Gutu and Hussein Bune (another leader from Ginnir district) usually do. They lack education; that's why they want to use the military approach to Oromo freedom. Our mission is to establish an association, under which we can teach our language, history, and culture. We are not here to shed blood like your uncles."

My uncle remembered his reaction. "It was as if I was hit by something enormous. I literally passed out. I couldn't see or hear my surroundings for minutes. Once I gathered a little bit of consciousness, the only question I remembered asking was, 'What about the two ships at the Berbera Port? What about the two ships at the Berbera Port? What about the two ships at the Berbera Port?'" There was no answer from the other side.

"I don't remember how I got home," he recalled. He realized he had been played by the people and organizations he believed in. He was devastated, not only because the OLF had betrayed his trust and actually stood for something different than what they had led him to believe, but also because his actions had exposed thousands of soldiers at the Luuq camp to hunger and disease, not to mention having disappointed his uncle. The OLF had used him to destroy the pioneer Oromo organization—the Dhombir veterans—a strong symbol for standing up to the tyranny of Haile Selassie's regime.

Until this time, Hangasu had been driven by his deep desire to liberate his people. He had given up government posts and joined the OLF with the original founders like Baro Tumsa, Magarsa Bari, Getachew Waqjira, and Nuguse Nagassa. He had connected the Oromo students and intellectuals with Bale movement leaders. He wanted to merge the vision of the Oromo students in the cities with the determination and bravery of the Oromo fighters in Bale.

Hangasu had experienced his fair share of disagreements with General Wako Gutu and his organization. The Bale movement leaders lacked vision and strategy. But Hangasu knew their intention was to achieve freedom for the Oromo masses someday. He had thought the OLF could fill the gap in vision and strategy. The OLF leaders were well educated and understood world politics. They could put together a coherent game plan.

But Hangasu discovered that the OLF of the 1980s had no interest in liberating Oromia. "Their first mission was to dismantle the Bale Oromo movement because that would establish them as the sole Oromo organization. Once they had Oromo hearts and minds, they would manipulate them as they wished, making deals on behalf of the Oromo people when it benefited them and their masters, cutting ties with whoever didn't fit their interests." said Hangasu.

The key strength of the OLF as an organization was the precision of its messaging to the Oromo masses. The organization conducted thorough background and historical investigations before approaching its targets. The way the OLF approached Hangasu in Somalia was a great example. The OLF understood Hangasu and everything he was trying to accomplish, which allowed them to adjust their message.

The OLF operatives had intentionally mentioned the two shiploads of arms at Berbera Port. Hangasu had connected with the plan at a visceral level because he was primed to receive it. It reminded him of his comrades Nuguse and Magarsa and their plan in 1975 to reroute two ships from Assab Port in Eritrea. The arms carried by the two ships would have been divided between the Oromo and the Eritrean fighters, except that the mission had been aborted when Nuguse Negassa was assassinated while returning from the Djibouti independence celebration.

The OLF operatives knew how Hangasu had worked in Ginnir and Dallo to prepare the Bale fighters to take advantage of the arms. They fabricated a similar plan, put it in front of Hangasu, and he immediately fell under their spell because he wanted so badly to get the weapons into the hands of the people who needed them most to intensify the struggle.

Right there and then, my uncle made one of the most crucial decisions in his adult life. He left the OLF after eight years as its primary leader in Bale and Somalia. "It was clear to me their war was against the Oromo, not against the Ethiopian government. The meeting at the Ruba Hotel in 1982 was the last time I was to associate myself with the OLF. I felt like I didn't recognize the organization anymore."

Hangasu went into self-imposed isolation. He cut off all ties with the OLF and tried to focus on his family. Around the time he left the OLF, his son, who was 18 months old, passed away, giving him all the more reason to focus on his family and take a break from politics. The lesson he learned was never to get involved with things he didn't understand or people he didn't know or trust.

Six months later, General Wako Gutu reached out to Hangasu and asked if he could join a mission to Ethiopia. Hangasu had just lost a son. His wife was a few months pregnant. He was tired of politics. Now his uncle was saying, "Please, I need you."

My uncle remembered the pain he'd inflicted on Wako and his men when he acted on behalf of the OLF. He wondered if this could be an opportunity for redemption—a chance to make things right. However, the timing was bad. His family needed him too. Throughout his life, every time he had been faced with a choice between family and the struggle of the Oromo people, he had chosen the struggle. He had refused to get married until the Oromo people obtained their freedom. After he was forced to marry, he left on a mission after only one month of marriage. This time was no different. Once again, Hangasu decided to accompany his uncle in the field, putting himself at risk instead of staying home and comforting his family.

*

In mid-1983, General Wako prepared an army of eight hundred men from different regions of Ethiopia, including Bale and Borana. The army was a mix of Oromo and Somali fighters. Right before leaving the Luuq camp, General Wako appointed a man named Haji Haraam as commander of the army.

Haji Haram was from the Digodi tribe; he was a Somali Ethiopian. People from the tribe approached both General Wako and Hangasu to say that appointing Haji Haraam was the wrong move. Haraam was suspected of being a double agent for the Somali and Ethiopian governments. People close to Haraam advised Wako not to trust him and certainly not to put him in charge. They pleaded with Wako to reverse his decision. Although General Wako would listen to different perspectives, in the end, he only implemented his own opinion.

Three days before Wako's army departed, the Somali general in charge of the Luuq camp told General Wako that they had received intelligence that the Ethiopian army was aware of General Wako's plans and were prepared and waiting for General Wako and his troops. The general asked Wako to delay his departure.

"We will not delay the departure," General Wako said. "If the Ethiopians know we are coming, they will run away anyhow. If not, we will make them run away!"

The commander of the Luuq camp tried again. "Wako, I don't think you understand. You and your men have never faced such an army before. They are waiting for you with tanks and convoys. Delay your departure by two or three months. I will help you cross the border safely." Wako was adamant and determined to leave. He turned to his men and said, "By the way, Somalians always lie like this." When the commander realized that General Wako would not be persuaded to stay, he wished him luck and left the meeting.

"We left Luuq on Friday morning. By Saturday morning after twenty-four hours of travel, we went back to the same place we started from, pretty much," Hangasu recalled. "Our road guide was working with the Ethiopian government. In fact, we later learned that his brother was the head of the Ethiopian army that was dispatched to finish us all. Our guide simply moved us around to place us right inside the Ethiopian army that was ready to ambush us." General Wako had been warned about Haji Haraam and about the Ethiopian army being ready for him, but he did not listen. "Once he made up his mind, it was almost impossible to change him. He was stubborn," Hangasu observed.

"Early that Saturday morning, it was dawn time, and it was still dark outside. We heard the closing of a vehicle door! It didn't make sense. We were in the middle of the jungle—there shouldn't be any cars around. This is a place called Malka Bari. Suddenly we realized that we were in deep trouble. A minute later, we were showered with bullets. We couldn't hear anything but bullets coming from all directions. We were unprepared, outnumbered, and outpowered. A few men and I stayed with General Wako," recalled Hangasu.

Their goal immediately shifted from fighting the Ethiopians to protecting General Wako at all costs. "A dead Oromo general was fine, but a captured one was not. He was the only Oromo general that had earned that title from his people. It was not given to him by any government."

*

Protecting him was not an easy task. To understand why, one must imagine both General Wako's physical build and his attitude. General Wako was approximately 6 feet, 8 inches tall with a strong body. He usually wore a tall white hat called a *kofia*. He was also stubborn and wanted to fight.

"I had no choice but to follow him," my uncle said. "I was prepared. If the Ethiopians got any closer to capturing us, I would kill him and myself. The idea of him getting captured was not acceptable to me. He was the head of this monumental struggle. It would have meant a big blow to the struggle.

"After ten or fifteen minutes of intense shooting, we went from eight hundred to forty-two men! Most had fled. Luckily, we escaped the Ethiopian tanks, but they pursued us. By this time, we were a small army with basically nothing except the one gun each of us carried. The road was great for us; it was a skinny road through the jungle. The Ethiopians had a much bigger army. They could not move as fast as we could. We traveled for seven days with very little sleep and no food or drink. For the seven consecutive days we were essentially on the run from the pursuing army, we ate one goat. One goat for forty-two people for one week. We drank salty, dirty water, and we ate wild fruits. When we reached a place called Goro Dugda, we could barely move due to starvation. Everyone lost at least half of their waist size. I was able to wrap my pants almost twice. Here at Goro Dugda, we got lucky. We met with our army in Ethiopia. People like Aliye Umar Aaga, Aliye Hussein Somo, Hussein Abdulla Gutu, and Sheik Kadir Tubbu. That was the best reunion. We settled into rest. They slaughtered a camel for us immediately."

The best part of a camel is also the quickest to cook: the fatty hump. The Oromos call this part *amanka*. The tradition was to chop the hump and liver into bite-size pieces (like chicken nuggets) and fry the meat in its own fatty oil. "We were given *amanka* and black coffee," Hangasu said. "It was like the best food I ever tasted in my life! After we ate, we got extremely tired and decided to sleep now that we were in a safe zone."

As Hangasu and the group slipped into sleep, the resident Oromo army celebrated their arrival. On the Ethiopian side, the news that General Wako Gutu had escaped the border encounter with the Ethiopian army spread everywhere. The Ethiopian army at the border directed the regional army to pursue Wako and his men.

"Less than two hours into our sleep, we were stormed with gunshots," Hangasu said. "The Ethiopian army caught us by surprise yet again. There was no time to grab anything else. We grabbed our only guns. We were lucky to have our people in the country. They fought hard! Sheikh Kadir Tubbu, the brave son of Madda Walabu, was martyred there. Hussein Jibri Elema was wounded on his hand. He was never able to use it again.

"We continued marching north until we reached Haro Dibbe. Here we met Mahmad Addow, Mahmad Dhabbar, and Abdullahi Qalla from the Gurra tribe. The governor of Haro Dibbe at the time, a man named Abduljalil Mahmad, heard about us. He sent us a message saying that he had heard about our encounter with the army. He said, 'I am happy you made it through. Please use this camel and food as gifts from me. However, the government is sending more troops your way. You are on your own. I can't help you.'" During the Bale Oromo movement, the guerilla army could often count on their people in rural areas and even some in the city, who seemingly worked with the government to provide support.

Around the same time, the Somali government sent a telegram saying that General Wako must immediately return to Somalia for his own safety. The Ethiopian government planned to go all-out to capture or kill him, going beyond anything they had done in the past. The Somali government shared that they had received two independent intelligence reports that corroborated one another. Given the urgency, Wako decided to return to Somalia. While they were in Ethiopia, they would recruit a few more people to replace the men they had lost. Most decided to stay and see their families; they would rather live hiding in their own country than go back to Somalia. Hangasu and Wako returned to Somalia.

*

While my uncle was in the midst of his self-imposed isolation and then his expedition with General Wako Gutu, the OLF worked to recruit the Oromo community in Somalia. The OLF's message was not in the form of reactive, impromptu motivational speeches, as were the messages from General Wako Gutu, Mahmud Rube, or Hussein Bune. The OLF's message was a calculated statement based on their understanding of their audience. Their message was well packaged:

You have fought enough. You lost your family members and your possessions during this struggle. You lost these things because you were led by people like Wako Gutu and Hussein Bune. They weren't educated. The days of spilling your blood are behind us. What we want is freedom, correct? There is a new way. All we need to do is sue the Ethiopian government in international court, which we have access to. Just like that, at the stroke of a pen, we will have our freedom. Nobody has to die. We will take care of this job for you.

Who would say no to that? These people had been waging a sustained war against the Ethiopian empire with meager support from the Somali government since 1963. The Oromo people in Somalia were torn by the war. They had gotten into the war out of necessity, and now there was no end in sight. They also saw what the Somali government was doing to the Oromo struggle, how they had hijacked the message and operations of the Oromo struggle. Wako Gutu and his group had no plan to minimize the Somali influence. The OLF's plan seemed like a much better alternative than continuing the armed struggle.

Everybody understood the parts about spilling no more blood and gaining freedom by pen. It sounded very good. One by one, group by group, people joined the OLF. By the time Hangasu and General Wako returned to Somalia six months later, almost everybody had joined.

General Wako Gutu's strength was his sincerity of purpose, his bravery, and the determination with which he pursued liberty for his people. The OLF's strength was its ability to communicate effectively and convince people. General Wako's organization slowly but surely became weaker and smaller until it consisted only of those who were personally loyal to him, those who couldn't abandon him due to kinship, and those who genuinely believed in his leadership and integrity. For the moment, the mission to Ethiopia was put on hold. The Somali government was preoccupied with its own internal conflict.

*

Fatuma (Fato), Hangasu's mother, missed her son. He had left Ethiopia in 1978, shortly after his marriage. Fato had heard that Hangasu had been imprisoned and then released. She knew him and knew that no matter what, Hangasu wouldn't easily give up the Oromo cause. Fato was a widow. Her only son was away, and she was not sure what he was up to. My mom, her only daughter, was by her side with seven children at the time. My oldest sister, Shebo, was dedicated to serving Fato. I did the same later in life in the 1990s.

Fato, my grandmother, tasked many merchants who traded between Ethiopia and Somalia to find Hangasu. When her cousin Hassan Haji Dawud went to Somalia for business, he did some searching and found Hangasu. He learned that Hangasu had three children and was doing just fine. Back in Ethiopia, the Oromo governor of the Borana zone, Godana Tuni, told Hassan to give Hangasu a message: "Tell our people to come back to their country. I will take personal responsibility for their safety *except* for two people—General Wako Gutu and Hangasu. It is better for the Oromo people to come back to their country and struggle within Ethiopia. The issue of Hangasu and General

Wako returning to Ethiopia is beyond me. That will be handled at the national level. I can't help them."

General Wako Gutu was the leader of the Bale Rebellion. The issue of his return to Ethiopia could not be handled at the regional level. Likewise, Hangasu had worked in the transitional government early in the 1970s. His return to Ethiopia had to be handled by the military. Hangasu couldn't just get in a car and go visit his mother; it was too risky for him.

When Hassan returned to Ethiopia and informed Fato about Hangasu's whereabouts, she could not contain her emotions. She decided to go visit him. Sometime in 1989, Fato managed to visit Hangasu in Qoryole, Somalia. She stayed with my uncle and his family for two months.

While Hangasu and his mother were reunited in Qoryole, Maryam set out to visit her own family in Ethiopia. She took her youngest son, Ahmednur, with her.

When Maryam left Ethiopia in 1980, she had trekked on foot through the desert to reach Somalia, walking fiercely alongside soldiers. When she returned to Ethiopia, she didn't have to walk. She rode in a car with merchants. The trip to Ethiopia took several days. She still had to be discreet so that authorities didn't discover her identity. She used an alias and a fake identification card. Maryam was able to visit her family and return to her husband and daughters in Somalia safely.

When Fato decided to return home to Ethiopia, Hangasu gave his mother a gift: his second daughter, Fatuma, who was 3. He had already named her after his mother. Fato took a piece of her son with her and returned to Ethiopia. Hangasu was certainly surrounded by women of strong will and bravery.

*

The Somali people are homogenous from a cultural, linguistic, and religious perspective. However, there are divisions along clan and subclan lines that dictate their allegiance more than their homogeneity in the broader ancestry. Soon after the 1977 Ogaden war defeat, the Somali government gave up the "lost territories" initiative and focused on its own internal matters. Particularly, in the late 1980s, the Somalian government was reluctant to engage with the Ethiopian Bale fighters in Somalia. Previously, Somalis were united against one external enemy—Ethiopia. As the Greater Somalia ambition failed, Somalis returned their focus to their old clan rivalries. Opposition to the Siad Barre military government grew among government officials and the military. As a countermeasure, the Siad Barre government created an informal network of trusted individuals and organizations comprised of his own tribe of Marihan. This measure enraged the other tribes, mainly the Majjerten and Isaaq tribes. Each disgruntled tribe organized itself and launched attacks against the Siad Barre regime. The Somali population at large was tired of nepotism and corruption of the Siad Barre government.

In 1991 General Siad Barre's government collapsed. Civil war broke out in Somalia. Various clans had banded together to oust Barre's regime. However, their goals were shortsighted and focused on ousting Siad Barre, not on the long-term vision to build a stable country. With Siad Barre gone, they turned against one another. Violent conflict intensified between rebel chiefs and warlords because they couldn't agree on how to share power. The conflict resulted in hundreds of thousands of deaths and many more injuries. Some people believed that, as Siad Barre saw his downfall, he fueled the conflict by opening all the arms warehouses in the country so his clan was fully armed. In the chaos of the collapse, other clans also got their hands on weapons. Whether he did it intentionally or the arms warehouses were robbed by the different clans, the free access to arms exponentially increased and prolonged sectarian conflict in the country.

CHAPTER TWENTY:
HANGASU RETURNS TO ETHIOPIA

WHEN THE CIVIL WAR BROKE OUT, my uncle lived in the Qoryole refugee camp in Somalia. Several months prior, the United Nations High Commissioner for Refugees (UNHCR) interviewed more than three thousand refugees at the camp. The purpose of the interview was to select those refugees who could not return to their home country because of the prosecution they would face from their government. Those who were selected would be given the opportunity to go to the United States or Europe. After a rigorous interview process, 110 families were granted the opportunity to go abroad. Hangasu's family was one of those lucky families. He was given a UN identification card and was told he would go to the United States.

As the civil war intensified, Hangasu decided to move his family to a safe place. After Siad Barre left power in 1991, his army ransacked all government belongings, including weapons and vehicles. The soldiers repurposed the military vehicles for commercial use. Hangasu thought if he could make it to a

Kenyan refugee camp, he would have the opportunity to go to the United States. "I rented a military vehicle to take me and my family to the Kenyan border," Hangasu recalled. "From there I would go to America. We took nothing with us other than the clothes we wore and baby food for our youngest daughter who was a few months old at the time." It took them one day to reach Kismayo. They stayed there for two more days searching for good transportation. On day three, Hangasu rented another car to take his family to the Somalia/Kenya border city of Leboy. They stayed there for about one month. At Leboy, the UNHCR determined what to do with a flood of refugees from Somalia and Ethiopia. Somali refugees were sent to Garesa, Kenya, and Ethiopian refugees were sent to Mersabet, Kenya. In the end, Hangasu was cleared to join the rest of the Ethiopian refugees in Mersabet.

"At the Mersabet refugee camp I was told to prepare to fly to the US in two weeks." Hangasu was grateful to escape the civil war with his family and to be headed to the United States. He was not sure what to expect, but he thought it would be better than escaping a civil war and struggling to feed his family in the refugee camp.

*

On June 4, 1991, Ethiopia's communist government, the Derg, was overthrown, and the Ethiopian People's Revolutionary Democratic Front (EPRDF) controlled the capital city of Finfinne. EPRDF was a multiparty coalition; however, the power resided with the Tigray People's Liberation Front (TPLF).

Back in the camp, the administrators broke the news to Hangasu and the other refugees: "There is good news and bad news. The good news is that the communist government of Mengistu Haile Mariam that drove you out is gone. The bad news—you are no longer going to the United States. Your case is dismissed."

The entire justification for Hangasu and others to go to the United States had been built on two things: first, the situation in Somalia was dangerous because of the humanitarian crisis. Second, Ethiopia was under the communist government that had ousted him and others in the first place, therefore he couldn't go back. However, now the communist government was gone. "We were told, 'Your cases were dismissed. Your country is free.' This was two weeks before the presumed move to America! Two weeks!" Hangasu said.

My uncle didn't know what to do. Would he go back to Ethiopia or stay in Kenya? He knew going back to Ethiopia meant involving himself in politics, which he had no appetite for at that time. After some thought, he decided to stay in Kenya. A month later, people reached out to Hangasu asking him to return to Ethiopia and be part of building the new government, or at least to advocate for the Oromo cause. General Wako Gutu urged him to return. Finally, his maternal uncle, Sheikh Yahya, visited him in the Kenyan refugee camp. Yahya had named Hangasu Ahmed-Berq when he was born. "Sheikh Yahya convinced me," Hangasu said. "He said this was what you fought for. The Derg government had fallen. This is an opportunity for the Oromo people to decide their own destiny. Your people need you. Who would represent your people if you stay here? Nobody from your region knows the Ethiopian system like you do. Please come back." Hangasu agreed to return.

When Hangasu returned to Finfinne, the city was familiar and strange at the same time. "After many requests to return home and help my people, I took my family and headed to Ethiopia," Hangasu said. "We arrived in Moyale, a border city between Kenya and Ethiopia. I left my family in Moyale to check out the situation in Finfinne. Fifteen years earlier, when I left Finfinne, I knew many people, and many people knew me. In 1991 when I returned, it was as if I didn't know a single soul in that city. It was very strange. The city and landmark places hadn't changed, but the people did. Other than my family and close friends, I only recognized one person from my time in Finfinne. And only one person recognized me on the streets. I guess we all changed. Some of the senior people I worked with in the past were retired and stayed home. The young ones had grown up and were unrecognizable. I stayed for three months by myself in Finfinne. It felt safe. Then I brought my family to join me."

Finfinne was and still is the center of politics in Ethiopia. Hangasu lived in Finfinne during his teen years and before joining the Oromo guerilla army in mid-1976. He remembered the city very well. It appeared the freedom he and his people—and the generation before them—had fought for was finally fulfilled. When he'd last exited Finfinne, it was a matter of life and death. He escaped under an alias. Now he entered the city without the fear of being killed.

"Politically, the country had changed in a big way, even in the short few months since the collapse of the Derg regime," Hangasu said. "Historically, the Ethiopian leaders claimed they were God-elect and were therefore unchallengeable. The communist Derg government was equally dictatorial. There was no room for discussion or dialogue. It was a one-way street. Challenging the government and standing for your rights was a crime. But that had changed. Now it seemed like there was an opportunity to stand for yourself and for your people. There was an opportunity to debate ideas. There was talk of an inclusive government and constitution." There had been no opposition parties in the history of Ethiopia until this time. If they existed, they were eliminated immediately, similar to what had happened during the early days of the communist government. Opposition was dealt with swiftly in Ethiopia.

Taking advantage of Ethiopia's new political climate, each ethnic group organized itself by forming political parties to share power in the government. More than two hundred political parties were established. Some had connections to their ethnic populations; the majority had no backing at all.

In 1991, hope was on the horizon. It seemed that, all of a sudden, Oromos were everywhere. Oromo language was used openly in the streets of Finfinne. Oromo flags flew all over. Other ethnic groups such as the Tigre, Amhara, Somali, and Gurage were equally visible. The Oromos celebrated in the streets of Finfinne and across the country. Music and festivities were commonplace. OLF cadres spread the organization's views through these ceremonies across the country.

After two decades of separation, General Wako Gutu and General Jagama Kello met in Finfinne. Last time they were together in 1970, Jagama sealed a peace deal with the Bale fighters led by Wako. He brought the protracted conflict to an end. Now Jagama was much older and still maintained a good stature as a retired officer. Likewise, Wako was much older and continued to be regarded as a national hero. Wako asked Jagama to partner with him to advocate for the Oromo cause. Wako told him, "This is our moment to lift our people from the century-long subjugation." Jagama refused. "I don't want to be involved in ethnic politics," he said. Jagama firmly believed in the unity of Ethiopia. He thought the demands by the different Ethiopian ethnic groups for their rights was a threat to that unity. Wako hoped for a broad-based coalition of the Oromo people to unite and demand their own rights.

Five Oromo parties were formed: the United Oromo People's Liberation Front (UOPLF) led by General Wako Gutu; the Islamic Front for the Liberation of Oromia (IFLO) led by Jaarra Abba Gadaa; the Oromo-Abbo led by Siraj Haji Isaaq Dadhi; the Oromo People's Democratic Organization (OPDO) led by Hassan Ali; and the Oromo Liberation Front (OLF) led by Galasa Dilbo (Leenco Lata was the Deputy Secretary General). By far, the OLF was the most influential and dominant Oromo organization at this time, enlisting support from all regions of Oromia. The OPDO and Oromo-Abbo were the least credible; the OPDO was considered a puppet for the TPLF, and Abbo was a puppet for Somalia (at least back when it had operated in Somalia). OPDO was established by the TPLF and Eritrean who were fighting against the Derg. Support for the UOPLF was primarily limited to the Bale and Arsi regions with additional support from Jimma, Ilubabur, and Shawa. Support for the IFLO came primarily from the Harar region where Jarra Abba Gadaa had started the movement.

Sheikh Yahya told Hangasu, "We lost it again."

Curious, Hangasu asked, "Why do you say that?"

"Other ethnic groups put forward one organization that represented them all," Yahya said. "They have one voice to bring change for their people. Oromos brought forward five organizations. By the time we negotiate an agreement amongst ourselves, others will have already gotten their share and divided up our share."

In essence, that summarized the fate of the Oromo people. After all that struggle, Oromos were unable to take advantage of the changes in Ethiopia because they were disorganized, divided, and poorly led.

While the Oromos were dancing in the streets and celebrating victory, the EPRDF (led by Meles Zenawi's party, the TPLF) held a national conference and established the Transitional Government of Ethiopia, seeking to form a broad-based political pact. Meles Zenawi was elected as the transitional government president. Those in the room recall that Meles Zenawi nominated Leenco Lata as transitional government president, but Lata excused himself voluntarily, saying, "I am not ready at the moment." Meles Zenawi accepted the nomination to lead the nation during the transition. With the prime ministership in hand, the EPRDF consolidated power in the country.

*

Back in the 1970s, both Hangasu and Adam Jilo were OLF members. Hangasu left the OLF in 1981 after the OLF's treacherous plot that dismantled General Wako Gutu's organization. After the fall of the Derg, Hangasu joined the UOPLF, General Wako Gutu's party. Adam Jilo stayed with the OLF simply because he wanted to be out of General Wako Gutu's shadow. Hangasu and Adam Jilo were still close, even though they had supported different organizations.

Now in 1991, the roles were reversed. Adam Jilo invited Hangasu back to the OLF. The OLF had significant influence with the transitional government, and Adam Jilo wanted to take advantage of this. He was tasked with recruiting Hangasu back to the OLF because he understood Ethiopian politics and was influential in Bale due to his family's history.

""Adam Jilo begged me to meet with Mr. Leenco Lata. I refused to meet. He said, 'My nephew, please don't waste this opportunity. It is a win-win-win. Win for you—you get to work with a strong organization. Win for me—I deliver on my task. Win for OLF—they need you to organize the people.'"

Hangasu responded, "I won't be tricked twice by the same people."

"Oh, my nephew, you are a fool not to take advantage of this opportunity," Adam Jilo replied. What Adam Jilo said about the wins may have been true, but Hangasu could not trust the organization. Without trust, he wouldn't commit.

In 1992, the OLF left the charter, meaning they declared that their party was no longer part of the new Ethiopian government. From the ruling party's perspective, this was a declaration of war against the government. At the same time, the OLF leaders didn't inform the army about their decision. The majority of their soldiers were captured by the TPLF and surrendered without firing a single shot. It was one of the easiest victories TPLF scored against the Oromo.

"The OLF's departure from the charter is a mystery to me to this day," Hangasu said. He didn't understand why a party that had the full support of the Oromo people and that had played a key role in the formation of the transitional government would all of a sudden give up.

The OLF deputy chairman, Leenco Lata, who had declared war on the government by withdrawing from the charter, left the country through Bole International Airport as a diplomat with a government visa. He moved to Canada. Tens of thousands of Oromos were jailed and tortured throughout the country. Thousands more were made to disappear by the TPLF government. The pretext for all of these killing and torture was that these people had supported or sympathized with the OLF.

A few months after leaving Ethiopia, Leenco Lata returned through the same airport, to advocate for and free his colleague

Ibsa Gutama from an Ethiopian prison. He was successful. Ibsa Gutama was freed. Leenco returned to Canada again. This was mind boggling to most Oromos. It made no sense that, after having killed and jailed Oromos for their association with the OLF, they would permit the leader of the OLF to come, free his colleague, and return home.

Hangasu said, "I wondered how was it possible that Leenco freely flew in and out of Ethiopia when most Oromos were in mass prisons because of the organization he led?" Meles Zenawi was asked by a journalist who was baffled by this event, "How come the OLF leader, the prime enemy of the Ethiopian state, comes and leaves freely?" Meles responded, "Mr. Leenco apologized for what he did. He is a citizen of this country. He has the right to come and go as he wishes." This made some Oromos question the relationship between the OLF and the TPLF. To most Oromos, it looked like Leenco Lata got a free pass. Nobody understood the reason.

Hangasu calls this an "OLF-TPLF drama."

"I was with this organization [OLF] from its inception; their intentions were never clear. They had connections with the same government they were supposed to fight. Many early leaders who believed in free Oromia were eliminated— Abdullahi Badow, Nuguse Negassa, Kinfe Haji Hindhesa, Magarsa Bari, Baro Tumsa, and nine executive central committee members."

When the OLF left the charter in 1992, they didn't just pack up and leave. They made sure other Oromo organizations left with them. The OLF understood their decision to leave would create a vacuum for other organizations to fill. For example, if General Wako Gutu stayed behind, he would fill the vacuum. He was a national hero, having fought both the Haile Selassie regime and the Socialist Derg. The TPLF considered him a national figure who should be respected.

Adam Jilo was tasked with convincing Hangasu again, this time to meet with OLF leaders to exit the charter, enter the jungle, and resume guerilla fighting. Adam Jilo said, "My nephew, please, please, please just meet with them. Don't agree to anything; just meet with them."

Hangasu responded, "I am very sorry, I can't." Then "I stood up and kissed Adam Jilo on his forehead." In Oromo culture, you are not supposed to say no to elders. This was especially true in the case of Adam Jilo because they were such close friends.

After they gave up on Hangasu, the OLF moved to other council members of the UOPLF who had the ear of General Wako Gutu. They sent messages to him. In addition, they asked Jamal Robale to convince General Wako to leave the charter on the basis that the TPLF had changed its agenda: "The TPLF tricked us, and they are eliminating key Oromo figures." (Wako Gutu's life was at risk as well.) Jamal Robale was an OLF leader and a good friend of General Wako Gutu. Wako loved Jamal Robale for his bravery and probably saw in him a younger version of himself. Wako considered the message seriously but wanted to verify the situation independently. He reached out to the head of the Ethiopian Parliament (a man from the Hadiya ethnic group). The man was a mutual friend of both Leenco and Wako. The man confirmed the reports that the TPLF had indeed changed its agenda and planned to kill key opposition leaders (including Wako), and added that the Hadiya ethnic leaders were leaving the charter too. Wako's suspicions peaked. He decided to go to Bale until things settled.

Before he left Finfinne, Wako and Mahmud Bune met with Hangasu. Wako said, "The situation in the country has changed. I am leaving. Let's go!" Hangasu knew what he was talking about. Instead of asking where, which he already knew, he asked, "Why?"

Wako responded, "Everybody is leaving. The OLF left."

With frustration, Hangasu protested, "I don't follow the OLF. They have their own reasons for leaving. You don't know why they left. Why do you follow them?"

Hangasu recalled the conversation he and General Wako had in 1991 at Awasa. "There was a huge smear campaign against him [Wako] when I returned from Kenya. The OLF was behind it. They said that Wako was a sellout, and he put his support behind the TPLF and the OPDO for two million birr. I met him in Awasa city. We stayed in a hotel. We asked everybody to leave us alone. I wanted to know everything. What did he know about the campaign against him? Was he guilty or innocent? After an all-night dialogue, he convinced me that it was a fabrication. The campaign was designed to minimize his credibility and brand in the country. We agreed there and then that our only option was to advocate for our people from inside Ethiopia. The new form of resistance: struggle must come from the inside, not armed struggle."

Wako made one last argument. "But you always stood with us, even in much riskier situations. Why do you refuse today?"

"You used to be on the right path," Hangasu responded. "Today you are not. In addition, you have no plan. What are we going to do now if we leave? What did we learn from our Somalia experience? They gave us weapons, but they hijacked our struggle, made it their own. This is a losing plan."

Mahmud Bune stretched out his hands to stop Hangasu from saying that final phrase. "Please don't say that," he said. It is considered a bad omen to mentions a loss as a group heads off to a mission. Only good wishes are made traditionally.

At this point, Hangasu stood and left the meeting. Wako's son Abdul Qadir Wako (aka Shanqo, who was kidnapped and jailed with his mother in 1963 when the Bale revolt began) followed him to the door. He said to Hangasu, "I speak for my friends as well. We are young. We crave for a fight, a battle, because we never had a chance to fight the enemy. [He missed both the Dhombir and Sowra wars due to his age.] We are determined to fight. What advice do you have for us?"

"In the Oromo culture, when you see something piteous you would say, '*hebo,*'" Hangasu said. "Your situation today—this exit from the charter—is *below hebo.*'" Meaning he was sorry for them. More than that, he was disappointed.

Wako decided to visit Robe, Bale, where he gave a short talk. The theme of his message was "We fought all tyrants in the past—Haile Selassie and Mengistu Haile Mariam. We stand for our people's rights. We will again fight those who don't respect our rights." He added, "We are not afraid of Woyane (TPLF)!"

That evening Wako and his team of eight men stayed at the Baqqala Mollaa Hotel in Robe. Wako planned to go to Dallo in the morning. Around 8 a.m. the next day, the Woyane army surrounded the hotel as Wako and his men exited. Wako was ordered at gunpoint to stay still. He refused to comply and challenged the soldiers—who were they to stop them? The TPLF soldiers and Wako's men pointed guns at each other's heads. Wako was outnumbered and underarmed, but he didn't care. To him, the number of people or weapons was not the issue; the only concern he had was if he was standing up for a just cause. A few minutes later, the TPLF soldiers were told to stand down by their superiors. Wako and his small team walked away and drove off to Dallo. That was it. As he exited Goba, Wako decided that this was war. This meant armed struggle from within the jungles of Bale. Wako's guerilla struggle—as unprepared as they were—started again.

The departure of General Wako Gutu and Leenco Lata was punctuated by contrast. Leenco exited Ethiopia through the Bole airport. Wako exited Ethiopia through Bale. In Ethiopia, there are two types of struggles—diplomatic resistance and armed struggle. Bole represented diplomatic struggle; Bale represented armed resistance. The OLF claimed that it advanced the Oromo struggle through armed struggle, but this wasn't the case. Their claim was an attempt to erase others' efforts, such as those of the Bale Oromo's Struggle for Freedom. In reality OLF's struggle was more of a diplomatic pursuit. OLF excelled at mass propaganda campaigns using multiple mediums ranging from word of mouth to print media and radio. OLF leaders took little risk while the Oromo masses bore the brutal retaliation of the Ethiopian government. General Wako Gutu was a militant man from a young age. He didn't know any way other than armed resistance. He took the same risks as his people. In fact, he usually took the greatest risks.

CHAPTER TWENTY-ONE:
HANGASU RUNS FOR OFFICE

I N DECEMBER 1994, THE NEW ETHIOPIAN constitution, which was based on the premise of the charter, was ratified. The constitution guaranteed the right of each ethnic group in the country to govern its own affairs through its own autonomous regional government within the framework of a federal Ethiopia. This was the basis on which the Oromia Regional State was established in 1992. Nine ethnically based regional governments (including Oromia—the largest of them all) constituted modern Ethiopia. By the end of 1994, ethnically based political parties were everywhere, preparing for the national elections that would take place in 1995.

To manage the elections and consolidate power, the ruling coalition, EPRDF, declared that each ethnic group could only have one representative political party. With the absence of OLF, the remaining Oromo organizations began talks to merge.

When the United Oromo People's Liberation Front (UOPLF) and the Islamic Front for the Liberation of Oromia (IFLO) merged, they chose their new leaders: Sheikh Ahmed

Haro as chairman (from the UOPLF) and Haji Umar Malka as vice chairman (from the IFLO). Hangasu was working behind the scenes to make things happen.

The two organizations published a manifesto with a theme of peaceful struggle. This was an important distinction because some of the key figures of the UOPLF (General Wako Gutu) and IFLO (Jaarra Abbaa-Gada) decided to continue the armed struggle. The two merged organizations wanted to be clear that they believed in peaceful struggle through elections. As such, they registered with the elections board as a legitimate organization.

Hangasu and his colleagues wanted to make a statement. They decided to inform their rival Oromo organization, OPDO, in a face-to-face meeting that they would compete with them in the general election in Bale. OPDO had the backing of the ruling party and was well positioned to win because they controlled all the resources. Hangasu and his friends could barely fund their transportation. However, they counted on the support of their people.

Hangasu recalled, "We got an appointment with Yonata Dibisa. He was the OPDO secretary at the time. On the day of the appointment, Sheikh Ahmed Haro, Mahmad-Hussein Garo, and I went to Yonata's office. When we got there, we were surprised with who we found there. Abba-Dula Gemeda, the defense minister of Ethiopia, was sitting on the main chair. Our appointment was with Yonata. 'Why is Abba-Dula here?' That was what went through all of our heads. Yonata was sitting on a side on a sofa."

On their way to this meeting, Sheikh Ahmed and Mahmad-Hussein told Hangasu not to speak. The two friends worried that he would get angry and lash out if OPDO mistreated them. They told Hangasu to "just listen, because if you speak, you will put us all in danger." Hangasu agreed. When they entered the office, Hangasu sat in the middle. Sheikh Ahmed sat to his right, and Mahmad-Hussein to his left.

Abba-Dula wasted no time. He leaned forward and said, "Why did you come?" There was silence. Abba-Dula is of moderate height but has a bulky and strong physique. He has intimidating red eyes, especially when he is mad. Right then, it seemed like he was fuming. By comparison, my uncle is short and lean, but he thinks on his feet. Under pressure he speaks confidently and authoritatively. My uncle looked to his left and to his right, hoping someone would respond to the question. His two friends were caught off guard and hadn't yet gotten over their confusion.

Using the silence as an opportunity, Abba-Dula continued, "General Wako Gutu! We had many heroes of our own. We were planning to demolish the Menelik's statue in Finfinne and replace it with his statue. We carried him in our heads as our *hero*. In turn, he left the charter and destroyed our children [troops in the battle]. You, too, wanted to fight but you lost. You had nowhere to turn. That's why you are here now."

Filled with emotion, Hangasu turned to his two friends and said, "Please respond!"

They both looked at Hangasu and said, "You should respond."

"But you told me not to speak," Hangasu said.

"You should talk now," they said.

Hangasu gathered himself, making sure his emotions were under control. He said, "Abba-Dula! I have one question: Is this *your personal office* or an Oromo people's office?"

"It is an Oromo people's office," Abba-Dula said.

"I am deeply saddened and sorry you represent this office while you still harbor these backward thoughts!" Hangasu said. "You said we lost. We didn't lose. We have a proud history. We have our people [implying OPDO lacked both]. Yes, General Wako left the charter. I don't represent him. But truth be told, General Wako fought the Haile Selassie regime three decades ago. Oppression by the EPRDF is not sweeter than oppression by Haile Selassie or Derg. He doesn't own villas and high-rises like you do. What was he going to do when you didn't let him live in peace at his hut, the size of a birdhouse, in Ganale? We don't carry guns and submit to slavery. He had the right to defend himself."

Hangasu took a little breath. Nobody intervened, so he continued. "You just called him [Wako Gutu] a loser. He advocated for you [OPDO] when everybody launched a smear campaign against you as sellouts. Because of you, he was called the same."

Now it was getting personal, but Hangasu couldn't stop. "We came to Yonata out of respect for this office. You know people out there in the street say Yonata, Kumsa, and *you* are not Oromos."

Abba-Dula sunk deeper and deeper into his chair as Hangasu went through their names one by one. "Right now, if you, Abba-Dula, attempt to raise your hand to shoot me, I will make you regret before you reach your pistol," Hangasu said. "At that point, Mahmad-Hussein and Sheikh Ahmed simultaneously stepped on my feet, signaling that was *enough*."

This was typical of my uncle. Nobody can intimidate him. He speaks truth to power, particularly upon provocation. He would silence his opponents as he had just done with Abba-Dula.

Hangasu took a quick breath again and concluded by explaining why the men had come to the office that morning. "All we are trying to say is, you are working with Tigre, Amhara, and southern nations and nationalities. We are Oromo too. Let's work together on things on which we agree, which are many."

Abba-Dula had had enough. He offered no response to Hangasu's series of charges against him or his party. He picked up his notebook, stood, and said, "I am late for my meeting. Anyway, your meeting was not with me. It was with Yonata. Bye." With that, Abba-Dula left.

Yonata finally stepped up. "Abba-Dula is a military person," he said. "We don't have a problem. If there is, we can fix it."

"He is no more a military man than us," Hangasu said. "He just has a problem seeing us." On that note, the meeting adjourned.

After the meeting, Hangasu and Haji Umar Malka decided to enter the 1995 elections to represent the Dallo district of

Bale. Hangasu knew the election wouldn't be easy. After all, he would be going against OPDO (which was backed by the TPLF government) in that region.

Hangasu hoped to bring the issue of Muslims' religious rights to the Ethiopian parliament. By giving the issue its proper platform, Muslims and people of other faiths could openly talk. "For example, why can't a Muslim be a head of state in Ethiopia?" Hangasu said. "If it is due to Muslims' own problems, they should fix them. However, if it is due to the oppressive system that marginalizes people of other faiths, the *system* must be fixed."

By April 1995, voters began registering for Ethiopia's first elections. TPLF prepared its Oromo (the Oromo People's Democratic Organization), Amhara (the Amhara National Democratic Movement), and the Southern Nations & Nationalities (the Southern Ethiopian People's Democratic Movement) wings to dominate the elections. Hangasu underestimated the power OPDO had in forcing its will and desire on the people. "OPDO opposed me from day one—100 percent."

Hangasu traveled to Bale to begin the campaign. He met his extended family members, friends, and old acquaintances. Everywhere he went, he was greeted with enthusiasm. He was able to engage the youth and the elders. Just about everybody in the region knew who he was. His brand was great. People instantly trusted him because of the sacrifices he and his family had made on behalf of the Bale people during the Haile Selassie and Mengistu regimes.

OPDO representatives in the region took note of what was happening. They were not happy about Hangasu's popularity. His opponent was Mohamed Abdi Gudal, who represented OPDO. Mohamed was less popular in Dallo and Madda Walabu simply because he'd never had the presence Hangasu had on the ground in those districts. In addition, the people in the region didn't trust or respect OPDO because they were considered TPLF puppets.

OPDO leaders were given specific instructions to make sure Hangasu didn't win the election. Suleyman Abba-Nasha was a secretary of the Bale zone representing the OPDO administration. Suleyman gathered the OPDO cadres in Dallo and instructed them to do anything necessary to make sure Hangasu lost the election. To make his point clear, Suleyman said, "If Hangasu is elected, it means OPDO has failed in a major way, and his victory has far more implications for OPDO in general. You must do everything in your power to assure he doesn't win. However, if somehow he manages to win, he should *never* pass the Rira Mountain *alive*." (Rira is situated between Dallo and Goba in the Bale region). Hangasu heard about this and continued his campaign as planned.

One week before election day, the OPDO representative in Bidire—a man named Assefa—accused Hangasu of recruiting and using OLF cadres on his campaign. Assefa complained about this issue to the head of the army in Bidire—a TPLF army commander addressed as Shambel, which was a military title. The Shambel was supposed to settle arguments between different parties and ensure the election took place smoothly (in favor of TPLF allies of course—but they wanted to be discreet). They wanted the election to be viewed as fair, even though they had no intention of allowing it to *be* fair. In principle, the army was "a neutral body." But in reality, the army was anything but neutral. Assefa was looking for an accusation that would stick and disqualify Hangasu from participating in the election. At that point, working with OLF (the organization that had left the charter and chose armed struggle) was a crime. If the Shambel believed Assefa, that alone could disqualify Hangasu from the elections.

Hangasu found out that Assefa accused four of his campaign managers in Madda Walabu of being OLF cadres. This kind of information reached Hangasu through informal networks. Everybody in the city knew and cared for him, so he got information quickly, even things discussed behind closed doors. Hangasu took the four representatives who were accused of being OLF members and set out to look for the Shambel. He found him standing and chatting with Assefa.

Hangasu approached the two men and introduced himself to the Shambel. "My name is Hangasu Wako, a native of this town, and I am running for a House of Representatives seat. I am taking part in the election because it was advertised as a free and fair election. OPDOs have not earned the people's respect. They could not convince the people about their vision. They have nothing to show that benefited our people. Now they are desperate, and as a result they turned to lies as their main campaign objectives."

"What lies?" the Shambel asked.

"Have you ever seen these guys?" Hangasu asked. He pointed to his campaign managers.

"Yes, I see them all the time. Their faces are very familiar."

"How long have you been in Bidire?" Hangasu pressed.

"I came to Bidire ten months ago. I see them from time to time."

"Assefa told you these men are OLF. You look for OLF in the wilderness, when OLFs are actually inside your *tuttas* [a coverall garment often worn by military men]."

"How so?" the Shambel asked, looking Hangasu straight in the eye.

"You worked with Assefa for the last ten months. He hid these OLF members from you, even though he knew they were OLF all along. Assefa is one of them. Now, in the eleventh hour and because they campaigned for me, he snitched to you conveniently. Ask him why he hid this information from you for the last ten months."

Desperate and nervous, Assefa spoke to Hangasu in Oromo language.*"Gaash Hangasu, maalif akkas nagoota, namicha kana duratti?"* meaning "Mr. Hangasu, why do you do this to me in front of *this* guy?"

Hangasu replied in Oromo language, *"Situ barbaade. Afaan Amaaraa, malee hin dubadhu—gooftaan kee si dhagahuu!"* meaning "That is what you deserve. I will only speak in Amharic so that *your master* hears everything!"

As he realized that Assefa had made up the accusations, the Shambel said, "It is true. OLFs are in our *tuttas*."

A week later, on election day, voters turned to the closest polling stations. This was the first election in the country's history. People were naturally excited, but they were also anxious. The government was cracking down on key figures, teachers, and government employees under the pretext that they were supporting the armed struggle. People were threatened with jail or death if they voted for a non-OPDO candidate. At the polls, OPDO soldiers stood and watched the ballot boxes, intimidating the voters. If the voter dropped the ballot in a non-OPDO candidate's box, the soldiers took note. Some people voted for OPDO to spare themselves. Others voted for candidates like Hangasu who were opposing the OPDO in defiance. Even with all the intimidation, observers predicted he would win. However, when the election results were presented, Hangasu had lost, and OPDO had won.

Hangasu was disappointed, but he was not naive. He knew OPDO cheated in the election. And it was not just in Bale. In May 1995, the ruling coalition won a "landslide victory" across the country. Many opposition political parties boycotted the election because they had been prevented from campaigning. International observers declared the elections to be free and fair, patting themselves on the back for a job well done. The election ended the transitional period, and TPLF took full control in Ethiopia. Human rights violations, including extrajudicial killings, arbitrary arrests, and denial of freedom of association and expression, continued.

*

Hangasu returned to Finfinne again to focus on his family, minimizing political involvement. Halima, his eldest daughter, didn't remember much about the election other than the fact that he lost. On the other hand, she remembered morning routines with her father. "My dad highly valued education," she said. "He enrolled us in a private Islamic school called Abadir. Preparation for school begins the night before. He taught us how polish our shoes and how to clean our uniforms (red sweater, white shirt, and black skirt). They must all be spotless. He personally inspected them before we left for school every morning. My mom would pack a lunch for us. My dad would give us bus fare because we had to take a city bus to get to our school. Abadir was not the closest school to us, so it took us two different buses to get to the school. He would put us on the bus and walk to the market. I used to feel like he was always there because he would put us on the bus, randomly stop by school unannounced, or wait for us at the bus stop to take us home."

My uncle made it a priority to educate his children. He'd closely observed the Ethiopian government during the Haile Selassie and Derg regimes, and he'd come to realize that education is the foundation for bringing change. He also firmly believed that opportunities come to those who are educated and that someone with an education could pursue opportunities others could not. Living in Finfinne was not cheap. He lived 500 kilometers from his hometown of Bidire where he could get access to his wealth (camels, cattle, goats, etc.) that was being kept by his sister, Zamzam. When he returned from the Kenyan refugee camp, he'd had to start with nothing.

During his time in Finfinne, he worked as a broker to make a living. He knew the city and the language. Merchants who came from the Bale and Borana zones didn't speak the Amharic language, nor did they know the city. Finfinne was a dangerous place for someone who visited from the province. Thieves were everywhere. The shop owners in the city would exponentially increase their prices if they knew the buyer was from the province and didn't know the market. Therefore, merchants from the south needed a trusted person to do their buying. Hangasu fit the profile, and people from his region naturally came to him and asked for his help buying things. Some would simply call Hangasu from the comfort of their homes or shops in the south to ask him to buy high-value commodities (milling machines, spare car parts, etc.) for them. He would buy the items and ship them to the owners.

Whatever he made from his job, he invested in his children. "When the economy got bad, we would experience austerity in a different way, but we were confident our schooling was always taken care of," Halima said. "For example, we might not get new clothes and would eat plain meals, budena [injera] with shiro, because meat was too expensive. Yet my dad never delayed or missed our school tuition. He always paid for the school in full and on time. I know this because otherwise we would have been yelled at or kicked out of school. I have seen it happen to other kids."

My uncle's children, my cousins, shared a few personal anecdotes about their father when they lived in Finfinne. His children felt that he was always there when it mattered to them. From these stories, it is clear that Hangasu was close to his children. His parenting style was slightly authoritarian though. When I asked, his children would say, "He is a bit strict." For example, he didn't allow sleepovers. His children remembered moving to new houses frequently. That was Hangasu's way of coping with Ethiopia's dynamic political situation. Other moves were driven by the fluctuation of his income. "The only constant thing was our school," Halima said. "No matter where we moved, we went to the same school. The only friends we had were from the school—no neighborhood friends." To compensate for that, Hangasu took his children to his relatives' houses often. Many of his maternal aunts and uncles lived in Finfinne.

Hangasu wouldn't allow Halima to visit her friends. Halima had a friend named Samira who was an only child. Samira's family was rich in Halima's eye because she had *everything*. One time, during Eid al-Adha, Halima and Samira wanted to take an Eid (holiday) picture together. Because neither of her parents were home, Halima was supposed to be watching Badru (her youngest brother, who was 3 at the time). Samira and Halima decided to take the picture anyway. They left home in a rush with Badru and went to the local photo studio. Halima and Samira were ready. They got their sunglasses, and Samira hung her fancy purse at her side. But Halima had forgotten to dress Badru before going to the studio. He didn't even have pants on. There was no way they could go back home to get him a pair of pants. It was too far, and they were running out of time. They could get caught by their parents. Halima had an idea. "I took off my sunglasses and put them on Badru. He doesn't have pants on, but these sunglasses were *super cool*! *And* we took a picture together."

Zahra, Hangasu's third daughter, remembers him as a hilarious man. "My dad always had a radiant smile," she said. "Nothing made me more joyful than seeing my father smile. I used to say, 'Oh God, please give me a husband that has a smile like my father.' So one day I approached my dad and said, 'You have a really nice smile and teeth.' Now I know this was a mistake, of course. He replied to me by saying, '*hin beeka*,' which means 'I know' in English, ha-ha."

Zahra's childhood memories of her father were filled with laughter. Zahra remembered one occasion in particular. "It was during Ramadan (the holy month of fasting in Islam). We were sitting and breaking our fast right after sunset. My older sister, Fatuma, was notorious for eating slowly. On average she ate like 15 calories a day and was eating like 0.3 calories per bite. My dad said, 'Look here, girls, there is no way ya gonna be models because ya too short, so please just stuff ya face and don't worry about gaining weight.' I don't remember if my sister was laughing as hard as me, but I had to run to the ladies' room, if you know what I mean. When he's saying this, he's laughing so hard himself, and that even makes it even funnier because he has the funniest laugh. It kinda sounds like a cat dying!"

These and many other stories from Hangasu's children show him as a personable and approachable person at home. He loved his children. He wanted to shield them from what was going on in the country. He would deal with the security concerns for himself. He didn't want them to worry.

In his mind, he was paranoid. He was always on alert. The government's indiscriminate killing was a common practice. As a public figure who challenged the government, he knew he was being watched. He slept very little. He anticipated that someday the government would make up some stories if it wanted to eliminate him. This concept didn't sit well with him.

CHAPTER TWENTY-TWO:
THE CRACKDOWN

ONE EVENING EARLY IN 1998, my uncle was walking home after a long day at the market in Finfinne. Three policemen stopped him and questioned where he was going. He explained that he was going home. The policemen searched Hangasu and discovered that he was carrying a handgun. The policemen arrested him on the spot. They inquired about his house and sent a team to search it. There they found two additional guns. However, the weapons were all registered. He hadn't broken any laws. Yet the police kept Hangasu in prison that night without any explanation.

The next morning, the deputy police commissioner of Finfinne, Colonel Ta'ime, visited Hangasu in prison. Ta'ime was an ethnic Tigre, Ethiopian's ruling party. It was uncommon to be interrogated by the deputy commissioner. Hangasu's case must have been a serious one.

That afternoon, Hangasu was brought to the interrogation room. Two officers were present: Colonel Ta'ime and the chief of the station. Ta'ime said to Hangasu, "Tell us what's going on."

Hangasu was already agitated. He thought his arrest had been planned. Why else was he being interrogated by a senior officer?

"I will tell you what's going on," Hangasu said. "We fought the Haile Selassie regime. We fought the Derg regime. We didn't fight you [TPLF] because we thought you were freedom-seeking people just like ourselves [the Oromo]. As soon as you took power and controlled the country, you forgot what it was like for others to fight for their own freedom and dignity. It bothers you that we still exist. You won't be in power forever. Your time will pass too. My wish is that someday you and I will go back to the jungle to resume the struggle again. We could have this conversation there."

Effectively, Hangasu had threatened Ta'ime. Ta'ime realized Hangasu was extremely angry and emotional. He patted Hangasu on the shoulder and said, "I am sorry. That was not my intention."

Ta'ime continued. "To tell you the truth, we are investigating recent attacks that took place in this city. We had a theory that these attacks were orchestrated by ex-servicemen. You happened to be part of a larger investigation. It was nothing personal to you or your people."

My uncle was released that afternoon without any charges but was told to report to the police station twice every day—once in the morning at 9 a.m. and again in the afternoon at 3 p.m. This was done to both intimidate and keep him under surveillance.

On his way home from the prison, Hangasu realized that it was not safe for him to stay in the city any longer. People were still being imprisoned indefinitely without any reason or, worse yet, made to disappear. He thought about what would happen to his family if any of those things happened to him. He consulted with Maryam. She had an idea. She wanted to get out of the country altogether.

Maryam called Hangasu's friend, Mohamed Adam Jilo, and explained her family's predicament. Mohamed lived in Minnesota in the United States. He was eager to help his friend.

He knew Hangasu wouldn't ask for help; that was just how he lived. Mohamed sent money and told them to find a way to get to Kenya, a regional hub for refugees fleeing persecution from their own countries.

To maintain the facade of compliance, Hangasu continued reporting to the police station twice a day. He would go in, sign his name, then leave. In between these reporting sessions, he planned their escape. He told neighbors and acquaintances that he wanted to move his children back to Bidire, his hometown in southern Ethiopia. He said this because people snitched on each other and could not be trusted. Hangasu sold some of his valuable furniture and shipped other pieces and household items to Bidire. All of this was done as publicly as possible to create a believable distraction.

A few days after the furniture was shipped, he moved out of his rental house and slipped under the radar into temporary housing arranged by his closest friend. The next day, Hangasu sent Maryam and three of their children to Moyale, the border city between Ethiopia and Kenya. He assigned one of his nephews to watch the family during the escape. After the family had made it safely to Moyale, Hangasu took the rest of the children and headed there. While Hangasu was on the way to Moyale, immigration officers in Moyale spotted Maryam and her children and confiscated their passports. The officers accused her of smuggling Eritrean children.

By the middle of 1998, the Ethiopian-Eritrean war had begun. Eritreans in Ethiopia were deported, and their properties were confiscated. This meant good business for immigration officers at the border. They could simply accuse anyone of being Eritrean to make a few bucks. That was what happened to Maryam and her children. When Hangasu arrived in Moyale, he talked to the officials and paid 400 birr (equivalent to $25 at the time) to get back his family's passports. Just like that, Hangasu was forced to leave Ethiopia again. But this time his main focus was to get his family to a safe place.

CHAPTER-TWENTY THREE:
LIFE IN EXILE

MY UNCLE'S TIME IN KENYA was punctuated by hardship. After narrowly escaping the brutal Ethiopian government, he settled in Nairobi, Kenya, with his family. None of them spoke Swahili. From his brief stay in Marsabet, Kenya, seven years prior, Hangasu remembered a few words of the language, but not enough to effectively communicate. Fortunately, his children quickly learned the language. His son Badru spoke Swahili just like the natives. He often acted as an interpreter in the market.

The economic challenge was not as simple to overcome as the language barrier. Hangasu had nine children, seven children of his own and two adopted. He had no income to support his family. The small amount of money he had saved before leaving Ethiopia was quickly spent. He rented a one-bedroom apartment; it was one rectangular 10-foot by 12-foot cell for his family of eleven. That was all he could afford. At night, there wasn't an inch in that room that wasn't covered by sleeping family members. A few kids slept at neighbors' houses.

Every space was optimized. Cooking items and other household equipment were moved outside before bedtime to make space for kids to sleep. There was only one bed. Children slept on the floor and under the bed. During the day, mealtime was handled in shifts. Children would eat and leave. Then the adults would follow.

Hangasu had gone to Kenya to save himself and his family, but his life was still at risk. The government consistently eliminated people like him—powerful rebel leaders. Living in Kenya didn't alleviate the fear of the Ethiopian government. The government could still hire an assassin to eliminate prominent Oromo leaders. It was natural to look over one's shoulder.

On top of that, another enemy struck in Kenya—poverty. The thought of what to feed the family and how to pay the rent on the one room the family occupied consumed Hangasu. He survived this difficult period with the help of friends, acquaintances, and strangers turned friends. This period of his life paralleled the time his family's property had been confiscated by the Ethiopian government. His family had lost everything, literally overnight. The community had risen to the challenge and helped his father get back on his feet again. Hangasu had a resilient mind-set and had learned how to live on meager resources. The hope that they might someday live in America and not have to worry about what to feed the family also kept their spirits up.

Kenya was open and diverse, so it was easy for Hangasu to find other Oromo immigrants and even old comrades to socialize with. One afternoon in the summer of 1999, my uncle asked me to visit General Wako Gutu with him. We lived in Kariobangi, and the general lived in Eastleigh—two neighboring towns in Nairobi. Kariobangi has a typical slum atmosphere with low-income apartments; it is also a major informal goat and sheep market, distributing meat throughout Nairobi. Eastleigh, on the other hand, feels more like Mogadishu. It is predominantly inhabited by Somali immigrants with shopping malls and restaurants everywhere.

My uncle wanted to visit the general because he had been ill for days. The trip consisted of a 15-minute jostling *matatu* minibus ride, followed by a brisk 10-minute walk. When we reached the residence, we found General Wako resting on his bed. My uncle entered his room first and greeted him; the general returned the greeting while switching to a sitting position. Then I entered. My uncle introduced me, saying, "This is my nephew. He is a student." I was 15 years old at the time. The general stood up and gave me a giant hug. He was an extremely tall man; I could barely reach his belly, but he bent down so I could reach his shoulders.

General Wako struck me as an extraordinary man. I didn't expect the giant hug or how he showed interest in talking to me. He held my hand and asked me to sit by him on his bed. We had casual small talk. Then his face turned serious as he looked up. "*Akako* [my grandson], you see my condition that I am getting old," he said to me. "We need people like *you* who are educated. How are you going to advance our cause using your education?" How was I supposed to respond? I was merely in high school— yet I was still considered *educated*!

Because of Ethiopia's systematic exclusion of southern Oromos and the ongoing conflicts, very few in my region obtained a high school diploma. The general must have realized the struggle for independence had to continue in a different form. He fought militarily with three Ethiopian governments (Haile Selassie, Mengistu Haile Mariam, and Meles Zenawi) throughout his life. His mission to liberate the Oromo people from the historic oppression was yet to be fulfilled. Wako hedged that the next generation would continue the struggle in their own way. All he cared was for the struggle to continue. His slogan was, "*Gabrummaa Hiddaan Buqqifna; dadhabnu ilmaan itti guddifna,*" meaning "We will uproot subjugation; if we were unable [in our lifetime], we will raise a generation that will do so."

When the general asked me in the summer of 1999, "How are you going to advance our cause using your education?", I didn't have an answer. At that time, all I could say was that I would think about it, which was enough of an answer that it pleased him. Now my answer would please him even more because I am advancing the cause by writing and sharing it with the world. The sacrifices he and his people made for the Oromo cause, for all the oppressed people in Ethiopia, have not been forgotten.

However, General Wako Gutu died in 2006 in exile (Nairobi, Kenya). His death deeply moved even his foes. His body was taken back to Ethiopia and buried in his hometown of Meda in Madda Walabu alongside his comrade and, at times, challenger, Colonel Adam Jilo, who also died in exile (Minnesota, United States) in 2005. But their legacy continues.

After two years of grind in Kariobangi, Nairobi, my uncle's family got the opportunity to move to America. That was a major milestone for anyone coming to the United States through Kenya. It was highly celebrated—a dream come true. Everyone offered well wishes. Most important, people would tell anybody who'd "won the lottery" of going to the United States to not forget those who stayed behind. Some heard that message, and others were deaf to it.

CHAPTER TWENTY-FOUR:
ST. PAUL

MY UNCLE CAME TO THE UNITED STATES in the fall of 2000, six years before that cold winter night when he asked me to give him a ride home from his job and I saw him mopping the floor of a Lake Street restaurant. He settled with his family in St. Paul, Minnesota. Minnesota is home to an estimated more than twenty thousand Oromo immigrants. Hangasu didn't choose Minnesota; it chose him. Minnesota happened to accept the cohort of refugees that Hangasu was a part of. Hangasu's family was hosted by Mohamed Adam Jilo (MJ) and Lutheran Social Services of Minnesota. MJ is a childhood friend of Hangasu who had moved to the United States in the 1990s. The two had a mutual friendship that transcended time. Matt, a refugee resettlement case manager, was the family's host from Lutheran Social Services. He was a good-looking young man in his early twenties, probably 6 feet, 3 inches tall with a modest build. He embraced Hangasu's family immediately and was determined to make their resettlement in Minnesota as smooth as possible.

Challenge struck right away. Hangasu's family size was twelve. It quickly became apparent that finding a place to stay would be a problem. MJ hosted the family for a few days, but he had his own large family already. Matt searched for housing, but he couldn't find anything. He reached out to his networks to find a place for the family, but to no avail. Many agents would have stopped there.

Matt was determined to find the family housing. He finally reached out to his colleague Mary at Luther Seminary. The two persuaded the seminary to allow Mary to host Hangasu's family until Matt found a permanent place for them.

Mary, who also lived at the seminary with her own family, took good care of the family. She invited them to dinner, stopped by to say hello before and after school, took the family grocery shopping, and gave them winter clothes. She even took the family to apply for jobs.

"I wished all Americans were like Matt and Mary. They are extraordinary people," said Hangasu.

After weeks at the seminary, Matt found Hangasu's family housing in St. Paul. Matt and Hangasu were excited that they had found a house that could accommodate the large family. It had four bedrooms—three bedrooms and a bathroom upstairs and one bedroom on the main floor. One bathroom for twelve people was a challenge by any measure, but the family improvised, and nobody complained. The house had major issues that the landlord neglected. One bedroom had a big hole in a wall. The furnace didn't work half the time. When called to fix the issues, the landlord was unresponsive. The family found a way to plug the holes and get through their first winter anyway. Despite these challenges, the family liked the neighborhood. They walked to a nearby grocery store. The children got outside and played in the neighborhood.

Perhaps the refugee family's biggest shock of moving from Ethiopia to Minnesota was, as one might imagine, the weather. They marveled at how the tiny snowflakes quickly piled up into a massive mountain.

Matt and Mary continued to visit the family at the new residence. They provided rides for the family to and from appointments. Matt and Mary were the first Americans the family got to know well. They showed genuine interest in getting to know the family and asked about their culture, language, and faith. Matt and Mary represented the American ideal that all are welcome and that there are opportunities here for those who want to work and reinvent themselves.

For my uncle, settling in the United States presented a stark contrast to living in his native country of Ethiopia. He'd first fled Ethiopia in his early twenties to escape the brutal communist government in the 1970s. The Somali government welcomed him with prison upon arrival, accusing him of organizing independent Oromo youth who'd refused Somalia's meddling in the Oromo struggle. He returned to Ethiopia when the Derg communist government was toppled to help rebuild his country. Within a few short years, the new ruling party, TPLF, consolidated the power in the country and marginalized all other groups. The TPLF government simply replaced the Amhara rule with the Tigray rule and continued human rights abuses—jailing, torturing, and killing innocent people without due process. Hangasu fled his country again, this time to Kenya. The neighboring countries such as Kenya, Somalia, and Djibouti weren't safe from TPLF's mercenaries. Ethiopian security officers and their partners in those countries frequently assassinate opposition that resides outside of the country's borders. Just because he'd left the country didn't mean Hangasu was safe from the TPLF brutality. Many political refugees from Ethiopia constantly looked over their shoulder.

"I had never fully slept until I came to the United States," said Hangasu. He appreciated the better life he and his family enjoyed in Minnesota. However, above all other improvements, he valued his family's safety and security most. For the first time in his life, he didn't have to worry about his and his family's safety on a daily basis. He wanted to make sure his children understood this: "Nobody will target us for simply being who we are if we abide by the law of the land."

The family wanted to move to a better house with proper running water, heat and air conditioning, and insulation. They needed a four- or five-bedroom house based on their family's size, but the rent was cost prohibitive. They constantly brought up this challenge with Matt and Mary. Matt went into problem-solving mode again. He found out about Twin Cities Habitat for Humanity. Habitat for Humanity's mission is to "Eliminate poverty housing from the Twin Cities and to make decent, affordable shelter for all people a matter of conscience." They do this by building homes for eligible applicants. Key eligibility requirements were that the applicant had lived in the Twin Cities for at least one year, cannot have owned a home in the last three years, and met the financial criteria. Matt encouraged the family to apply. Hangasu's family was the perfect applicant.

The process consisted of filling out the application form, and if the applicant met the requirements, someone from Habitat would conduct a phone interview to confirm what was on the application and to perhaps dig a little deeper on certain responses. If that looked good, an in-person interview was conducted at the applicant's home. Hangasu's family made it all the way through to the home interview. The family's hope for building and owning their own home in the United States grew by the day. What was even more important to them was that buying a house from Habitat was not like buying any other house on the market. The founders of Habitat for Humanity, Linda and Millard Fuller, believed in building simple, decent, and affordable houses free of mortgage interest. Habitat doesn't make a profit on sales. The principle paid by the homeowner is put back into the community to build another house for the next needy person. To Hangasu and his family, this was unbelievable. Not only would they be able to own their house, but they would buy it interest free. As a person committed to the teaching of his faith, Hangasu had been worried about mortgage interest. Giving and taking of interest is prohibited in Islam. When he heard about Habitat's interest-free mortgage, he was ecstatic.

The Habitat for Humanity interviewer concluded that the family's housing needs were obvious. The house they'd rented for the previous three years was in bad condition, and they met the Twin Cities residency requirement. However, there was one hurdle. Hangasu's income was below the minimum requirement, which meant he couldn't afford to pay the mortgage. This was a critical requirement; owners must be able to repay the loan. The Habitat interviewer, a young lady named Lisa, was torn about the decision to accept or reject the family's application. She witnessed the family's predicament and really wanted to help, but she had to follow the eligibility guidelines. It was difficult for her to inform the family of the decision, but she gathered herself and made the call.

I was living with my uncle during this time. I was also serving as the family's de facto interpreter. Lisa called me. I could hear genuine sadness in her voice. "I am so sorry," she said. "Everything looks great, but the family's income is below the minimum guideline."

I was shocked. I shouted, "No!" Hangasu had been sitting beside me when the phone rang. From my reaction, he gathered there was bad news. I didn't translate immediately. Instead, I continued the conversation with Lisa.

Lisa stated her interest in finding a way to help the family but explained she was stuck.

"There is new information," I said. "I started a part-time job last week. Could you add my income and see if we can meet the income guidelines? Getting a rejection would devastate this family."

Lisa was relieved to hear this news. She asked about my wages and the number of hours I worked per week and did a quick calculation. She was encouraged by the rough estimates; however, she needed the check stub to verify the income. The application was put on hold pending income verification.

When I ended the call, everybody in the house turned to me to learn what Habitat had said. When I explained, the family turned to prayer. "Oh, God, we need this. Help us." The next two weeks felt like months. When I finally presented the pay stub to Lisa, the extra income had put the family slightly above the minimum family income requirement. That was all Lisa needed. She quickly got the okay from her selection committee and called to congratulate Hangasu's family. The family celebrated with more prayers, thanking God.

One week later, Lisa called again. She'd found the location where their new home would be built. She offered to show it to them. The family could accept or reject the location. If they accepted the location, their house would be built there. If they skipped the location because they didn't like the neighborhood, they would be given only one more choice.

When they saw the lot where their new house would be built, their dream of owning a home seemed real. Their eagerness to move to their own home made it okay for the family to accept the location.

After the family accepted the location, Habitat began construction. Habitat houses are built by volunteers. The families who are selected must contribute their time to build their own house or other Habitat houses. This is called a "sweat equity" requirement, typically ranging from 350 to 450 hours. The number of hours is determined based on family size. In the case of Hangasu's large family, they were required to complete 450 hours of sweat equity.

The rest is history. In the summer of 2003, the family moved into their own home that they'd helped build. At the open house, Hangasu thanked Twin Cities Habitat for Humanity and the countless volunteers who continue to support this amazing cause! Hangasu and Maryam could now invite their relatives to visit them.

*

Hangasu gathered all of his children for a family talk. It was a mixed lecture and discussion. He began by saying, "We are in the United States, a place everybody hopes to live. Many only dream of being here. We can't squander this opportunity. We need a plan as a family."

Next, he turned to the older children and asked, "What should be our priority now that we are here?" He knew what he wanted, but he wanted to engage his children in the discussion. A few things were suggested: education, work to improve their livelihood here, support our relatives in Africa. Everybody emphasized a hunger for education. Hangasu summarized the opinions and revealed that he too believed education must be the family priority, especially for the children. "Therefore, let's agree today that a bachelor's degree is a minimum educational expectation in our family," he said. All nodded in agreement.

Hangasu himself was a middle school dropout, and Maryam never received a formal education. But because of his father's leadership position in the Bale Oromo movement and his own involvement in politics, Hangasu had seen the importance of education. He knew the Bale Oromo movement would have advanced more easily if they'd had access to education. Their lack of understanding of the enemy they were fighting and of the broader national politics hampered their success. He knew that education was a tool for individual, community, and societal development. Hangasu assured his children that prioritizing education would help them achieve all the other things they'd discussed, such as improving one's life and helping relatives back home. "If we miss out on the education, none of the other things matter," he said. "We won't be able to help ourselves, let alone help others."

He promised every child that if they followed through with education, he would help them with everything at his disposal. "Live here in my home as long as you need," he told them. "I will cover both our expenses here and our families' stipend abroad. You don't have to worry."

Many young immigrants wish their parents recognize the importance of education and support along the way. Many are pressured by their parents and relatives to provide for them as soon as they hit the United States. Feeling the mounting pressure and responsibility, these immigrants enter a low-wage workforce and never have the chance to consider school. Their situation forces them to neglect education. That, in turn, makes it difficult for them to pull themselves out of poverty.

Hangasu delivered on his promise. To lead by example, he and Maryam registered for an evening English as a Second Language (ESL) class at Hubbs Center for Lifelong Learning in St. Paul. During the day, he worked for St. Paul Public Schools in the Food Services department. This gave him the opportunity to supervise his children while monitoring who they befriended, what they ate, and more importantly, how they were doing academically. Of course, it was a nightmare for the children. They felt Dad was always watching, and that kept them largely out of trouble. But with Hangasu's insistence on the importance of school and Maryam's gentle love and nudge at home, all high school–aged children graduated and attended college.

When there was a challenge at school or home that Hangasu and Maryam didn't understand, the children turned to each other for mentoring. Their parents understood the importance of education at a macro level, but they had no idea about the day-to-day challenges of attending middle school, high school, and college in Minnesota. In most cases, older siblings stepped into the parent role and attended their younger siblings' school conferences; they also comforted and advised each other. In this arena, Halima played a pivotal role in supervising and guiding her younger siblings. As of this writing, eight of Hangasu's children have earned bachelor's degrees in the fields of science, engineering, social sciences, and public health. Two of the eight earned master's degrees as well. The rest are in the process of completing high school or pursuing their college degrees. Hangasu and Maryam look at their children's achievements as their own. They celebrated every educational milestone with their children.

In addition to supporting his children's education, Hangasu played a major role in establishing the Oromo Community in the Twin Cities of Minnesota. He articulated a vision that brought people together. He also brought decades of experience in the Oromo people's needs and dreams.

*

Immediately after arriving in the United States, Hangasu filed sponsorship papers to bring over his relatives. He started sending money to the poor and orphan children he knew in Ethiopia. Hangasu stepped in and partnered with his uncle Muhammad Haji Ibrahim to keep Zakiya Sheikh Yayha in school after her father's death. Sheikh Yahya was Hangasu's maternal uncle. Zakiya was able to graduate from high school and college. She is currently working as a nurse in the Borana Zone of Ethiopia. Zakiya is only one example of what Hangasu did for many children in Bale.

Hangasu also championed broader community initiatives. He planted the seed for building a school for the people of Koba Adi. When community leaders in a small village outside Nagele Borana asked for help to build a school for their children, Hangasu donated his own money. The following year when I visited the country, my uncle asked me to visit the school and listen to the community. Touched by the stories, I worked with many individuals in my network and built three rooms of the school—one fifth- and one sixth-grade classroom with one administrative office in the middle. A year later, the community used the remaining funds to build seventh- and eighth-grade rooms. The community's life turned around. Suddenly there was hope for the children to pursue education and lift themselves out of poverty.

A few years later, Hangasu moved on to another project designed to help students in rural Ethiopia. His tactics were always impressive and unconventional. He realized students lacked school supplies. He thought about things he could do with the few resources he had. He began collecting backpacks. After work, he would go to Savers, thrift stores, and the Salvation Army. At least once a week, he would purchase backpacks and store them in his basement. Every time he traveled to Ethiopia or saw any of his family members or colleagues, he would ask them to take a suitcase full of backpacks and distribute them to children in their hometown.

In 2016, Hangasu and a few of his friends established a nonprofit called the Burqaa Guddinnaa Foundation. The foundation focuses on building the identity of Oromo children by exposing them to Afan Oromo culture and history; it also performs humanitarian work in Ethiopia to expand the educational opportunities. Through the foundation, the Oromo community in Minnesota funded the construction of temporary schools and the purchase of school supplies for students whose families were displaced by internal ethnic conflicts. Hangasu would match a backpack for every student who received notebooks and pens. He also engaged youth such as Ahmed Abdo Adam Jilo (grandson of Adam Jilo) and me to ensure the long-term continuity of this humanitarian work.

In the end, Hangasu wants to be remembered as the "one who tried to be of service to his people." In Minnesota, he is an advocate for the revival of the Oromo language and the teaching of his people's history. In Ethiopia, he is mobilizing his community to educate their girls and boys. He has committed to providing educational materials—pens, pencils, notebooks, and backpacks—to as many students as possible.

*

Hangasu's journey filled my thoughts that cold winter night in 2006 as I gave him a ride home from his job at the Lake Street restaurant. His journey is in many ways my journey and the journey of my community. He left Ethiopia before I was born. As I was growing up, my mother and grandmother talked about him regularly. They were concerned about his safety because of his involvement in the Oromo struggle.

Before I met Hangasu in person, I heard him on the Ethiopian National Radio in 1992, right after he returned to Ethiopia after spending thirteen years in exile in Somalia. During the interview, he talked about his vision to be part of rebuilding the country, to make it a country that protects the dignity of all of its citizens. As an 8-year-old boy, I was proud of him. Later that year I met him in Bidire. I felt like I knew him already. He encouraged me to stick to school and do my best. When he was forced to leave Ethiopia the second time in 1998, he brought me along to Kenya and then the United States.

On a personal level, he was mopping floors because his education and experiences were deemed irrelevant in the United States. He wanted to make sure his children could compete for a better life. He has a dream of a decent life for his children, and he demands education from every young person in his community. He views his children as his single biggest accomplishment.

For his community, Hangasu knows education is necessary but not sufficient to succeed. He came from a pastoral community. Collectivism is important to him. He often says, "Without an education, a person is blind. But education is not enough. People who are educated and organized can determine their own destiny." For Ethiopia to move forward as a nation and bring about positive social change, Hangasu is convinced education, organization, and genuine leaders are critical.

He inspired me to do something for our community. He and I, with the support of our family and friends, built schools in Ethiopia. Since then I brought solar light to schoolchildren in rural Ethiopia so those kids, especially girls, could study and do their homework at night after completing their daily chores and responsibilities. While investment in education is important for everyone, empirical evidence shows a girl's education benefits the next generation.

My uncle is a man of strong will. When he spoke, people listened. He is thoughtful. He is a thinker. At the completion of the book project, my uncle is 64 years old. He lived far more than half of his life in exile. That's the price of the struggle. It is a privilege for me to share his story.

Although there is more to be done—personally and collectively—we are both proud of the progress we've made so far.

EPILOGUE

THE TWIN CITIES OF MINNESOTA has the largest concentration of Oromos outside of Ethiopia. Actual population data is difficult to obtain, but it is estimated that more than twenty thousand Oromos live in the Twin Cities. That's why Minnesota is referred to by many Oromos as "Little Oromia." A street in Minneapolis, Oromo Street, was dedicated in recognition of the people.

On October 20, 2013, Oromos in Minnesota, in coordination with Oromos elsewhere in North America, decided to celebrate the fiftieth anniversary of the Bale Oromo Revolt. The event took place at the O'Shaughnessy Education Center Auditorium at St. Thomas University in St. Paul, Minnesota.

The event began with a brief video message from General Wako Gutu. The video was recorded in the 1990s after he'd been forced to leave Ethiopia. Here is an excerpt:

> "My people! We are here because we want to talk about our history and our current situation. I greet all of you—wherever you are, in the

country or abroad. We are in the jungle because
we demand our freedom. Freedom is not free.
Freedom doesn't come without bloodshed. You
must know this. We [the Oromos] occupy
eleven provinces [of Ethiopia]. Those who
oppressed us and continue to oppress us occupy
only one province. What is this? How do we
accept this? What would God think of us? What
would the world think of us? What would we
think of ourselves? How can one group from
one province oppress the people of eleven
provinces? How can three million people
enslave thirty-three million people? My
comrades! Open your eyes! Raise your head!
Stand up for your dignity like other human
beings."

General Wako Gutu had died in 2006. His legacy had not.
One of Wako's longtime comrades, Haji Muhammad Haro (also
known as Qoncora), said, "I felt like he was speaking to me right
now" after watching the video. Many people in the audience
expressed a similar experience, which shows how highly Wako
is regarded in his society.

Numerous Oromo professionals and youth leaders spoke at
the event. Hangasu led the most important part of the
conference, the veterans' roundtable, where he facilitated
discussion among the elders. It was the first public forum where
these elders could share what happened to them and how they
responded to the systematic subjugation. Their stories were
simultaneously painful and inspiring. This is where the idea of
capturing these people's history emerged for me.

*

At the same time, Ethiopia was undergoing a difficult
period. One Saturday afternoon in the summer of 2014, I visited
my uncle at his house in Minneapolis. He was listening to

satellite television such as OMN (Oromia Media Network) and ESAT (Ethiopian Satellite Television) to stay on top of news and events that were taking place in Ethiopia. Maryam had just finished making the afternoon coffee. I joined them for a cup of coffee. My uncle likes his coffee with black seed oil. He added three drops for me and three for himself. He then started to fill me in on what was happening in Ethiopia. The Oromo youth protest had expanded rapidly across the country. The government responded with a ferocious crackdown on protesters, the way it always dealt with objections. The country was a mess.

My uncle dresses well, even when he is at home. He has a long red henna-colored beard with a trimmed mustache. His eyes and smile project wisdom. Given all the chaos in Ethiopia, I asked him what it would take to stabilize the country and put it on the right trajectory. Without hesitation, he said, "TPLF must relinquish power." He paused and sipped his coffee. "If TPLF did that, the Tigray people must be protected from retaliation for what they have done in the last twenty-three years."

"OK, if TPLF relinquished power, who should step forward?" I asked.

"In theory it doesn't really matter who," he said. "There is an Oromo proverb: '*Sunsuma jirjiiraniif, nyaati hin mi'aahu*,' meaning 'Simply because one changes the stove, the food doesn't all of a sudden become delicious.' I have witnessed the last three Ethiopian governments closely. At their core, they are all the same; the fundamentals are the same. Not even the socialist government of Derg was able to change it. It is primarily a system problem. Under the current Ethiopian system of government (the unwritten rules), elect an angel if you like; you will get the same result—corruption, torture, human rights abuses, jailing, killings, control of the country's resources in the pocket of few.

"The change of a leader is necessary but not enough. Change of the system must be a priority." He delivered this point with utmost conviction. He was excited to discuss the topic.

When I asked him if he could imagine who from the current Oromo leaders could lead such a systematic change, Hangasu quickly dismissed all of the opposition leaders outside of Ethiopia. His reasoning was that these so-called opposition leaders in the diaspora have no foundation in the country nor credibility. He emphasized, "The next leaders must come from *within* the country."

He then started naming the stereotypical Oromo leaders from the different Oromia regions. He finally got to the Jimma region. "If you ask me today where we should look for the next Oromo leader who can unite Ethiopians, I would say look in Jimma," he said. "The Oromo people from Jimma are wise, diplomatic, patient, and effective. I spent a lot of time with the people of Jimma. They never get angry. If you were to insult a wise person from Jimma, he would not insult you back. In fact, he wouldn't directly respond to you. Instead, he would turn to your friend and say, in the most respectful manner you've ever experienced, 'Is he [referring to the person who made the insult] OK?'

"By doing that, he has demonstrated he can maintain his composure in a hostile environment, and yet he is still laughing. He would at least win over your friend with his charm. Imagine your friend is an entire room full of the audience." He smiled as if he could visualize the person he was talking about.

According to Hangasu, the people of Jimma master the art of communication. They can see the big picture, and at the same time, they can navigate the minutiae. That is a potent tool for any leader anywhere; only a few master it.

Hangasu's hunches were prophetic.

The Oromo youth protest pressured the ruling party to relinquish power by demanding human rights and political change in the country. Protests around the country got out of control. The government was unable to govern. The acting prime minister, Hailemariam Desalegn, resigned.

Unexpectedly, a small group within the Oromo People's Democratic Organization (OPDO) fully embraced the Oromo youth's grievances. This small group, led by Lamma Magarsa and Abiy Ahmed, joined the youth protest by opposing the government they had been a part of for twenty-seven years. The OPDO leaders saw the opportunity to take their people to victory and seized it. By joining the youth movement on the street and fighting the system from the inside, they exposed themselves.

Lamma and Abiy showed courage and political adroitness in the face of a violent enemy. While Jawar Mohammed (a Minnesota-based prominent Oromo activist) fueled the protest by mobilizing Oromo youth on the streets of Ethiopian cities through social media and Lamma and Abiy employed political maneuvering and alliance building to negotiate for positive change in the country. In essence, Abiy and Lamma accomplished what none of the earlier Oromo movements could not. They had an organization, however weak. They embraced the populist uprising, made it their own, and turned against the government they'd previously aligned with to bring positive changes to the country. Finally, it all came together: popular uprising, politically savvy and genuine leaders, and organization.

When Hangasu asserted the right leader for Ethiopia should come from Jimma, he did not know about the wise young man from Jimma who was not on any Ethiopian or Oromo's radar. Four years later, the ruling coalition of Ethiopia elected Abiy Ahmed Ali as prime minister. He instantly united Ethiopians from all walks of life. Eighteen months after stepping into the position, Abiy received international recognition via the Nobel Peace Prize for decisively ending the war between Ethiopia and Eritrea.

My uncle never expected he would see such a change in Ethiopia within his lifetime. From his perspective, the country has the right leader with Abiy at the helm. Now the question remains: Will he change the system to build a new Ethiopia that embraces its diversity and unleashes its potential? And will the people of Ethiopia let him?

*

Despite the challenges, I'm an optimist. Abiy Ahmed and Lamma Magarsa saved Ethiopia from the brink of collapse. So far, they have demonstrated a strong will to establish lasting democracy in the country. They've shown Ethiopians and the world that Oromos are builders of nations. The Oromo people have gained the dignity of living alongside all nationalities in Ethiopia as equals. What determines the sustainability of the new era of liberty, equality, and economic growth will be the endurance of the law and the organization that protects the people's interests. Therefore, their chief priorities must be the application of law that is just and the establishment of an institution that guarantees the continuity of this change.

The challenge is that Ethiopia has not reconciled with its history as of yet. Unresolved historical wounds could still put the current positive momentum and growth trajectory at risk.

Ethiopia's history is a point of pride for one or two ethnic groups and a point of calamity and ruin for everybody else in the country. This tension, if not dealt with properly, could cause the country to slide back from its current progress.

Unfortunately, the country has no golden history where all or even a majority of its citizens would say was an exemplary period. In Ethiopia, the golden period will be in the future if all of its citizens are willing to work for it. It appears to be possible under Abiy Ahmed's leadership.

As Nelson Mandela once said, "Young people are capable, when aroused, of bringing down the towers of oppression and raising the banners of freedom." Beyond the usual and historic ethnic strife in the country, Abiy Ahmed's biggest challenge ahead is figuring out how to turn his nation's youth into an asset.

The median age in Ethiopia is 18. Young Ethiopians are credited for bringing about the change that brought Abiy Ahmed to power. The big question for Abiy Ahmed and his government is how well he can channel the energy and talent of his country's youth toward the nation's development.

Youth fueled the Oromo struggle that dismantled the status quo; now the same youth will be expected to lift the country out of poverty. However, to do that, young people need the right training, opportunity, and a conducive environment in which to operate. Abiy can't do it alone. All Ethiopians must participate. Perhaps the Nobel award will encourage the international community to provide the right kind of assistance for Ethiopia. The assistance should primarily focus on skill development, vocational training, and job creation while also advancing environmental and cultural sustainability.

As a nation, the Oromo people have a lot to celebrate. For the first time in Ethiopia's history, Oromos managed to lead the country. This victory came with the compounded sacrifices of the Oromo people for more than a century. The rise of Abiy Ahmed and Lamma Magarsa made all the Oromo people's early struggles and sacrifices worthwhile. Time will tell if this transition will be successful. But this has been a great start.

Perhaps the biggest victory for the Oromo people is still in progress. That is, little by little Oromos are realizing that their strength lies in their numbers. They must not allow anyone to divide them. The unity of the Oromo people is not only good for the Oromos, but also for Ethiopia and the entire region. Good people united for the sole purpose of improving the situation for all will be an unstoppable force.

In the words of Wangari Maathai, "You cannot enslave a mind that knows itself. That values itself. That understands itself."

ACKNOWLEDGEMENTS

Writing this book was both challenging and rewarding. It would not have been possible without the extraordinary support of many people. It is because of their effort and encouragement that I have now a legacy of writing a book to pass on to my children where one didn't exist before. I want to thank the individuals who helped me make this book a reality.

First, I am deeply grateful to my publisher, Bill Burleson at Flexible Press. Bill, thank you for partnering with me on this book. I was so lucky to find you. I'm impressed by your vision for structuring the book and the tireless work in making this manuscript relatable to the readers. Your commitment to supporting local authors and faith in the book has encouraged me to push this book to completion. I am also grateful for your philanthropic partnership with me in investing fifty percent of profits from this book's sale in purchasing educational supplies for school children in Ethiopia.

I am indebted to my friends, Laura Murphy and Charles Nguyen, for taking on this book project with me and for spending countless hours editing the manuscript and making the time to discuss a way forward. I love how you two conspired to make this book a success. I could not have done this without you. Thank you, that true friendship!

I want to express my gratitude to my editor, Daniel Schuette. You worked with me on this manuscript every step of the way. Your feedback was insightful and meticulous. I am also grateful to my editor, Vicki Adang. Thank you for your careful and thoughtful final copyediting.

I want to thank my buddy, Santiago Vallejo. You played a critical role in helping me synthesize my ideas and in crafting the title of this book. I also want to express my appreciation to my friend Lauren Lombard for taking the book cover portrait of my uncle and me. I'm very grateful, Lauren.

My longtime friend, Dave Meitz, thank you for generously offering to edit the early manuscript and providing me with valuable feedback. Thank you to Sam Bohrman for your help with developmental editing. Your feedback helped me organize my thoughts better.

I am deeply grateful to my teacher, Professor Stephen Wilbers. You connected me with my publisher, Bill, and you "wilberized" this manuscript! Thank you for your incisive editorial suggestions and for the time you invested in me.

Finally, I owe immeasurable gratitude to my wife, Halima, mother of our children Adam, Hakima, Sakina and Muhammad. Thank you for your constant stream of love, encouragement, and unwavering support! This book would not have been possible without you.

ABOUT THE AUTHOR

Abdul Dire is an Ethiopian-born philanthropist, author, and tech leader at a Fortune 500 company.

Abdul honors his connection to his homeland by helping the next generation of Oromo immigrants understand their multidimensional identity through the study of history, culture, and language. He honors the sacrifice of those who came before him with his work to improve access to education in Ethiopia, including building a school, distributing solar electricity to villages, and providing school supplies.

Abdul has a B.S. in Materials Science and Engineering and an M.S. in the Management of Technology from the University of Minnesota. He lives in Minnesota with his wife and four children.

BIBLIOGRAPHY

Adejumobi, Saheed A. *The Greenwood Histories of the Modern Nations: The History of Ethiopia*. Connecticut: Greenwood Press, 2007.

Ademo, Mohammed. "Commemorating 50 Years of Oromo Struggle led by General Waqo Gutu." *OPride*. October 15, 2013. https://www.opride.com/2013/10/15/commemorating-50-years-of-oromo-struggle-led-by-waqo-gutu/.

———. "Remembering Ethiopia's Hidden Genocide: Aannolee." *OPride*. August 28, 2011. https://www.opride.com/2011/08/28/remembering-ethiopias-hidden-genocide-aannolee/.

BBC News. "Abiy Ahmed: Ethiopia's Prime Minister." *BBC*. October 11, 2019. https://www.bbc.com/news/world-africa-43567007.

Boahen, A. Adu. *General History of Africa, Vol. VII: Africa Under Colonial Domination 1880–1935.* United Nations Educational, Scientific, and Cultural Organization (UNESCO). Berkeley: University of California Press, 1985.

Challi, Nasise. *Oromiya Today: A Pocket Guide.* Finfinne: Oromiya National Regional Government, President Office Directorate of Protocol & Public Relations, 2008.

Gedamu, Yohannes. "Ethiopia's Abiy Ahmed and the Survival of the Ruling EPRDF: Will Ethiopia's New Prime Minister Manage to Introduce Change and Push the Country Towards Democratisation?" *Al Jazeera.* May 28, 2018. https://www.aljazeera.com/indepth/opinion/ethiopia-abiy-ahmed-survival-ruling-eprdf-180528082306152.html.

Lata, Leenco. *The Ethiopian State at the Crossroads: Decolonization and Democratization or Disintegration?* Asmara: Red Sea Press, 1999.

Mazrui, Ali A. *General History of Africa, Vol. VIII: Africa Since 1935.* United Nations Educational, Scientific, and Cultural Organization (UNESCO). Berkeley: University of California Press, 1993.

Melbaa, Gadaa. *Oromia: An Introduction to the History of the Oromo People.* Minneapolis: Kirk House Publishers, 1999.

Reiss-Andersen, Berit. "The Nobel Peace Prize 2019." *Norwegian Nobel Institute.* October 11, 2019. https://www.nobelpeaceprize.org/.

Schulze, Peter B. *Yabegaw Mebrek (The Summer Thunder).* Addis Ababa: Shama Books. 2009.

Tareke, Gebru. *Ethiopia: Power and Protest. Peasant Revolts in the Twentieth Century.* New York: Cambridge University Press, 1991.

Made in the USA
Monee, IL
04 March 2022

REMEMBERING
MARY

During this Christmas season in which we remember Christ's birth, may we also be mindful of Mary. We do not worship her, pray to her, or see her as an intercessor for our sins, but we can and should learn from her. At some moment when the tree lights are dim, children are sleeping, and wrappings have been set aside for another day, we would add to the blessings of the season if we took some time to consider her role in it. We could read of how she exhibited faith in the midst of what should have been a time of great fear. We could study how she submitted to and glorified God during a period of great personal sacrifice. And we could admire her quiet reverence for sacred things. Mostly, we could observe that these very characteristics we cherish in her were then reflected in the life of our beloved Savior. During this season in which we try so hard to emulate Him, even if it means giving up our shoes and walking in bare feet, may we remember that those qualities that were given to Him by His Father in Heaven were also nurtured in Him on this earth by a woman, a mere mortal, a mother.

Mary Holland McCann, the daughter of Elder Jeffrey R. and Sister Patricia T. Holland, has a BA in English from Brigham Young University. She is married to Lee McCann, and they are the parents of five children.